Contents

5 Beyond Manga

6 The Players

7 The Information

THE ROUGH GUIDE TO

Manga

by

Jason S. Yadao

ROUGH
GUIDES

www.roughguides.com

Credits

The Rough Guide to Manga

Additional contributions: Simon Richmond, Abe Chang
Editing: Kate Berens, Ruth Tidball
Design: Link Hall
Cover design: Diana Jarvis
Layout: Umesh Aggarwal
Picture research: Chloë Roberts, Kate Berens
Proofreading: Jason Freeman
Production: Rebecca Short

Rough Guides Reference

Director: Andrew Lockett
Editors: Kate Berens, Peter Buckley, Tracy Hopkins, Matthew Milton, Joe Staines, Ruth Tidball

Publishing information

This first edition published October 2009 by
Rough Guides Ltd, 80 Strand, London WC2R 0RL
375 Hudson Street, New York 10014, USA
Email: mail@roughguides.com

Distributed by the Penguin Group:
Penguin Books Ltd, 80 Strand, London WC2R 0RL
Penguin Putnam, Inc., 375 Hudson Street, New York 10014, USA
Penguin Group (Australia), 250 Camberwell Road, Camberwell, Victoria 3124, Australia
Penguin Books Canada Ltd, 90 Eglinton Avenue East, Suite 700, Toronto, Ontario, Canada M4P 2Y3
Penguin Group (New Zealand), Cnr Rosedale and Airborne Roads, Albany, Auckland, New Zealand

Printed and bound in Singapore by SNP Security Printing PTE.

The publishers and author have done their best to ensure the accuracy and currency of all information in *The Rough Guide to Manga*; however, they can accept no responsibility for any loss or inconvenience sustained by any reader as a result of its information or advice.

288 pages; includes index

A catalogue record for this book is available from the British Library

ISBN: 978-1-85828-561-0

1 3 5 7 9 8 6 4 2

Introduction

Flash back to 1997 for a moment, when I was toiling away at my journalism degree at the University of Hawaii. It was the latter part of a significant period in American comics, a time when several universe-shaking events happened one after the other: Superman died, Batman had his back broken, Wolverine had his indestructible adamantium ripped out of his body by Magneto, Green Lantern Hal Jordan went crazy... it was an interesting time to be a comics collector.

Mind you, I had no idea at the time that comics existed with perfectly good, mature stories that didn't involve superheroes, like Dave Sim's *Cerebus*, Jeff Smith's *Bone*, and the Hernandez Brothers' *Love and Rockets*. I had grown up on a steady diet of full-colour comic stories with Archie, Richie Rich, Little Lulu, Looney Tunes and Disney characters. The only other types of comics I knew about were the hero-versus-villain slugfests, and I wasn't really interested in those... that is, until newspaper stories started hyping the "momentous" changes to the Superman and Batman franchises. I dutifully followed along with those stories as four Supermen showed up, as a new, more violent Batman ripped through Gotham City, and finally as the status quo was restored to those series.

And that was the problem for me and comics in 1997: I was bored with the status quo. It was around this time that a friend offered me a copy of a comic called *Maison Ikkoku*, written and drawn by someone named Rumiko Takahashi and translated from Japanese to English.

It blew my mind. Here was something refreshingly different. Characters weren't beating one another up over acts of villainy, there were no galaxies to save, and the pages weren't in colour – everything was rendered in black and white instead. The story was at turns humorous and poignant, a romantic tale whose outcome remained in doubt until its final pages. I was hooked, and my friend and I took turns buying each new volume as they came out until the series concluded.

I had no idea at the time that this first contact with what I later learned was called manga would eventually lead to my writing a weekly column about it (and its animated counterpart, anime) for the *Star-Bulletin* – one of Honolulu's two daily newspapers – and now a Rough Guide on the topic, too. It's certainly testament to how the industry has expanded during the last decade or so. Back in my *Maison Ikkoku* days, I had to look for new volumes in the corner of a rack at one particular comics store. Now, any respectable bookstore will have at least a small section devoted to some of the more popular titles. And while I've since learned that there are galaxy-saving, good-versus-evil stories like those of the superhero comics I left behind, there are so many other different types of stories told in manga as well.

Manga itself is changing, too. No longer taken solely to mean "black and white comics from Japan", the term has come to represent an entire style of sequential art. While Japan is naturally manga's heartland, creators in Asia, Europe, North America and elsewhere are producing manga worthy of notice as well, usually known as "global" or "original English language" manga.

The Rough Guide to Manga is a chronicle of manga's evolution. We'll start with the origins of manga in Japan and how the industry took off in the 1950s with the work of a former doctor turned cartoonist. We'll go on to chart the rise of manga through its golden years and subsequent gradual decline – a decline that dovetails into the industry's growth elsewhere in the world (covered in Chapter 2).

In Chapter 3 we take a closer look at what manga's all about today, exploring the medium's unique vocabulary, one that reflects the traditional working practices of artists and editors. Also in this section is a thorough exploration of the basic categories and genres of manga, revealing that manga's not just schoolgirls or robots (or pornography), but that it encompasses a huge variety of subject matter for audiences of all ages and both genders.

Japanese animation and manga have always had a close relationship, with almost sixty percent of anime based on manga series; manga based on anime is less frequent but also exists. This – and manga's relationship with live-action film and with videogames – is outlined in Chapter 5. We devote an entire chapter to the publishers of English-language manga, which not only offers highlights of their publications but also provides an overall view of the manga industry within English-speaking territories. This is followed by a selection of resources: recommended manga books, websites and conventions; plus a glossary of terms.

Right at the heart of this book is the Canon, in-depth reviews of fifty must-read manga, ranging from the 1950s to the present day. Inevitably these selections are subjective and likely to inspire a good deal of controversy: ask me on ten different days which titles ought to be included, and I would likely give you ten different lists. The list of alternate titles that didn't make it onto this list would make a pretty good Canon in its own right. We've covered most of these in shorter reviews dotted throughout the guide and especially in the Canon chapter, where they accompany pieces on a handful of individual manga creators.

Whether you're new to manga altogether, an anime fan considering reading the comic that inspired your favourite TV series, or even a hardcore otaku, you'll find something in this book that you will enjoy. I've learned a lot about manga over the two years I spent writing this book, and I hope you will too.

Jason S. Yadao

How to use this book

Translating names

In any book about an essentially Japanese art form, there are inevitably a few points you need to know to avoid linguistic confusion. For instance, in Japan a person's family name is listed first, followed by their given name. So you may sometimes see the name Tezuka Osamu. In this book we use the Western convention of given name followed by family name, hence Osamu Tezuka.

When it comes to the names of manga themselves, we've used the published English-language title wherever possible, with the transliterated Japanese title given where there's no (official) English translation.

Pronunciation hints

Learning the Japanese language, particularly from an English perspective, can take years to truly master. The basic scripts, hiragana and katakana, have 48 different characters apiece, and there are seemingly several gazillion more characters derived from Chinese ideograms, known as kanji. But even if you can't read the language, you can learn how to pronounce Japanese words without sounding like a fool. The key is in the vowel sounds:

> **a** is an "ah" sound, as in "bar"
> **i** is a long "ee" sound, as in "elite"
> **u** is an "ooh" sound, as in "lunar"
> **e** is a short "eh" sound, as in "method"
> **o** is an "oh" sound, as in "zone"
> **ō** is pronounced twice as long as a normal o, as in "shōnen" or "Tōkyo". This vowel sound is sometimes denoted in English by "ou", for example in "shoujo".

Key to abbreviations in reviews

pub denotes the publisher and is followed by the region of publication – UK, US, Jp (for Japan) or Aus (Australia)

ser refers to the magazine in which the manga was originally serialized, with dates where appropriate

vols refers to the number of volumes to date of a manga, with individual regions specified where appropriate

age is the recommended US age rating where this is given on the manga itself, namely 13+, 16+ and 18+. Where there's no rating given, it's because the publisher doesn't use ratings or the manga is suitable for everyone – read the review itself to get a better idea of suitability.

Acknowledgements

It's both simple and difficult to write an acknowledgements section – simple because you have in mind a whole list of people you want to thank, difficult because you have a feeling of dread lurking in the background that you're going to forget someone. First of all, thanks to Sean Mahoney, who believed in my work enough to offer me the opportunity to write what you're now reading, and to Kate Berens, Andrew Lockett and the rest of the Rough Guides team for helping to nudge, poke, prod and otherwise will this project to completion. Thank you also to Simon Richmond and Abe Chang, who helped polish up the Manga Chronicles, Manga Goes Global and Beyond Manga sections respectively, as deadlines grew tight. This book also wouldn't be a reality if not for the help and support of Wilma Jandoc, my dearest friend and colleague who will always be the Tag-Team Partner in Anime and Manga Fandom for me. Thanks also to my other friends who kept me sane and laughing throughout my many months of book-writing: Charlene Robinson, Christina Chun and Jackie Carberry. A special nod to people who helped and supported me throughout my career: my mom and dad (of course!), Brandi-Ann Uyemura, Tracy Orillo-Donovan, Jim Borg, Gary Chun, Lucy Young-Oda and my Mililani Missionary Church family. And of course, I must thank Carrie Higa, the friend whose copy of the first volume of *Maison Ikkoku* started me on a journey that I never could have imagined would have included writing a book available worldwide. Much love to you all.

Rough Guides would like to thank Chloë Roberts for tireless work on the pictures; Link Hall for design and last-minute font work; Jane Lui and Evelyn Dubocq at Viz Media for assisting with the cover; and Mr Yohei Tanahashi at Kodansha Ltd, Amy Huey at Dark Horse, Kaoru Morimura at Tuttle-Mori, Jessica at Vertical, Adam Arnold at Seven Seas, Colin Turner at Last Gasp, Peter Goodman at Stone Bridge, Rumana Haider at Simon & Schuster UK, Andrew Whelan and Vy Nguyen at Tokyopop, Amiram Reuveni at Fanfare/Ponent Mon and Frank Pannone at Media Blasters for their help in the production of this book.

Manga Chronicles

the story of manga

For manga's most recent fans, the story of Japanese comics begins within the last decade, in bookstores around the world, their shelves stacked with the latest volumes of top-selling titles, such as *Fruits Basket*, *Naruto* and *Death Note*. Another wave of fans date themselves back to the 1980s and 90s, when *Dragon Ball Z*, *Sailor Moon* and several series by Rumiko Takahashi ruled far more modest sales charts. Then there are the hardcore fans who confidently claim that it all began when the God of Manga, otherwise known as Osamu Tezuka, created a character named Tetsuwan Atom, better known by his Western name – Astro Boy. The truth, though, is that the history of manga goes back further even than the contribution of Tezuka, significant though it was. How much further is a topic of dispute, but there's no doubt that today's manga is the result of centuries of artistic and stylistic influences.

The seeds of manga

The Japanese have been culturally attuned to reading stories through pictures down the centuries. It can be argued that the stylistic seeds of what eventually would be called manga were planted as far back as twelfth-century Japan in the form of **emakimono**, narrative "picture scrolls" with occasional text. *Emakimono* usually depicted people, animals or religious figures in a series of pictures that told a story, often rendered in ink with light washes of colour. Text was used only when necessary to explain what was going on. Readers viewed these scrolls, which sometimes stretched as long as eighty feet, a portion at a time from right to left. The most widely celebrated example of this art is *The Tale of Genji*, the tenth-century royal court romance attributed to Murasaki Shikibu and adapted to various forms of media over successive centuries. A manga version by Waki Yamato was even published in Japan by Kodansha between 1980 and 1993, and partially translated into English by the Kodansha Bilingual imprint.

For the purposes of manga history, though, scholars usually point at the **Chōjū jinbutsu giga** ("Scrolls of Frolicking Animals and Humans"), often shortened to *Chōjūgiga*, a set of four scrolls attributed to **Sōjō Toba**, head priest of a Buddhist sect near Kyoto. Differences in the quality of art have called into question whether Toba was solely responsible – some accounts date the first two scrolls to the early twelfth century and the last two to the mid-twelfth century, which would make it nearly impossible for him to have done them all unless he lived an exceptionally long life – but whoever the artist was, he had a great sense of humour. The first scroll depicted anthropomorphized animals engaging in human activities like gambling, watching cock fights, archery contests and water sports. The second scroll depicted fifteen different types of real and fantasy animals. The third and fourth scrolls satirized people at play, with animals mocking them.

As enjoyable as *emakimono* may have been, though, they were only seen by the clergy, aristocracy and select powerful warrior families. Art for the masses would not become possible until woodblock printing technology made large-scale production possible during the rule of the **Tokugawa shogunate** (1603–1867). It was during this era that the *shinōkōshō* class system came into play: warriors (*shi*) held the highest prestige during this time, followed in descending order by farmers (*nō*), artisans (*kō*) and merchants (*shō*). But while artisans and merchants were oppressed socially, the two classes prospered symbiotically; using woodblock printing tools, the artists could make a living selling their art to merchants, who in turn sold the art to other people.

Generally considered the closest relative to modern manga are **kibyōshi**, which hit their height of popularity in the late eighteenth century. Literally meaning "yellow covers", these illus- trated picture books contained around ten pages of drawings accompanied by explanatory captions and were produced from woodblock prints. While the subject of early *kibyōshi* were primarily children's stories, the format soared in popularity when artists took on the issues of the day through the use

One of manga's precursors: the "frolicking animals" of the *Chōjū jinbutsu giga,* thought to be by Buddish priest Sōjō Toba.

of satirical caricatures. The frequent targets of those jabs – the military government – were not amused, and when government reforms to reverse what was seen as moral decay were mocked in *kibyōshi* in 1787, authorities promptly launched a mass crackdown and censure of the art form.

The precursors of the manga art best-known outside of Japan are **ukiyo-e**, a print style that rose to prominence in Edo (modern-day Tokyo) in the latter half of the seventeenth century. The term *ukiyo-e* has been translated as "illustrations of the floating world", thought by some scholars to refer to Yoshiwara, Edo's theatre and brothel district. Indeed, there's quite a bit of *ukiyo-e* that depicts actors and courtesans of the era. But in an essay titled "From Shadow to Substance: Redefining Ukiyo-e", Sandy Kita proposed an expanded definition as being art that depicts the "here and now" as viewed by artists, which included landscapes, flora and fauna, and depictions of factual history and fictional heritage.

Two *ukiyo-e* artists would prove influential in this stage of manga's artistic development. **Katsushika Hokusai** (1760–1849) popularized the term "manga", meaning "whimsical sketches", as a description of his work, using it as the title of a series of sketchbooks released between 1814 and 1878. There was no story to speak of in these books; the closest Hokusai's manga gets to telling a story is in illustrating the Buddhist parable of blind men trying to describe an elephant. Instead, its pages were mostly

Otsu-e and Toba-e

Some of the earliest mass-produced art in Japan to feature caricatures was *otsu-e*. The name is derived from the place where these simple paintings were sold, in and around the post town of Otsu, which lay on the Tōkaidō Road running between Edo (present-day Tokyo) and Kyoto. Stands were set up along the road to sell these paintings, created by anonymous artists and their families, as souvenirs to passing travellers. The earliest *otsu-e*, dating from the first half of the seventeenth century, depicted Buddhist religious themes, but several decades later the subjects had broadened to include secular satirical cartoons, renderings of beautiful women, and – most popular of all – drunken goblins.

Toba-e, prints that originated in Osaka in the early eighteenth century, featured an art style that recalled the *Chōjūgiga* with its exaggerated caricatures. The defining work in this style was the *Tobae Sankokushi* by Shumboku Ooka, depicting long-legged, impish men in an everyday world.

Early Western influences

The arrival of US Commodore Matthew Perry on Japanese shores in 1853 and the subsequent signing of a treaty that opened the country's ports to the rest of the world offered a key opportunity for **cultural cross-pollination**. The start of what is known as the **Meiji Restoration** (the passing of power from the shogun back to the emperor and the subsequent changes in Japan's political and social structure) was a period when Japan, self-isolated from the world for centuries, became a sponge for other cultures and technology.

Equally so, it didn't take long for Japan's artists to start making an impact abroad. Old *ukiyo-e* prints, used as packing in tea boxes sent from Japan, found their way to European art lovers and artists, who were astounded by the otherworldly beauty of what they saw. The impact of this art, which can be seen in the works of Impressionists such as Renoir and the prints and posters of Toulouse-Lautrec, created a movement known as **Japonism**. With its growing popularity abroad, *ukiyo-e* that once was relegated to the lower classes became elevated in the eyes of the government, which saw this style of art as a tool to promote lucrative trade with Western markets.

Western visitors to Japan also provided inspiration. Print artists in Yokohama

© Simon Richmond

The first work to be called "manga"? Hosukai's artwork on display at the Kyoto Manga Museum in Japan.

filled with whatever subjects caught the artist's fancy at the time, including people, gods, monsters, animals, architecture and the environment.

Tsukioka Yoshitoshi, also known as Taiso Yoshitoshi (1839–92), produced even more extravagant and innovative *ukiyo-e* works, which he preferred to call *kyoga*, or "crazy pictures". In Yoshitoshi's art, one sees a vibrant glorification of often blood-filled violence that certainly has echoes in modern manga.

Charles Wirgman's expat magazine influenced a new style of cartooning in Japan, known as *ponchi-e*.

would assist in the evolution of Japan's highly developed style of caricature towards what we know today as manga.

Charles Wirgman (1832–91) was an artist and the chief foreign correspondent for the *Illustrated London News*, the world's first illustrated magazine, who was sent to China to cover the Second Opium War between the Chinese Qing Dynasty, France and the UK in 1857. After three years there, Wirgman moved on to Nagasaki and would remain in Japan for the rest of his life. He sketched scenes of daily life for *Illustrated London News* readers that are thought to have inspired many British travellers and merchants to strike out for Japan.

In 1862 Wirgman began publishing *Japan Punch*, a humour magazine modelled after the British *Punch* and aimed at his fellow expatriates. The ten-page issues, published intermittently through the 1860s, 70s and 80s, employed a whimsical style and often satirized Japanese politics, society and customs while examining the roots of Japanese–Western conflict. Meanwhile, Japanese art students were introduced to and began to emulate Wirgman's style through his oil painting classes.

The second expat to make a mark was **Georges Bigot** (1860–1927), a French newspaper and book illustrator who moved to Japan in 1882 and began drawing caricatures for his own satirical magazines. His greatest contribution to Japanese cartooning would come in 1887 with *Toba-e*, a magazine he

producing the city's *ukiyo-e* counterpart, *yokohama-e*, began depicting everyday scenes of foreigners going about their business in the port city. But it was two European expatriates in particular who co-created with the philosopher Nakae Chōmin. Bigot is believed to be the first artist in Japan to employ narrative sequential panels in his cartoons. *Toba-e* lasted for only three years, but in that time Bigot managed to draw caricatures that were so damning of the excesses of the Meiji Restoration that the magazine had to be circulated in secret.

Although aimed primarily at Western expats, the works of Wirgman and Bigot inspired some Japanese artists to adopt the new styles for their own newspapers, magazines and political cartoons. As this happened, the term **ponchi-e** – cartoons in the style of the Japanese *Punch* – was coined. Honda Kinkichiro is credited as the first Japanese artist to draw a multi-frame cartoon – six panels in a July 1881 issue of the weekly satire magazine *Kibidango*. Four years later, the first serialized frame comic strip – Beisaku Taguchi's *Enoshima – Kamakura Chōtan Ryokō* was published in the weekly magazine *Marumaru Chinbun*.

Style takes shape: 1900–45

At the dawn of the twentieth century new American comic strips, such as the Yellow Kid and *The Katzenjammer Kids*, began to filter into Japan, further inspiring local artists to emulate this Western way of telling stories. One such artist, **Rakuten Kitazawa** (1876–1955),

is considered by manga historians to be the founding father of the art form as it's known today. Kitazawa started his career in 1895 at *Box of Curios*, an English-language magazine published in Yokohama. In 1902, while working at the daily Japanese newspaper *Jiji Shimpo*, Kitazawa created the first serialized Japanese comic strip with recurring characters, *Tagosaku to Mokube no Tokyo Kembutsu* (*Tagosaku and Mokube Sightseeing in Tokyo*). Three years later he began publishing a full-colour weekly cartoon magazine, *Tokyo Puck*, which regularly focused on international events and was translated into English and Chinese. Among his beloved characters were the street kid Donsha and flapper girl Haneko. Kitazawa's contribution to manga art can't be underestimated, especially since he founded a school in 1934 to train cartoon artists.

Another pioneer of the modern manga scene is **Ippei Okamoto** (1886–1948), who worked for the *Asahi* newspaper and was the founder of Nippon Mangakai, Japan's first society of cartoonists. Ippei helped introduce a wider local readership to the blossoming American newspaper comic strip format in the 1920s through helping arrange the Japanese syndication of George McManus's *Bringing Up Father* and Bud Fisher's *Mutt and Jeff*. A translated version of *Bringing Up Father* was first serialized in November 1923, but the format really took off when Japanese newspapers took on their own artists

Tales from America: The Four Immigrants Manga

Around the time newspaper-style comic strips were growing in popularity in Japan largely thanks to foreign expatriates, a Japanese expatriate was working on a comic of his own. Yoshitaka Kiyama emigrated to the United States in 1904, adopted the Western first name of Henry, and took up classes at the San Francisco Art Institute while working at a variety of jobs. His artwork earned him several awards between 1915 and 1920, a number of exhibitions in San Francisco, and even a scholarship from the New York Art Students League.

But it was an exhibition he held in San Francisco in February 1927 that gives him a place in Japanese manga history. It was at that exhibition that he displayed what he called *Manga Hokubei Iminshi* (*A Manga North American History*), 52 comic-style episodes depicting the lives of Kiyama and three of his friends in San Francisco over a twenty-year period, beginning with his arrival. Kiyama tried to get a newspaper to publish his work, but its novelistic length – 104 pages – was likely a key factor in his lack of success.

Courtesy of Stone Bridge Press

Instead, he published the comic book himself, going back to Tokyo in 1931 to get it printed and returning to San Francisco with copies of the newly retitled *Manga Yonin Shosei* (*The Four Students Manga*). It came complete with forewords and praise from influential figures such as the Japanese consul general for its documentary-style veracity (each of the manga's characters speaks in his native tongue, be it Japanese, English or even Chinese) and humour.

And that might have been the end of the story were it not for Frederik L. Schodt's finding the book in a library in Berkeley, California, in 1980. Seventeen years later, he began translating it for an English-speaking audience, and in 1998 Stone Bridge Press released the book as *The Four Immigrants Manga: A Japanese Experience in San Francisco, 1904–1924*. And so what was arguably the first manga – if not the first graphic novel of any type – to be released in the US was reintroduced, for a new generation to appreciate.

who worked in the new American style of four-panel cartoons, known in Japanese as **yonkoma** manga.

Yutaka Aso's *Nonki na Tosan* (*Easygoing Daddy*), a four-panel strip that debuted in the *Hochi* newspaper in January 1924, was a direct artistic successor to *Bringing Up Father*, but with a Japanese cultural spin. **Shigeo Miyao**, thought to be one of the first artists to specialize in children's comics, tweaked the formula further, compiling his strips *Manga Taro* (*Comics Taro*) and *Dango Kushisuke Man'yuki* (*The Adventures of Dango Kushisuke*) in book form. The latter, about a samurai-superman, became a bestseller and was reprinted over one hundred times.

Manga prototypes

The early twentieth century also saw the emergence of **magazines** aimed at children that served as prototypes for modern-day manga magazines. While today's magazines often devote hundreds of pages solely to manga, these early magazines mixed in comic strips and single cartoons with articles illustrated with photographs and illustrated stories, all printed in considerable amounts of colour. Magazines from the 1930s like *Shōnen Club* (for boys), *Shōjo Club* (for girls) and *Yonen Club* (for younger children) were already targeting specific audiences, a trait that has carried over to modern publications.

© Simon Richmond

Norakuro (*Black Stray*), seen here at the Kyoto Manga Museum in Japan, featured in one of the first tankōbon.

The comic strip stories originally published in these magazines were also compiled in hardcover books, known as **tankōbon**. Among the most popular were Suihō Tagawa's *Norakuro* (*Black Stray*), about an anthropomorphic stray dog's rise in the Japanese Imperial Army, first published in 1931. From the same era also came Keizo Shimada's *Boken Dankichi* (*Dankichi the Adventurer*),

© Theo Wargo/WireImage/Getty Images

Astro Boy: Osamu Tezuka's enduring character has come to symbolize manga around the globe.

about a boy who rises to power on a Pacific island; and the sci-fi adventure *Kasei Tanken* (*Mars Expedition*) by Taro Asahi and Noboru Oshiro, about a boy who dreams about travelling to Mars.

All of these developments in Japanese comics occurred against a backdrop of **social change** and an ideological shift in government. While there were a few sources of artistic countercultural thought during this time, influenced primarily by Marxist theory from the Soviet Union, these soon were muzzled by the government's "Peace Preservation Law", which intimidated artists and their editors into self-censoring their work. The collapse of financial markets worldwide in 1929 crippled the Japanese economy, widening the gap between the government and its people. Growing unrest over this situation eased the way for an expansion-minded military to take control of a weakened government.

The content of comics in the 1930s through to the end of World War II shifted accordingly. Many cartoonists who were once anti-government either willingly fell in step in support of the army and its goals of Japanese colonial expansion in the region or were threatened by social ostracism, detentions and censorship into promoting the new goals. Following the bombing of Pearl Harbor in 1941, many cartoonists found themselves surplus to requirements as the nation's resources were diverted to the war. Those that continued to work did so either on uncontroversial family-friendly comic strips or propaganda that elevated the status of the Imperial Army while vilifying the Allied forces.

Tezuka's impact: 1945–59

Following the nation's unconditional surrender in 1945, most Japanese – intent on rebuilding their lives after the devastation of the war – had little time or money for publications of any kind, including manga. This hit the big pre-war publishers hard, as did Allied occupation force censorship of certain subjects: art forms, including manga, had to steer clear of topics that might inspire a resurgence of militarism, which put a temporary stop to political cartoons.

Even so, people were hungry for entertainment that could help them forget about the past or distract them from the present. Catering to this need, a cottage industry of new publishers emerged in Osaka, printing cheap, long-format story comics called **akahon** ("red books") for their red-ink covers and selling them from street stalls. It was in *akahon* that a young medical student called Osamu Tezuka would make his first distinctive mark in manga history.

While he might be universally known today as the "God of Manga", perhaps the most divine blessing bestowed upon this prolific artist was that he came along at just the right time in manga history. When the nineteen-year-old Tezuka

made his *akahon* debut in 1947 with the release of **Shin-Takarajima** (*New Treasure Island*), a kids' adventure story created with his cartoonist friend Shichima Sakai, the impact on the struggling Japanese comic market was undeniable. In a grim post-war world hungry for novelty, *Shin-Takarajima* was a sensation, selling around 400,000 copies, without the benefit of publicity.

Shin-Takarajima was far from perfect: the published version reportedly was trimmed down from Tezuka's original draft of 250 pages to 60. Tezuka himself banned reprints until later in his career, and even then the version released was one largely redrawn to adhere closer to his original vision for the book. And its initial sales most likely had more to do with *akahon* being the most affordable form of entertainment at the time rather than because of the quality of the story or its presentation.

All this said, it's generally recognized that while earlier artists may have pioneered the cinematic style of manga, Tezuka refined it in *Shin-Takarajima*, with the art appearing like dynamic still frames of objects in motion, shot by a camera at different angles.

Shin Takarajima (New Treasure Island)

Shichima Sakai (story), Osamu Tezuka (story and art); *pub* Ikuei Publishing (Jp, 1947), Kodansha (Jp, 1984 reissue); *vols* 1

Tezuka's first bestselling book thrilled readers with the adventures of Pete, a boy

Osamu Tezuka

Manga artist / anime director, 1928–89

"Please, please let me continue to work…" These were reportedly the last words from a man who during his life had produced no fewer than 150,000 pages of manga for around 600 different titles, not to mention scores of animated works, and had acted as a global ambassador for the art form in its crucial boom years from the 1950s through to the 1980s. Small wonder that Osamu Tezuka is commonly referred to as the "God of Manga".

Tezuka's skills lay in his ability to innovate and adapt, paying tribute to what already existed while taking those conventions to another level with his artistic style. He was a fan of the Disney and Fleischer animated films that had made it into the country, and the art he drew – with what would soon become the trademark of Japanese cartoon art, big-eyed characters – paid homage to the character designs of those films. He was also obsessed with perfection in his art, often revisiting his earlier works to change the order of the story chapters and tweaking the artwork whenever they were reprinted.

The characters themselves were like a travelling troupe of virtual actors, with Tezuka as the director (indeed, he would frequently insert a caricature of himself into his series, always wearing his trademark beret). The Tezuka **"star system"** took secondary characters like Mustachio, Dr Ochanomizu, Hamegg and Spider and placed them in different series, sometimes with different names and occupations – like actors taking on different roles. The storytelling mechanism was influenced heavily by his frequent visits as a youth to see the famed Takarazuka Revue, an all-female theatre troupe in his home town of Takarazuka that specialized in performing lavish, Broadway-style romantic musicals.

What also helped drive Tezuka's popularity was his ability to provide audiences with exactly what they wanted. At the start of his career, epic stories like *New Treasure Island*, *Princess Knight* and *Astro Boy* captivated the post-war, entertainment-starved audience. As the children who read his manga aged and manga began edging towards grittier fare influenced by the *gekiga* movement, Tezuka responded with more complex, adult-oriented series, delving into such subjects as the human psyche, religion and spirituality.

His sphere of influence extended beyond manga, too. *Astro Boy*, first broadcast on Japanese TV in 1963, was the realization of his dream to become an animator like Walt Disney. While his studio, Mushi Productions, struggled financially from the day it opened to when it went bankrupt in 1973, Tezuka gained much respect and won awards for experimental shorts such as *Tales of the Street Corner* (1962); the *Fantasia*-inspired *Pictures at an Exhibition* (1966); *Jumping* (1984); and his final film, *Self Portrait* (1988). He also pioneered animation for adults in the late 1960s with *Arabian Nights* and *Cleopatra*.

who discovers a treasure map left by his deceased father and sets out with his dad's friend, Captain, to find the treasure, encountering hordes of pirates and savage tribesmen along the way. The version published in 1947 was heavily edited by Tezuka's collaborator; for the reissue, Tezuka relied on his memory to restore most of the cut material, bringing the work closer to his original vision.

A maturing audience

After the Treaty of San Francisco, between the Allied powers and Japan, came into force in 1952, officially ending World War II, many government restrictions were removed, including those relating to press censorship. Along with his fellow artists Tezuka was now free to produce the types of stories he wanted to, not necessarily targeting children as his audience.

Tezuka saw the potential for more complex, adult-oriented stories told in manga form. "I also believed that comics were capable of more than just making people laugh," Tezuka wrote in his autobiography. "So in my themes I

Busting the Tezuka myths

Tezuka's status as "God of Manga" has led to several myths about his influence on the medium:

✦ He pioneered manga's cinematic style of laying out frames – in fact, this way of drawing cartoon action was already evident in Sakō Shishido's *Spiido Tarō* (*Speedy Tarō*) in 1930, and was refined by Katsuji Matsumoto in his seminal shōjo manga of 1934, *Nazo no Kurōbaa* (*The Mysterious Clover*). Noboru Oshiro's work from the same era also hinted at cinematic influence.

✦ He invented shōjo manga – this had actually existed as a distinct category since 1903 with the publication of *Shōjo Kai* (*Girl's World*) magazine, which carried illustrated novel serializations, and *Shōjo* magazine, which carried the manga *Anmitsu-hime*. Also see Katsuji Matsumoto's work mentioned above.

✦ He was the first to produce an extended manga series – an award that rightly should go to Rakuten Kitazawa, who created the first serialized Japanese comic strip with recurring characters – *Tagosaku to Mokube no Tokyo Kembutsu* (*Tagosaku and Mokube Sightseeing in Tokyo*) – in 1902; or to Shigeo Miyao who had an extended serial with *Manga Tarō* in 1912; or Suihō Tagawa's *Norakuro* books, which were smash hits in the 1930s.

incorporated tears, grief, anger, and hate, and I created stories where the ending was not always 'happy.'"

Such themes were incorporated into his follow-ups to *Shin-Takarajima*, including the sophisticated sci-fi trilogy *Lost World* (published in 1948), *Metropolis* (1949) and *Kurubeki Sekai* (*Next World*, 1951). Even though these titles featured child characters and had a "cartoony" rather than realistic appearance, they appealed to more mature readers and helped form a defining line between the older generation that considered manga to be "kids' stuff" and stopped reading around middle school and the younger generation that took manga for granted as a medium for all ages.

Tezuka wasn't the only mangaka (manga artist) catering to this growing market, which thrived particularly in the rental libraries, or **kashihonya** (see box, below), often patronized by older manga readers. Such manga, which featured more adult and action-oriented themes and had more realistic characters and art, became known as **gekiga**, or "drama pictures". Coining that word and defining the movement was artist **Yoshihiro Tatsumi**, who created a monthly serial, *Kage* (*Shadow*), to showcase *gekiga* in 1957. Several of Tatsumi's stories in *Kage* offered a raw, unfettered look at a Japan still wounded deeply by its losses in World War II and struggling to recover. The term *gekiga* is still used

From kashihonya to tachiyomi

In the immediate post-war years few people had spare change to buy manga, so fans turned to the services of pay libraries, or **kashihonya**, where lenders let patrons borrow books and comics for a small fee based on the length of time they were borrowed. In many cases customers got their manga fix standing in the store or on the pavement nearby and reading, an activity known as **tachiyomi** (a combination of the characters for "standing" and "reading"). Such businesses remained popular well into the 1960s when they began to die out as incomes rose and people could afford to buy their own manga.

Even in these more affluent times the *kashihonya* concept hasn't entirely disappeared. Highly popular are manga coffee shops where patrons have on-site access to vast libraries of manga titles, supplemented by drinks, Internet and videogames, all for a flat, time-based fee. Meanwhile the free activity of *tachiyomi* is very much alive and kicking, as a visit to any Japanese bookstore or one of the millions of 24-hour grocery stores will prove.

today to describe underground, avant-garde works.

Manga monthlies

As the same time that Tezuka was producing his early *akahon* works, he was also being commissioned by two new monthly magazines – *Manga Shōnen*, published by Gakudosha, and *Shōnen* magazine, published by Kobunsha – to create what would become two of his career-defining series. *Jungle Taitei* (*Jungle Emperor*), the series that Western audiences would later know as **Kimba the White Lion**, went to *Manga Shōnen* and became the first single-story manga serialized in a magazine, starting in 1950, while *Shōnen* received *Tetsuwan Atomu* (*Mighty Atom*), the series that would become **Astro Boy** in the West, starting in 1952.

Eventually the demand for Tezuka's comics was such that he would move in 1953 from Osaka to Tokyo, the centre of publishing in Japan, where he would set up a studio in the city's **Tokiwaso** apartment complex a year later. Other mangaka who would also go on to become legends in the industry soon joined him at Tokiwaso – people who also got their start in *Manga Shōnen*.

While the magazine would only run for eight years from its debut in 1947, **Manga Shōnen** was significant in that it featured predominantly manga rather than the comic/prose combination that had been the blueprint for post-war children's magazines. Secondly, while most of it was professionally produced, audience participation was invited for the first time, with the magazine hosting regular contests where readers could submit short samples of manga stories for evaluation. The best were sent winners' badges, some even rewarded with publication and, perhaps, a shot at being commissioned to create a regularly serialized story. Artists who got their start this way include the creative duo Fujiko Fujio (*Doraemon*), Leiji Matsumoto (*Galaxy Express 999*) and Shōtarō Ishinomori (*Cyborg 009*).

Publishers also started to target girl manga fans, in what would become the **shōjo manga** market. Shosuke Kuragane's *Anmitsu-hime*, which ran from 1949 to 1955, followed a princess (*hime*) with a mouthwatering name (*anmitsu* being a popular Japanese dessert) and her life with her royal family and attendants (who also had names derived from foods). The theory behind *Anmitsu-hime* was that the tale would provide a fantasy escape for an audience living in a world where such luxurious food items were still in short supply, and it seemed to work, lifting sales of Kobunsha's *Shōjo* magazine to 700,000 copies.

Ever with his finger on the pulse, Tezuka also created the genre-defining shōjo manga series called *Ribon no Kishi* (*Princess Knight*) in Kodansha's *Shōjo Club* magazine in 1953. Soon afterward, two girl-targeted monthly magazines would debut: Kodansha's *Nakayoshi* in

Machiko Hasegawa, one of the earliest women mangaka, portrayed with her titular character Sazae-san.

December 1954 and Shueisha's *Ribon* anthology in August 1955. They are both still published today and are considered national institutions.

But while these series and magazines were all aimed at girls, at the time the people creating them remained predominantly male. One of the few female mangaka from this era was Machiko Hasegawa, creator of the comic strip *Sazae-san*, about the exploits of a housewife and her extended family. The strip, which debuted in the *Fukunichi* newspaper in 1946 and was picked up by the *Asahi* newspaper in 1949 when Hasegawa moved to Tokyo, ran through until 1974 when the artist retired.

Sazae-san

Machiko Hasegawa; *pub* Shimaisha (Jp, reprints until 1993), Asahi Shimbun (Jp, reprints 1993–), Kodansha International (US, selected comic strips, 1997); *ser* various newspapers 1946–74

Pioneering female mangaka Hasegawa's Sazae-san is one of the most famous manga characters in Japan. As post-war Japanese society – and especially the roles of women – evolved, so too did the adventures of Sazae Fuguta, a "liberated" woman of the 1940s who marries Masuo, a 28-year-old salaryman. Even though the story of their life together mirrored contemporary life in Japan, from the food rationing and American occupation in the late 1940s through the hippie and feminist movements in later years, the characters themselves never aged. The four-panel strips were turned into an anime series in 1969 that is still going today, making it the longest-running animated TV series in history.

Jungle Taitei (Jungle Emperor Leo) / Kimba the White Lion

Osamu Tezuka; *pub* Gakudosha (Jp, 1950–54), not licensed for English translation; *vols* 3

Leo is a white lion borne from tragedy. His father is killed by a hunter in the African jungle; his mother gave birth to him at sea while being held captive on a ship en route to an overseas zoo. Seeing no hope for herself, Leo's mother tells him to swim back to Africa and take his rightful place as king of the jungle. The ship later sinks in a storm, taking her with it, but Leo does make it back to Africa. Now, with the help of a human boy named Kenichi, Leo hopes to establish an animal kingdom that protects weaker animals. *Jungle Taitei* would go on to become the first animated TV series to air in colour in Japan, as well as one of the first Japanese animations to air in the US (as *Kimba the White Lion*).

Ribon no Kishi (Princess Knight)

Osamu Tezuka; *pub* Kodansha (Jp, 1953–66), Kodansha International (US, 2001); *vols* 6

Tezuka's first series aimed at a female audience features a character with a rather conflicted identity: Sapphire, a princess who has both a boy's and a girl's mind thanks to a trick played by an angel. The problem is that while she's a girl in appearance, the law of the land already has decreed that she should rule the land… as a *prince*. What's worse is that Duke Duralumin has a son that he wants to inherit the throne and will stop at nothing to reveal Sapphire for what she really is. The all-female drama troupe Takarazuka Revue was an inspiration for this story. Also worth noting is the glittering star Tezuka inserts in every pupil.

Advent of the weeklies

By the late 1950s, with Japan's economy well on the way to recovery, more people could afford to buy more manga more often. At the same time, radio and television were becoming increasingly popular, and publishers realized they would have to ramp up their publication schedules from the monthly model so as not to lose readers to other forms of entertainment.

On the same day, 17 March 1959, rival weekly magazines **Shōnen Sunday** (a Shogakukan production) and **Shōnen** (from Kodansha) launched, both failing in an attempt to be first on the market. Like *Nakayoshi* and *Ribon*, the magazines are still published today. They remain competing publications but in a rare alliance between the two, as part of their fiftieth anniversary celebrations in 2008–09, each magazine featured a cross-promotional cover image of boxer Ippo, from the *Shōnen* series *Hajime no Ippo*, shaking hands with young detective Conan Edogawa, from the *Shōnen Sunday* series *Detective Conan / Case Closed*.

The success of the weekly manga magazine format over the monthlies may have been a financial boon for publishers, but it was a bane for the manga artists, who were subsequently required to churn out four times as much material. As the manga industry skewed more towards producing titles for younger readers,

Real-life inspiration

During his career Osamu Tezuka tackled a wide variety of subjects, mostly fantastic and springing from his own imagination. Occasionally, though, he took inspiration from real life and incorporated historical figures into his manga or created manga based on other people's works that he felt passionately about. Here's a few of the well-known subjects from lesser-known series in Tezuka's catalogue of work (at least those published in the English-speaking world).

Adolf Hitler

During the war there was a community of European Jewish refugees living in Kōbe, a port city not far from where Tezuka lived in Takarazuka. It's very likely that Tezuka knew about this community and its circumstances and that this knowledge inspired his series *Adorufu ni Tsugu* (*Tell Adolf*; 5 vols, 1983–85; published in English as *Adolf* by Viz's Cadence Books, 1995–96). This epic tale of mysterious murders and political intrigue spanning decades features three Adolfs – the real leader of the Nazi Party, and a German boy and his Jewish friend living in Japan at the onset of World War II. This is one of Tezuka's most adult-themed works and, although the story tends towards melodrama, it is also a gripping thriller with a moving conclusion.

Crime and Punishment

In 1947, while at college, Tezuka had a bit part in a stage production of Dostoyevsky's *Crime and Punishment*. This exposure to the great Russian novel inspired him to create his own manga version of it in 1953, entitled *Tsumi to Batsu* (published in a bilingual Japanese/English edition by *Japan Times*). Tezuka's manga retained the dark, philosophical themes of the original but simplified the story so children could understand it and changed the ending. It was the only manga version he drew of an already published novel.

Ludwig von Beethoven

Tezuka once wrote: "I feel that my personality is very similar to that of Beethoven. He was moody, naïve, egocentric and he had a short fuse. We also share one very peculiar thing: we're both compulsive 'movers'. Beethoven loved moving houses and so do I." At the end of his life Tezuka started working on *Ludwig B* (1987–89, untranslated), a biography of his favourite composer from early childhood, when he was a prodigy already suffering pain in his ears. The series had yet to be completed when Tezuka died.

artists who wanted to work in a more mature style had to seek publication elsewhere, mostly in the rental titles carried at *kashihonya*. More importantly, though, this shift to faster production led to the slow demise of more costly and complex colour printing and the thoughtful political and editorial cartoons that once defined comics in Japan.

Tetsujin-28

Mitsuteru Yokoyama; *pub* Kobunsha (Jp, 1956–66); not licensed for English translation

Mitsuteru Yokoyama's manga was the first to feature in a starring role that mainstay of manga and anime: the giant robot. In this case, the robot is the 28th in a series of robots that were designed to defend Japan during the war – hence the title, meaning "Iron Man 28". Afterwards, the robot's mission was changed from fighting to peacekeeping. Under the control of a young boy, Shotaro Kaneda, it fights crime around the world… that is, if its remote control doesn't fall into the wrong hands. The animated adaptation of this story would air in the US in the mid-1960s as *Gigantor*.

Maturity and diversity: 1960–79

As the industry headed into the 1960s, it was clear that more artists would be needed to meet the surging demand for manga, from both readers and the publishers who needed to fill pages in their anthologies. Within a few years of the creation of *Shōnen Sunday* and *Shōnen*, there were five shōnen weeklies and two shōjo weeklies in print. The most notable of these newcomers both debuted in 1963, when the publisher Shōnen Gahōsha launched *Shōnen King* and Shueisha started publishing the first shōjo magazine to go weekly, *Margaret*.

While a market would always exist for the younger readers, manga publishers became concerned about holding on to teenage and young adult readers who were growing out of the kids' fare that shōnen and shōjo publications offered. There was little available that bridged the gap between these series and the much more adult-themed works of the *gekiga* artists.

In an effort to keep older readers engaged, the savviest manga publishers began to turn to *gekiga* artists to provide new, more mature material than was typically run in their mass-market magazines. Some took up the offer, and those creators, with their more unconventional approaches, helped shōnen in particular expand its readership and reach new highs in copies sold. In 1965, *Magazine* editor Masaru Uchida invited *gekiga* artists to ply their craft in his pages; the result was a sales boom in both child and teen readership, with circulation approaching 1 million a year later.

However, the heavy workload, potential for editorial interference and lack of creative freedom were costs that not all *gekiga* artists were willing to pay, regardless of how much money publishers offered. One such artist who chose to go in a different direction was **Sanpei Shirato**. A key figure in the early *gekiga* movement, he had survived the collapse of the *kashihonya* market of rental manga to create a few period pieces for *Shōnen* magazine, but creatively he wasn't happy working for such a mainstream publication.

In the summer of 1964, Shirato helped to finance a new avant-garde magazine being set up by a small publisher, Katsuichi Nagai. Nagai was so impressed with a proposal that Shirato had for a new series about ninjas, *Kamui Den* (*Legend of Kamui*), that he agreed to create a monthly magazine to showcase it and other similarly cutting-edge and experimental manga works. The magazine was called **Garo** after one of Shirato's characters, and his series' popularity helped the publication become a hit among the older, more intellectual audience that the publication courted.

Specifically, what made *Garo* different from the likes of *Shōnen* was that the artists retained total editorial control over their work, a model that appealed to mangaka who didn't want to turn out mass-produced cartoony or action-adventure pieces but instead wished to explore the medium intellectually and on a more personal level. This resulted in a magazine that not only contained a wide range of drawing styles, few of which conformed to the fashions of the time, but also a publication that was equally happy to publish works by female artists who – despite the rise of shōjo titles – were still finding it hard to break into the male-dominated industry.

Garo's sales figures were never significant enough to make much of a dent in the overall manga market, its circulation peaking at eighty thousand copies in the early 1970s, a fraction of *Magazine*'s million copies. But its very existence had an effect on the industry nonetheless, inspiring Osamu Tezuka to publish his own avant-garde monthly manga magazine, **COM**, in January 1967. In COM's five-year life, it featured not only some of the master's most ambitious manga, including episodes of his life's work *Hi no Tori* (*Phoenix*; see p.171), but also launched other promising young artists.

Back to politics

Kamui Den, as it turned out, was the right manga for the right period in Japanese history. Its themes of class struggle against injustice and corrupt authority were perfect for an emerging college student resistance movement who, like their contemporaries around the world, railed against the issues of the day, such as the growing conflict in Vietnam and the continued existence of American forces on Japanese soil. By the late 1960s, editors at several

Serving the public for thirty years

Befitting a series with such a long name, *Kochira Katsushika-ku Kameari Kōen-mae Hashutsujo* (*This is the Police Station in Front of Kameari Park in Katsushika Ward*) by Osamu Akimoto is also the longest continually serialized manga. The first chapter of what's more handily known as *Kochikame*, introducing middle-aged policeman Kankichi Ryōtsu, appeared on 21 September 1976 in *Weekly Shōnen Jump*, and Akimoto has not missed a week since. More than 150 volumes have been collected of the series to date, which, strangely enough, has never made actual police work a central part of its story. Sure, Ryōtsu has superhuman strength from time to time, but it's rarely applied to his work, focusing instead on his never-ending quest to get more money by whatever crackpot scheme necessary. The story can also be considered a homage to the working-class districts of Tokyo from thirty or forty years ago, with their sense of community and kindness.

The series celebrated its thirtieth anniversary with the release of a special compilation, *Chō-Kochikame* (*Super Kochikame*). More than eighty manga creators, including Akira Toriyama, Takao Saito and Monkey Punch, contributed drawings, and Ryōtsu made cameo appearances in every series running in *Weekly Shōnen Jump* at the time. Publisher Shueisha also permanently installed two life-size bronze statues of Kankichi Ryōtsu at the north and south exits of Kameari station.

Sadly, don't count on Ryōtsu's adventures ever becoming available in wide distribution for an English-speaking audience. (There have been a couple of attempts at unauthorized scanlation – translations of the original manga – but these are no longer available.) The costs involved in licensing and producing such a large amount of manga are astronomical, and the amount of translation involved is likely to discourage even the wealthiest publishers. The only official English translation that exists to this day is a small portion of the series that was reprinted in the May 1996 issue of *Mangajin* magazine.

magazines were encouraging manga with **political and social themes**, resulting in series like *Harenchi Gakuen* (*Shameless School*) by Go Nagai, where male students and teachers seemingly learned more about the "three G's" (girls, gambling and a nice gin and tonic) than the traditional "three R's" of reading, writing and 'rithmetic. Just as rebellious teens and young adults turned to rock music to set themselves apart from their parents' generation, so too did they identify with these convention-breaking manga.

Also Japan's economic recovery inspired many to throw off the shame imposed on the nation following its defeat in World War II. In this context it's easy to see why readers also embraced the classic boxing manga *Ashita no Jō* (see p.80) by Tetsuya Chiba and Asao Takamori for the way the hero fought his way to fame and respect.

Mirroring the concerns and actions of their audience, some of the top manga artists at the time also became involved in the social changes Japan was going through. In 1969, for instance, artists Shōtarō Ishinomori, Fujiko Fujio, Shigeru Mizuki and Kogi Asaoka all aligned themselves with workers fighting factory exploitation and students battling the US–Japan Security Treaty.

This loose alliance between college revolutionaries and mangaka did not go unnoticed by the authorities. Between 1968 and 1970, bans on certain manga series were called for by local branches of the Parent Teacher Association, and protests against commercially available manga were organized. The government also started cracking down on the violence and more mature themes that were being introduced into children's stories, creating the Youth Policy Unit in 1967 and placing suspect manga on a "Harmful Designation List".

The continued prosperity of the Japanese economy would eventually dampen down student protests. Manga publishers were also forced to tone down the content of their mainstream publica-

tions, but some artists refused to let their series go quietly. When Nagai's publisher, Shueisha, drew the Youth Policy Unit's ire over *Harenchi Gakuen*, for instance, he agreed to end his series… but not before he depicted his opponents in the PTA storming the school and promptly getting annihilated in a climax that killed off both friends and foes alike.

For girls, by girls

In the midst of this drive to produce more mature stories (and the ensuing controversy), a quieter, albeit equally significant, revolution was taking place in the area of shōjo manga. As more female fans who had grown up reading manga during the 1950s came of age in the 1960s, they began to realize that the artists who were telling "their" stories were all men. While there were a few women who were working in the industry, their repertoires were rather limited, with most of their stories focusing on primary school girls in humour, horror or tragic settings.

The artist often cited as one of the strongest influences on the "**for girls, by girls**" movement, though, would be an up-and-coming teen artist who entered and won a talent competition in 1964. **Machiko Satonaka** was sixteen when her first work, *Pia no Shōzō* (*Portrait of Pia*), debuted in *Shōjo Friend* and earned her Kodansha's award for new artists that same year. Satonaka was confident that she knew better what female manga

The magnificent 24s ride into town

Within shōjo manga circles the year **1949** (which, according to the Japanese way of counting years, is known as Shōwa 24 – the 24th year of the reign of the Shōwa emperor, Hirohito) is key. That was the year that a fresh crop of female manga artists who began to make their mark in the late 1960s – women such as Moto Hagio, Riyoko Ikeda, Yumiko Oshima, Keiko Takemiya and Ryoko Yamagishi – were born. Manga scholars have dubbed this otherwise non-aligned group the **Hana no Nijūyon-nen Gumi** (Flowers of the Year 24 Group) for the collective artistic impact they had on the medium. Specifically genre defining was their more florid, floral style of presentation – a softening of the hard lines employed by their male counterparts and removal of the traditional borders that surrounded the action. For more on genre styles, see Chapter 3.

readers wanted than did male artists twice her age. In tune with the growing feminist sentiments of the era she also wanted to work in a profession that would not just give her independence but also allow her to be considered on an equal level with men.

Satonaka's success proved an inspiration as more female mangaka began contributing their work to manga magazines. Yoshiko Nishitani's high school romance series, including *Mary Lou*, *Jessica no Sekai* and *Remon to Sakuranbo*, were among the first to feature teenage girls as central characters – a staple of shōjo manga today. Manga also became the focus of other creative women artists and writers who switched their attention from the still male-dominated worlds of movies and television.

The stories told by these artists were predominantly stories of love gained, love lost and love longingly pined for. Yet, while the plots may not have been ground-breaking, the techniques used to tell them – as pioneered by the **Year 24 Group** of artists (see box, above) – were becoming increasingly complex and unique to the genre. One series in particular, Riyoko Ikeda's *Rose of Versailles* (see p.178), which incorporated real historical figures and a cross-dressing, androgynous lead character, not only changed the way love stories have been depicted in shōjo manga ever since but also was a contributing factor in the rise of the popular shōnen-ai (boys' love) genre.

It wasn't just the way romance stories were told that helped shōjo manga mature. Different, unique shōjo stories were being told as well. A few years after Japan's women's volleyball team captured the gold medal in the 1964 Olympics, women's athletics appeared on the story-telling radar for the first time with Chikako Urano's volleyball-based series *Attack No. 1* in 1968. *Tsuru-hime Ja!* (*Here's Princess Tsuru!*) in 1973 by Yoshiko Tsuchida, an understudy of male gag-manga artist Fujio Akatsuka, proved that women could tackle this hyperactive, nonsensical genre just as well as men.

The accelerating evolution of shōjo manga in the 1970s was, in effect, a microcosm of what was taking place in the industry during that decade. Women were proving that they could tackle different types of stories from their own perspectives, and the way they were telling those stories – sometimes by adopting shōnen manga conventions – attracted a crossover male audience to their work as well.

In addition, the manga generation from the 1940s and 50s had grown up and was now producing its own stories based on a diverse array of personal interests and experiences. Manga, rather than film or television, had become the preferred pop culture venue, being easily and cheaply accessible at bookstores, newsstands, train stations and coffee shops. Magazines were available for all different tastes and interests, often collecting several twenty- to thirty-page stories in a thick, 200- to 400-page stapled collection that could be as chunky as a typical phone book.

Manga, in short, was diversifying and adapting in the boom times of the Japanese economy. That diversification would prove to be a mixed blessing as the industry headed into what would turn out to be its peak period in Japan.

GeGeGe no Kitarō

Shigeru Mizuki; *pub* Kodansha (Jp, 1965–69), Kodansha International (US, 2002); *vols* Jp 9, US 3

Originally published under the title *Hibaka no Kitarō* (*Graveyard Kitarō*), this whimsical manga has as its hero Kitarō, one of two remaining members of the Ghost Tribe and a leading advocate for peace between humans and *yōkai* (a supernatural being in Japanese folklore, similar to a ghost). With the assistance of wise Daddy Eyeball, who is both Kitarō's father and a giant eyeball, the rodent-like *yōkai*/human Ratman, and a host of magic-imbued gizmos, one-eyed Kitarō fights monsters and does good deeds. While Mizuki's story is aimed at a shōnen audience, his art has a more realistic look owing to his experience working on *gekiga* series.

Apollo's Song

Osamu Tezuka; *pub* Shonen Gahosha (Jp, 1970), Vertical (US, 2007); *vols* 1

Chikaishi Shogo has never known love in his life and has become quite the violent delinquent. In an effort to prevent him from striking again, the police place him under the care of Dr. Enoki. Enoki subsequently subjects Shogo to a series of electrotherapy sessions, during which Shogo meets the goddess of love and undergoes the trials of love. Thus Shogo experiences a never-ending, Sisyphean cycle of romance, repeatedly thrust into a new situation in a different time, falling in love with a woman and subsequently losing her. Tezuka's favourite theme of the cycle of life and death is on display here, as are his ideas on the essence of love and sex.

Mazinger Z

Go Nagai; *pub* Kodansha (Jp); *ser* Weekly Shōnen Jump (1972–74); *vols* 5

Go Nagai, who cites among his early childhood influences *Tetsujin-28* and *Astro Boy*, came up with his own robot idea while sitting in traffic one day, imagining ways the drivers around him might escape the gridlock. His creation, a giant robot that could be controlled from the inside by a human, essentially established the mecha genre as it exists today. The series' hero, high school student Koji Kabuto, is living a normal life until evil forces destroy his home and mortally wound his grandfather. Before dying, the grandfather tells him of a powerful giant robot he was working on that has the power to do whatever he wishes. As the new pilot of the Mazinger Z, Koji battles Doctor Hell and his collection of mechanical menaces intent on world conquest.

The Genius Bakabon

Fujio Akatsuka; *pub* Kodansha (Jp, 1967–76), Kodansha Bilingual (US, 2000–01); *vols* 21 Jp, 3 US (suspended)

The Simpsons of its day, *Bakabon* features a family made up of a lovable dolt of a father, an sensible mother, a mischievous son (Bakabon) and a baby sibling who is a child prodigy. When it was first published in 1967, the series caused a stir for its fast-paced, anarchic, gag-laden humour – much of which seems pretty tame by today's standards. A typical plot involves either Bakabon and his dad coming up with outrageous solutions to what should be straightforward problems or dealing with the neighbours who make fun of their idiocy by trying to devise ways to fool them.

Buddha

Osamu Tezuka; *pub* Ushio Shuppansha (Jp, 1972–83), Vertical (US); *vols* Jp 14, US 8; *ser* various

Osamu Tezuka was fascinated by the cycle of life and death, and one of the lengthier series in the second half of his career was a retelling of the story of the life of Prince Siddhartha, the man who would later be revered as Gautama Buddha, and the prince's spiritual journey contemplating life, ageing, disease and death. While Tezuka has been lauded for the way the series brings the story of Buddha to life in a sequential art form, it should be noted that the series shouldn't be taken as biographical canon. Tezuka added fictional characters to the story and enhanced some of the historical figures for dramatic effect; traces of his earlier cartoony art style also pop up from time to time.

Manga for the masses: 1980–96

By the 1980s, the manga industry had matured to the point that there now existed a story for virtually everyone's tastes. Three of the core genres – shōjo for young girls, shōnen for young boys, seinen for the older male audience – had been established by the mid-1970s, while a fourth – josei manga, for women who wanted more mature plots – emerged as a distinct genre in the late 1970s. (For more on the main categories and genres of manga, see Chapter 3.)

The dōjinshi revolution

In the 1980s and 90s manga fans increasingly started to move beyond reading to creating. Fandom had grown to such an extent that conventions hosting hundreds of thousands of visitors were held to trade **dōjinshi**: self-published manga. Many dōjinshi use the characters from the amateur creator's favourite manga in new adventures and spins-offs from the original plots. So accurately are they drawn and so professionally are they put together that dōjinshi are often difficult to tell from the real thing.

Even though such publications flagrantly ignore Japanese copyright laws – not to mention sometimes depicting star characters in sexually compromising positions their official creators would never dream of placing them in – the dōjinshi scene has been allowed to flourish for a couple of reasons. Japan is largely a consensus-based society where direct confrontation is avoided – lawsuits are usually the very last, rather than the first resort of disgruntled citizens and corporations. Manga publishers and artists are also wary of alienating the most enthusiastic and, to a large extent, influential sector of their readership with heavy-handed tactics. Besides, these über-fans are not only serving up good ideas that manga publishers may capitalize on but also feeding the talent pool needed for the industry. Hence artists of the calibre of Rumiko Takahashi got their breaks in the industry by working on dōjinshi.

The highlight of the year for dōjinshi fans and creators – and the largest lovefest for manga and anime generally – comes in the form of Comic Market or **Comiket**, a three-day convention held twice a year at the Big Sight convention hall in Tokyo. The event, for fans by fans, debuted in December 1975 with about 600 participants and has since grown to an average attendance of 500,000. And that's just the visitors; there are an estimated 35,000 individuals and groups selling dōjinshi, model kits, videogames and unofficial memorabilia, with both original works and tributes to existing manga and anime series represented. The variety is so vast that a catalogue is usually available weeks in advance, listing exact locations of vendors and the genres in which they are working.

Many professional artists got their start as artists selling dōjinshi at Comiket, the most famous example being CLAMP. Many other artists, knowing full well what the professional manga industry entails as far as the work they would be asked to do, choose to remain dōjinshi artists for life, yet still generate professional-quality work. Some professional artists even come full circle and return to sell dōjinshi to eager fans who are more than willing to snap it up. And since much of the material sold at Comiket has limited print runs and likely never will be available to the public again, an added layer of frantic competition is added to the whole affair.

Thus, the groundwork had been laid for a new generation of artists to bring a fresh artistic and creative sensibility to the table, blurring the lines between genres like never before. Popular series like Akimi Yoshida's *Banana Fish* and Rumiko Takahashi's *Ranma ½* in 1987 (see p.87 and p.175) drew male readers to shōjo titles and female readers to shōnen titles, respectively.

Publishers also started to more narrowly **target audiences** than at any other point in the industry's history. A magazine targeted at eleven-year-old boys, for instance, would be fundamentally different from one aimed at a boy two years older. Those publications, of course, would be even more different from a publication for a commuting office worker. There were manga for administrative assistants, housewives, people who played the Japanese pinball game *pachinko*, people who played mah-jongg… if there was an interest out there, there was likely at least one series that covered it.

Even though much of the market was controlled by the "Big Three" publishers – Kodansha, Shogakukan and Shueisha – according to manga scholar Frederik L. Schodt, by 1984 there were around seventy different publishers of manga magazines in Japan and nearly fifty publishers of paperback book collections.

With manga widely accepted as a way of telling entertaining stories, the art form also started to be used to educate and inform. Student **textbooks** appeared in manga versions. Shōtarō Ishinomori, creator of the seminal 1960s manga *Cyborg 009* (see p.106), got in on the act with *Japan Inc.*, a manga about the Japanese economy released in 1986 which sold more than 500,000 copies. Even when a manga wasn't intentionally instructional it could have that effect – for example, the growing popularity of josei manga could be seen as partly due to the titles that showed women how to deal with relationship problems that weren't dealt with in other media.

For readers this was manga's **golden age** since the magazines' low production costs allowed them to be priced to sell by the millions. Workers could buy one of the dozens of magazines available at the starting point of their commute, read it along the way and dispose of it when they arrived at their destination. The most successful titles were industries unto themselves, first moving from magazines to collected paperback editions (either tankōbon, or the more compact and cheaper pocket versions called bunkobon).

Dedicated manga bookstore chains sprung up around this time to accommodate the growing number of collections. If a particular title was a hit, animated and live-action adaptations on television and in movies, as well as a good deal of merchandising, would soon follow. The market had a combined value estimated in the $6–7 billion range – three times as much as generated by the domestic movie industry.

Despite the occasional blip, new records for circulation were set every year, peaking in 1995 at 1.34 billion copies. The 400-page-plus *Shōnen Jump*, alone, was selling in excess of 6 million copies a week, powered along by its hit series such as Akira Toriyama's epic *Dragon Ball* (see p.116) and the basketball saga *Slam Dunk* by Takehiko Inoue (see p.182). Even in this boom period, though, signs were emerging that the good times wouldn't last forever. Publishers were always scrambling to find the next big thing, and when one publisher found it, the others would fall in line, getting their artists to develop something similar to capitalize on the original series' success. Short-term gains were the priority with little regard for long-term success.

Also the effects of the bursting of Japan's economic bubble were about to come into play. From the late 1980s, a highly speculative real estate market that had driven land prices to record highs and spawned risky bank loans gradually collapsed in on itself, taking a good portion of the Japanese economy with it. The impact on manga sales, like other areas of leisure spending, was noticeable.

At the same time, declining birth rates in Japan signalled an ageing population, a demographic time bomb that would inevitably affect manga's core markets of children and teenagers. In March 1995, respected news magazine *Aera* ran an article entitled "The Beginning of the Twilight of the Manga Industry", which pointed at the declining growth in the shōnen and seinen markets and concluded there might be limits to what had seemed just a year or two earlier to be a recession-proof industry.

Apocalypse Meow

Motofumi Kobayashi; *pub* Softbank Publishing (Jp), ADV (US); *ser* Combat Magazine (1991–2005); *vols* Jp 4, US 3; *age* 16+

It's the Vietnam War as no one – except, perhaps, author Kobayashi – could have possibly imagined it: with a corps of American bunnies fighting a force of determined Viet Cong cats. It would seem as if a story involving anthropomorphic combatants would be light-hearted, but Kobayashi uses a great deal of historical research as the foundation for his story. It's among the best series from ADV Manga's early days.

Five Star Stories

Mamoru Nagano; *pub* Kadokawa Shoten (Jp, 1986–), ToysPress (US); *ser* Newtype; *vols* ongoing

Amaterasu, the god of light, sits in the middle of this complex sci-fi epic about interplanetary conflict, which spans several millennia, multiple solar systems and characters who regularly cross into different dimensions. It is the destiny of Amaterasu and his bride, Lachesis, to rule the Joker Star Cluster of solar systems, which once was united but has fallen into disarray. The relationships and chronologies become so complex that the English translations come with background essays, character profiles and timelines to help sort everything out. Most of the appeal, though, lies in Nagano's fantasy worlds, expanded versions of the universe depicted in an anime he co-created with *Gundam* director Yoshiyuki Tomino in 1984.

Magic Knight Rayearth

CLAMP; *pub* Kodansha (Jp), Tokyopop (US); *ser* Nakayoshi (1993–96); *vols* 6

CLAMP's first breakthrough hit came with this mahō shōjo story of three middle school girls, with nothing in common, whisked away into an alternate world. As it turns out, Hikaru, Umi and Fuu are the prophesied Magic Knights, a trio destined to save the kingdom of Cephiro through their combined elemental powers of fire, water and wind, and the help of giant robot-like mechanisms known as the Mashin. The series has two major story arcs, the first of which includes a rather compelling twist to what came before.

Mai the Psychic Girl

Kazuya Kodo (story), Ryoichi Ikegami (art); *pub* Shogakukan (Jp), Viz (US); *ser* Weekly Shōnen Sunday (1985–86); *vols* 3

The Wisdom Alliance, a secret organization, has managed to manipulate a number of world events toward a doomsday scenario. To complete the job and send the world into total chaos, though, the group has turned its attention toward gaining control of a number of psychic children around the world… and Mai, a Japanese schoolgirl whose powers of telekinesis and telepathy have only just begun to emerge, is naturally a target. Mai must now defend herself, her friends and her family from agents who will stop at nothing to capture her while she explores her newfound, highly destructive abilities.

Future challenges: 1996 to the present

From being *the* big thing of the 1990s, in the last decade and a half, manga in Japan has matured into one of the many options available for entertainment. Japanese youths have turned away from the manga their parents once read towards the shiny technologies that drive contemporary pop culture: cellphones, the Internet and videogames. The stereotype of the commuter reading a thick manga magazine is increasingly being replaced by one of the commuter peering intently at a phone screen, watching a video, web-browsing or text-messaging friends and colleagues.

Responding to such changes in the domestic market, publishers have started offering manga for download to mobile phones in chapters costing around ¥50 each. Known as **keitai** manga (*keitai* is the Japanese for mobile phone), this new format offers stories frame-by-frame, with the ability to pan across an image. Readers can control the speed at which they watch, turn speech bubbles on and off and, for a more stimulating read, the phone will vibrate at key moments. Hundreds of titles are available covering old favourites such as Leiji Matsumoto's *Galaxy Express 999* as well as stories developed specifically for release via *keitai*. Despite initial teething troubles (there had been complaints that it was impossible to see the art, that it was cropped incorrectly, or it took too long to download and scroll through) sales stood at ¥22.9 billion in March 2008, up eighty percent from the previous year.

Also chipping into the sales of traditional manga has been the increasing

Japanese foreign minister Masahiko Komura at Doraemon's inauguration as Japan's first Anime Ambassador in 2008.

number of stores selling **secondhand** volumes at reduced prices, and the rising popularity of manga *kissa*, or manga cafés (see box on p.14). On top of all this, there's a growing perception among fans that the stories have fallen into a rut, and rely on mimicking past hits.

While to outsiders the numbers remain impressive (for 2008 the Japan Magazine Publishers Association reported that Shueisha's *Weekly Shōnen Jump* regularly shifted around 2.78 million copies per edition, while Kodansha's *Weekly Shōnen Magazine* sold 1.77 million copies), the fact is that manga sales in Japan have been declining every year since 1996. In 2007 the Tokyo-based Research Institute for Publications recorded that manga magazine sales had tumbled to 745 million copies in 2006, down almost half from their peak a decade earlier. It also reported that in the same year the industry made ¥481 billion ($4.1 billion), a drop of at least ¥200 billion from 1996.

Now more than ever it has become clear that if manga is to rekindle the kind of growth figures and profits achieved in the past, then the source for this would have to be overseas markets. In a timely move the Japanese government in 2008 drafted in two superstar manga cats, Doraemon and Hello Kitty, as **overseas ambassadors** for Japanese pop culture – hardly Batman and Robin, but maybe just the kind of superheroes that manga needs in the twenty-first century.

Black Lagoon

Rei Hiroe; *pub* Shogakukan (Jp), Viz (US, UK); *ser* Sunday GX (2002–); *vols* ongoing; *age* 18+

Manga's equivalent of a summer blockbuster action movie, a series where you jump in, turn off your brain and prepare to be thoroughly entertained. A group of mercenaries aboard the titular torpedo boat – Dutch the Boss, Benny the Mechanic and Revy Two Hand – takes on the unlikeliest of travelling companions: Rokurō "Rock" Okajima, an office worker whose company disavowed his existence after the crew took him hostage. So while Rock tries to negotiate his way through the crew's frequent smuggling jobs throughout southeast Asia, everyone else prefers to let their actions do the talking. Rei Hiroe loves to draw guns and women, so it's no surprise to see that when gun-toting Revy hits a scene, the bullets will start flying and the body count will start rising.

Cromartie High School

Eiji Nonaka; *pub* Kodansha (Jp), ADV (US); *ser* Weekly Shonen Magazine (2001–06); *vols* Jp 17, US 13 (suspended); *age* 13+

Takashi Kamiyama, an above-average student, transfers into Cromartie High School and instantly becomes the smartest person at the school. That's because it's populated by a wide range of juvenile delinquents, all brawn and tough talk but with very little brainpower. In fact, no one really notices that enrolled among their ranks is a silent muscleman with an uncanny resemblance to the late Freddie Mercury; a gorilla; and a robot, Mechazawa. This series' deadpan gags come packed in easy-to-read, six-page stories. Nonaka parodies the juvenile delinquent manga popular in the 1970s and 80s here, right down to the static close-ups that Tetsuya Chiba used in his manga at the time. The series won a Kodansha Manga Award for shōnen in 2002.

Love*Com [Lovely Complex]

Aya Nakahara; *pub* Shueisha (Jp), Viz (US, UK), Madman (Aus); *ser* Bessatsu Margaret (2001–); *vols* 16; *age* 16+

The classmates of Risa Koizumi and Atsushi Ōtani nickname the pair after a popular comedy duo comprising one tall and one short member. In this case, Risa is the tallest girl in the class, while Atsushi is the shortest boy. In trying to get away from each other and date other people, though, they end up uniting to help each other get what they want... and in the process learn that they have much more in common than they realize. The concept may be simple, yet Nakahara manages to capture all the ups and downs, from light-hearted comedic moments to uncertainty over their feelings for each other.

The series won the 49th Shogakukan Manga Award for shōjo in 2004.

Vampire Knight

Matsuri Hino; *pub* Hakusensha (Jp), Viz (US, UK), Madman (Aus); *ser* LaLa (2005–); *vols* ongoing; *age* 16+

Yuki Cross and Zero Kiryu are members of Cross Academy's Disciplinary Committee, a group tasked with keeping the squealing, fawning girls in the high school's Day Class away from the elegant, beautiful boys in the Night Class. Unbeknownst to the Day Class, the Night Class boys are also vampires, a secret that must be protected in a world of vampire/human conflict. While the opening panels suggest a romantic school comedy, Matsuri Hino instead builds a dramatic story of vampires, tragic secrets and doomed love. Hino's male character designs have a wispy, effeminate look to them, and scenes of Zero, who's slowly becoming a vampire, biting human Yuki for her blood are sensually paced.

Yotsuba&!

Kiyohiko Azuma; *pub* MediaWorks (Jp), ADV (US, vols 1–5), Yen Press (US, UK, vols 6 onward); *ser* Dengeki Daioh (2003–); *vols* ongoing

For his first series after *Azumanga Daioh* (see p.85), Kiyohiko Azuma moves away from the four-panel format to tell short stories in more traditional multi-panel manga. Little green-haired girl Yotsuba, along with her dad, Koiwai, have just moved to a new neighbourhood, and now Yotsuba wants to learn about everything in her new surroundings… As their neighbours, sisters Asagi, Fuka and Ena, quickly find out, Yotsuba's naturally inquisitive mind and her tendency to apply what she's learned to the extreme make for some entertaining adventures. Azuma creates again a world full of bubble-eyed, innocent-looking girls, but this time adds more multi-dimensional male characters like Koiwai and his best friend, Jumbo, so called because he towers over the other characters in height.

Manga Goes Global

from Japan to the world

As manga's domestic market has shrunk since the 1990s, a steadily rising overseas audience has seeped in to fill the gap. In 2006, the Japan External Trade Organization (JETRO) estimated the overall value of Japan's manga exports at ¥50 billion (approximately $429.7 million).

For neighbouring Asian countries, such as Korea and China, sharing similar cultural backgrounds and history, manga's appeal is easy to fathom and native versions have existed since the early twentieth century. But manga's popularity in the West is a more complex story, one that is partly tied up with the success of anime – Japanese animation.

Manga in Asia

Just as manga's artistic style was initially shaped by political cartoons imported from the West and adapted by local artists around the turn of the nineteenth century, so too were the styles of its closest Asian relatives – **manhwa** in Korea and **manhua** in China. As Japan's imperialist ambitions grew, Chinese and Korean cartoonists began to satirize the threat of Japanese annexation, but after subsequent occupation they ended up producing pro-Japanese propaganda in the 1930s.

With Japan's defeat at the end of World War II, Chinese and Korean artists were free once more to pursue their own paths, and both manhua and manhwa would flourish soon afterward. However, political circumstances within the two countries, as well as a gradually resurgent Japan and its growing manga market, ensured those renaissances were short-lived… but not before several key artistic distinctions between the three forms had developed.

Korea's manhwa: the first 70 years

Today, **South Korea** is second to only Japan in Asian comic production – a fact that underlines the two countries' long history of enjoying stories told in a dynamic mix of pictures and words. Koreans saw their first single-panel editorial cartoon in 1909, drawn by Do-young Lee in the newspaper *Daehan Minbo*. Hard on Japan's annexation of Korea in 1910, artists Dong-sung Kim and Suk-joo Ahn had their four-panel cartoons satirizing the Japanese published. Ahn also created a style known as manmoon manhwa – sketches paired with short essays.

Another early manhwa artist to hit the big time was Soo-hyun Roh, whose strip "Imbecile's Vain Efforts" was made into a movie. However, by the 1930s the Japanese occupiers were doing their best to destroy Korean culture, even to the point of replacing the Korean language with Japanese. Manhwa of the time concentrated on non-political humour or legendary figures. With the advent of war, Korean cartoonists, just like their Japanese brethren, were recruited to provide propaganda material.

Following World War II Korea was liberated from Japan, but it would be another decade before manhwa was able to flourish. Korea's occupation by US troops, followed by the rift between rival independent governments that led to the Korean War (1950–53), ensured that artists would be employed primarily to draw propaganda for the various factions for several years to come. The most popular series at the time – including the first Korean comic book to emerge, Young-hwan Kim's single-volume *The Rabbit and the Turtle* – reflected an atmosphere of gloom and often tore at readers' emotions.

By the mid-1950s, the manhwa industry in South Korea started showing signs of diversifying for different audiences, much like its Japanese counterpart at the time. **Manhwabang**, or manhwa rental libraries, became highly popular and fuelled an industry-wide boom until a military coup placed Chung-hee Park in power in 1961. Park imposed strict censorship on printed material, including bans on depictions of males and females in the same panel and "extravagant" fashions, such as miniskirts, ribbons, flowers and other fripperies. This affected not just the look of manhwa but also the kind of stories artists were permitted to tell.

The strong nationalist sentiment and cultural identity that formed after Korea regained independence from Japan had extended to national law, which banned imports of anything related to Japanese culture – including manga. Even so, in the 1960s, manga began infiltrating Korea at an underground level as local artists took stories from Japanese comics and rewrote them as Korean titles.

Manhwa post-1979

Park's assassination in 1979 led to a gradual easing of restrictions on manhwa, and the industry boomed as a broader range of titles featuring more true-to-life characters and plots were published. The government also began to see the economic potential in the industry, establishing agencies to promote the art both at home and abroad and encouraging the setting up of courses to teach manhwa production.

Even so there were still fundamental problems that hampered the industry's development. Rentals of manhwa continued to outpace sales and so publishers were unwilling to risk long-running series. Meanwhile, a trade agreement with Japan allowed manga a legitimate route into the country. Young Koreans flocked to manga in droves, all but abandoning their native manhwa save for a handful of long-running general and shōjo-style titles.

Seeing the success that manga was having overseas, manhwa publishers began to target foreign markets. For Western publishers, there did appear to be benefits to translating manhwa over manga: it's read front to back and left to right, so there's no need to reorder the panels; South Korea's censorship laws limit the amount of sexual and violent content, making series easier to market to a broad overseas audience without the need for editorial input; and the art style of some titles tends to be more realistic, hence appealing to the graphic novels audience.

However, in 2005 manhwa titles published overseas were estimated to be earning the industry around $3.25 million – a drop in the ocean compared to the value of the export manga market. Although they had been initially keen to exploit this new source of content, Western publishers of manhwa have since fallen away, leaving only a handful of translated titles now available.

Banya: The Explosive Delivery Man

Young-oh Kim; *pub* Haksanpub (SK, 2004–06), Dark Horse (US); *vols* 5

In this cracking sci-fi fantasy adventure, one of Korea's top ten bestsellers, neither rain nor snow nor world-rending conflict between humans and a race of monstrous creatures known as the Torren will stop the delivery team of the Gaya Desert Post Office from making their rounds. Chief among them is Banya, a shōnen-style Mad Max who takes innumerable risks but has yet to come up against a delivery that he couldn't make.

Faeries' Landing

Hyun You; *pub* Daiwon C.I. (SK, 1998–), Tokyopop (US); *vols* 19

Although it's nominally set in modern-day Korea, Faeries' Landing has plenty to keep fantasy fans transfixed. It all starts off a bit like one of Rumiko Takahashi's manga with its sixteen-year-old male protagonist becoming hitched by convoluted means to the beautiful faery Fanta, as well as her rival Medea who curses the hapless boy to suffer through 108 failed relationships. Much of the original Korean folk tale references were ditched for the English translation.

Priest

Min-woo Hyung; *pub* Daiwon C.I. (SK, 1998–), Tokyopop (US); *vols* ongoing

A gothic horror tale, inspired by the Japanese computer game *Blood* and with a distinctive angular art style. The plot, which takes place in the American Wild West, the time of the Crusades and the modern day, centres on Ivan Isaacs, a deceased priest who continues to battle evil, even though he's sold his soul to the devil. Alliances are realigned when the opponent is a fallen angel, Temozareal, whom Ivan resurrected and unintentionally unleashed upon the world.

Ragnarok

Myung-jin Lee; *pub* Daiwon C.I. (SK, 1995–), Tokyopop (US), Madman (Aus); *vols* 10, on hiatus

The manhwa on which the massively multiplayer roleplaying game is based takes Norse mythology as its source. A warrior named Chaos finds out he's the reincarnated form of Balder, the God of Light, when the reincarnated form of Fenrir the Wolf God asks for his help in bringing about Ragnarok, the prophesied fall of the gods and the rise of the age of man. The game's popularity is such that Lee has apparently put the planned forty-volume manhwa on hiatus to work on story expansions.

Unbalance x Unbalance

Dall-young Lim (story), Soo-hyon Lee (art); *pub* Daiwon C.I. (SK, 2005–), Infinity Studios (US); *vols* ongoing

This school-based drama, which zones in on a tricky student–teacher relationship, provides an insight into modern Korean life. The mildly rebellious student hero Jin-ho Mung is one point of a romantic triangle with the virginal homeroom teacher Hae-young Nah and the half-Korean, half-British Caroline, Nah's teaching assistant. The art style reflects manga's influence.

China's manhua: 1867–1950s

In China, Western-style satire and caricature was introduced via **China Punch**, the country's own version of Britain's *Punch* magazine, in 1867. Cartoonist

Tse Tsan-tai is credited with drawing the first political cartoon in "The Situation in the Far East", in 1899. From this start the development of a local cartoon tradition was somewhat slower than in Japan and Korea. It wouldn't be until 1928 that China's first manhua magazine, the eight-page *Shanghai Sketch*, was first published. At the height of its popularity it was selling around three thousand copies a week and it helped encourage some seventeen other manhua publications to be launched in China's most cosmopolitan city during the 1930s.

History then interrupted manhua's development across China, with Japanese occupation of parts of the country in the 1940s. Following the end of World War II, on mainland China, the Chinese Communist Party eventually came to rule, a movement that would result in the Cultural Revolution of the 1960s and severe crackdowns on artistic and journalistic expression. By contrast, in the non-Communist-controlled Chinese territories of Hong Kong and Taiwan, art was allowed to flourish.

Before the 1950s, reading *lianhuantu*, a form of illustrated storybook, was a popular pastime in both territories, as was reading the manhua produced in Shanghai. When the supply of material from Shanghai was cut off, readers turned to the four-panel comics that were starting to appear in newspapers. Topics that were taboo in mainland China could be freely disseminated in Hong Kong (and to a lesser extent in Taiwan), and soon there were manhua for a wide range of ages and interests.

Several of them adopted the artistic style of American comics and animated movies of the era, all freely available in those territories. In 1958, Hui Guan-man's comedy wartime comic strip "Uncle Choi" was published in Hong Kong's bestselling *Cartoons World* magazine, a series that would run until the mid-1970s.

Manhua from the 1960s onward

Because of the wartime experience of Japanese occupation, locals were initially unreceptive to manga, but during the 1960s, with memories fading and a new generation coming up, manga's influence began to be felt in both Hong Kong and Taiwan.

Animated TV programming from Japan began airing in Hong Kong around 1967 and brought with it an increased awareness of Japanese properties and a demand for new stories featuring those characters. Manhua artists obliged with **pirated versions** of Japanese manga. *Science Wonder Boy* from 1966 had character designs and stories that not only copied Mitsuteru Yokoyama's seminal *Tetsujin-28* but also Tezuka's *Astro Boy*. *Ding Dong*, a pirated version of *Doraemon*, began running in the 1970s.

Such pirated titles would gradually dwindle to negligible levels as authentic manga became more available. Spurred on by the success of the Hong Kong movie industry's kung fu flicks, one subject that local artists developed independently was manhua devoted to martial arts. The **violence** depicted in some of these manhua became so excessive that in 1975 the Hong Kong government saw fit to introduce the Indecent Publications Law.

One general style difference with manga that has developed is that manhua tends to be printed in full colour. A good example of how manhua looks is *Chinese Hero: Tales of the Blood Sword* by Ma Wing Shing, first published in 1980 in Hong Kong's *Golden Daily* newspaper and one of the territory's most successful series, selling over 200,000 copies in compilation book form. The kung fu action drama mainly takes place in the US and has been praised for the realistic detail of its artwork and skilful use of colour.

Chinese Hero is one of the few manhua titles to have made the leap into English-language translation, beginning with the series' second season, since the first is packed with incidents of racism and anti-Western expressions that may well have alienated its potential audience. Among other manhua available in English translations is the historical romantic drama *Real/Fake Princess* by Yi Huan and originally published in Taiwan.

In the International Manga Awards (see p.54) it is notable that the top prize winners for the contest's first two years were both from Hong Kong: Lee Chi Ching for *Sun Zi's Tactics* in 2007 and Lau Wan Kit for *Feel 100%* in 2008. Runners-up in both years also hailed from Hong Kong.

Journey to the West

Western artists from Charles Wirgman to Walt Disney may have had a great influence on manga, but the reciprocal influence of manga on the West has taken far longer to develop, partly because of the still prevalent attitude that comics are largely for children, and partly because of the medium's subject matter often being so culturally specific to Japan.

Mainstream acceptance has developed just in the past decade or so, mainly piggybacking off the success of **anime** (animated films, TV and DVD series made in Japan), which sparked demand from fans and a rush for publishers to snap up associated manga for translations. The prevailing trend has been for the United States to get an English-translated series first, with those series then trickling down to eager fans in the UK, Australia, New Zealand and other English-speaking territories. Meanwhile, in other European countries such as France and Belgium, both with venerable and respected histories of comics (where they are known as *bandes dessinées*), the embrace of manga has been more enthusiastic.

As the full breadth of manga has filtered out to the world, so too has the artistic style of Japanese comics begun to have an impact on how foreign artists draw and present their stories – a reversal of the process whereby manga developed under the influence of Western comics – to the point where there is now a recognized subset of the medium known as **international**, **global** or original English language (**OEL**) manga.

Anime leads the way

When Americans got their **first translated taste of manga** in 1965, a time when the market for weekly manga anthologies was booming in Japan, it was with the comic *Astro Boy*, published by Gold Key as a spin-off from the hit animated children's TV series. Even though the characters were recognizable as those created by Osamu Tezuka, the comic resembled the edited, US-localized versions of the show, rather than the show as it had first screened in Japan three years earlier or, indeed, Tezuka's original manga stretching back to the 1950s.

The success of the TV version of *Astro Boy* in Japan saw many other manga go on to become animated series, and a new industry became established. It was through the growing popularity of these **imported anime**, in their localized versions, that manga would eventually start to be noticed in the West and that a demand for the printed originals would grow. Even so, to begin with, Western audiences weren't necessarily aware of their Japanese origins when watching *Gigantor* (formerly known as *Tetsujin-28*), *Kimba the White Lion* (in

Japanese-inspired American comics

Before US publishers started translating manga directly, some cut their teeth on home-grown titles that incorporated the characters and sometimes the plots of the Japanese print originals. *Shogun Warriors* published by Marvel in 1979 was one such title – it introduced many American kids to manga and anime's giant robot stars such as Mazinger Z, Raideen, Getter Robo, and Grendizer (aka Goldorak), well known for over a decade to the Japanese.

As with *Astro Boy* two decades earlier, the TV success in the 1980s of *Robotech* (three different anime series – *Macross*, *Southern Cross* and *Mospeada* – edited together to form a single 85-episode series) inspired the Comico comic *Robotech*; the first edition of the comic actually ran under the title *Macross*.

GASP!

I-it's the lady I was just talking to. What happened to her?!

Hey, I-lady?

She's... she's DEAD!

Help! Mamaaa!

Some-body's coming...

H-hey, mister! Help! This lady's dead!

Gasp!

An unflinching account of the Hiroshima bombing and its aftermath, Keiji Nakazawa's *Barefoot Gen* was one of the first translated manga released in the US.

Japan *Jungle Emperor*) or *Speed Racer* (in Japan *Mach Go Go Go*). In the US the syndicated series *Battle of the Planets* (an adaptation of the anime *Science Ninja Team Gatchaman*) in 1978 and *Star Blazers* (adapted from *Space Battleship Yamato*) in 1979 were the first to be widely acknowledged as Japanese animation.

There's a simple reason why anime broke into the US before manga. Localizing TV shows for foreign markets meant overdubbing the original Japanese dialogue with a translated script in the new language, whereas translating the printed page involved numerous considerations on top of the actual translated script, not least of which was how to fit new text onto a page while keeping the original art intact, how to reorder the way panels were printed (the Japanese read books from back to front and text from top to bottom), and whether to colourize the black and white images.

Manga makes its mark

Some of the earliest promotion of **untranslated manga** in American fan circles came courtesy of Richard Kyle and Fred Patten, who from late 1972 until 1975 imported and sold manga through mail order and on the premises of their comic bookshop Wonderworld Books in Long Beach, California. In his book *Watching Anime, Reading Manga*

Patten tells how he had contacted publishers throughout Europe and Japan to propose carrying their comics; while the Europeans were eager to do business with them, only one publisher in Japan, Akita Shoten, expressed an interest, and this was only because an employee there wanted to practise his English.

The 1970s also saw the first full-story manga to be translated into English and published for distribution in the US. Released in May 1978 by the New York-based War Resisters League, this was Keiji Nakazawa's **Barefoot Gen**, the semi-autobiographical story of a boy who survives the Hiroshima atom bomb (see p.88). The volunteer activist group viewed the manga as having an anti-war message consistent with its own goals. Five years later another Nakazawa title, *I Saw It*, was published by San Francisco-based Educomics as a fifty-page full colour American-style comic.

Apart from at speciality comic stores, in the 1970s and early 80s fans of manga could also get their fix at Japanese product stores in the Japanese districts of major American cities. Spotting an opportunity, in 1980 one such store – **Books Nippan** in Los Angeles, the American subsidiary of Japanese bookstore chain Nippan Shuppan Hanbai – started to import extra quantities of anime and manga specifically for the burgeoning fan market. While the store's initial efforts primarily focused on the market in Southern California, a mail-order department soon was established and promoted in anime fan club bulletins. Books Nippan also tried its hand at publishing translated manga, debuting the 88-page *Manga* anthology in the early 1980s, as well as a *Star Blazers* "anime manga" based on the TV series in 1984.

As American readers began to thrill to manga, so too did some local comic book artists become enamoured of the medium's distinct art style, which played with ideas that were little exploited in the US comics industry at the time (see box overleaf). Manga's storytelling technique didn't rely on richly coloured, meticulously detailed still-frame shots, but on more simply drawn yet dynamic characters, with multiple frames used to depict a single action and a raft of visual devices used to keep the eye moving from one panel to the next. There was a certain energy in manga – that same cinematic energy that Tezuka developed and honed many years earlier.

Frederik L. Schodt's book *Manga! Manga!*, first published in 1983, tapped into the growing fascination with Japanese comics. It was the first English-language book on the subject and contained translations of episodes from four seminal manga, including Tezuka's *Phoenix* (see p.171) and Riyoko Ikeda's *Rose of Versailles* (p.178). Two years later Antarctic Press would start publishing *Mangazine*, featuring **fan-produced comics** drawn in the Japanese style – if American fans couldn't get the original

The manga influence

Several American comics writers and artists have acknowledged being influenced by manga:

✦ Wendy Pini cited Tezuka's style as an inspiration for *Elfquest* in early promotional materials for the series in 1979.

✦ Frank Miller, creator of *Batman: The Dark Knight Returns* and *Sin City*, tipped his hat to the Kazuo Koike/Goseki Kojima samurai epic *Lone Wolf and Cub* (see p.147) as a major influence on his DC Comics series *Ronin* in 1983. (Miller would later go on to draw several covers for the American *Lone Wolf and Cub* translations.)

✦ Jo Duffy and Tom Palmer, working on Marvel Comics' *Star Wars* in 1983, depicted a disguised Lando Calrissian as the galaxy-traversing space pirate Captain Harlock, one of Leiji Matsumoto's iconic anime and manga characters.

✦ Ben Dunn's *Ninja High School*, which started in 1986, clearly owes a debt to the works of Rumiko Takahashi.

manga then they would start drawing their own.

Meanwhile over in **Europe**, fans of anime shows such as the romantic soap opera *Candy Candy*, the giant robot show *Grendizer* (renamed *Goldorak*) and Leiji Matsumoto's *Captain Harlock* (renamed *Albator*) were beginning to get the opportunity to read about their favourite characters in translations of the original comics sold on French, Italian and Spanish newsstands.

An industry takes shape

With the market for translated manga growing slowly but surely off the back of increased general interest in anime, Books Nippan joined forces with Saito Productions in Japan to bring out *Golgo 13 Graphic Novel Series No. 1: Inside the Wolf's Lair* in 1986. That same year, young entrepreneur and one-time hippy Seiji Horibuchi, who had been living in San Francisco since 1975, saw an opportunity to market manga in the US and managed to persuade the president of the Japanese media company Shogakukan to part with $200,000 to help him do so: this was the origin of what would become **Viz Media**, one of the largest publishers of English-translated manga.

Another key figure in the rise of English-translated manga is the

Canadian **Toren Smith**, a writer of comic books who got hooked on manga when a friend showed him some samples in 1982. In 1986 he moved to Japan to found Studio Proteus, which would go on to become one of the major producers of translated manga. One of Studio Proteus's first successes was *The Dirty Pair*, a manga drawn and written by Smith and Adam Warren and based on the characters originally created by Haruka Takachiho. It followed the adventures of a voluptuous duo dispatched to solve crimes and mysteries, but who often end up leaving a trail of destruction in their wake. Smith would later work with US publishers Eclipse on Masamune Shirow's *Appleseed*.

Also in 1986 Mike Richardson established **Dark Horse Comics**, a company that would rise to become the third largest comics publisher in the US (after Marvel and DC Comics); among its first releases were translations of the manga *Godzilla #1* and Jōji Manabe's *Outlanders*, a project that came about with the help of Toren Smith.

By the latter half of the 1980s translated manga was really starting to come into its own in the US, albeit presented in the traditional comic-book format that readers were familiar with. Pages were "flopped" so that they could be read left to right and colour was added. First Comics' version of the samurai saga **Lone Wolf and Cub** (see p.147) would shift 100,000 copies in 1987, becoming the first stateside manga publishing hit. Among

the first manga translations published by Eclipse/Viz were the *Top Gun*-esque *Area 88*, Sanpei Shiratō's ninja drama *Legend of Kamui* and the *X-Men*-ish *Mai the Psychic Girl*.

Meanwhile, anime director and *Nausicaä of the Valley of the Wind* author Hayao Miyazaki, impressed with an article Smith wrote criticizing *Warriors of the Wind*, the English adaptation of his *Nausicaä* movie, asked Smith to do a translation of the manga for Viz. Viz, for its part, kept plugging away, releasing Naoki Urasawa's *Pineapple Army* and Yoshihisa Tagami's *Grey* in 1988.

All these early publications by the US manga publishing upstarts sold in respectable numbers but it would be the established stalwart Marvel who would have the biggest hit with its colourized translation in 1988 of Katsuhiro Ōtomo's **Akira**, its sales boosted by the success of the movie anime of the same name.

By the time the early 1990s rolled around, Viz and Dark Horse had cemented their position as the dominant players in the translated manga market, which numbered several other new publishers, including Antarctic Press, Studio Ironcat and Central Park Media (see Chapter 6).

Spreading the word

With a steady stream of titles being released, there now were enough manga

Licence to print

When a series is generated that could potentially attract interest outside of Japan, one that's sold well and often has been collected into tankōbon (paperback book collections of the chapters that run in magazines), prospective publishers enter the picture and try to negotiate a deal that will result in the licensing of a property, or the awarding of exclusive rights to a particular publisher. It's a highly competitive process, as everyone knows which are the hot properties and is willing to pay top dollar to get them. Some publishers even begin to make offers while stories are still being serialized in magazines.

It helps to have established connections in the industry beforehand, as well as the skills necessary to negotiate in Japanese culture. Trust and status are also key, with the Japanese publishers more likely to deal with established publishers abroad than up-and-coming operations. Adam Arnold of Seven Seas once wrote: "There's tons of gossip, publishers trying to undermine each other, infighting, and bitter rivalries – all for the purpose of winning that prized licence or the affection and favour of the biggest and best Japanese publisher." There are already a number of special relationships between US and Japanese publishers, with Viz jointly owned by Shogakukan and Shueisha, Del Rey allied with Kodansha, and Yen Press working closely with Square Enix.

Assuming that a publisher gets the desired licence, the next step is to translate the pages from Japanese into English. Considerations that must be made include whether to stick with straight translations or translate and then adapt into more natural-sounding English, all while keeping the original art intact as much as possible. If an anime adaptation exists, the question also arises of whether the anime's translation of certain names should be retained, or whether the manga version should strike out on its own. For instance, in *Excel Saga*, Viz ended up translating the dog's name as "Mince", whereas ADV Films, in its translation of the anime, retained the untranslated name "Menchi".

Once the script is done, it gets sent to a layout department, which plops the newly translated dialogue into new bubbles. The process is easier with unflopped manga, where pages retain their original right-to-left orientation, but even so there still remain questions of how much and what to translate. Sound effects, for instance, can be left untranslated, or explained in notes at the bottom of the page. For more on the conventions and techniques unique to manga, see Chapter 3.

to warrant **English-language magazines** on the medium: in 1992 *Mangazine* changed format to concentrate on anime and manga news, gaining a sister publication, *Dojinshi: The World of Japanese Fanzines*, an anthology of cartoons by Japanese fans, later that year. Also launched in 1992 was *Manga Newswatch Quarterly*, started by Indiana resident Mark Paniccia, with Viz publishing *Animerica* in 1993, followed by its first manga anthology, *Manga Vizion*, in 1995.

Comic book **conventions** (cons) had been a feature of the fan scene in the US since the 1970s but by the early 1990s there were enough fans to warrant cons devoted specifically to manga and anime. One of the largest of these early gatherings, the four-day **AnimeCon 91** held in San Jose, California, was organized by Toren Smith and Toshio Okada from the Japanese anime studio Gainax and attracted more than 1700 fans from across North America. The Japanese guests who attended included Kenichi Sonoda (the author of *Gunsmith Cats* and *Riding Bean*, also known at the time for his character design work on the anime series *Bubblegum Crisis*) and *Outlanders* author Jōji Manabe.

Technology also came into play in spreading the word about manga. The proliferation of video cassette recorders (**VCRs**) allowed tapes of anime to be traded among fans, spurring an interest in the associated manga. The success of computer games coming out of Japan, also

featuring manga characters, was another factor that further boosted demand for the original printed product.

At the same time the **Internet** was emerging, providing an ideal platform for fans to swap information and views. The web became a place where fans could build virtual shrines to their favourite series, while Usenet forums like rec.arts. anime and rec.arts.manga predated the thousands of online forums and chat rooms devoted to manga today.

Breaking the stereotypes

The late 1980s and early 1990s saw manga, albeit in a largely Westernized version, introduced successfully to an English-speaking audience. However, the titles chosen for translation by publishers also tended to play safe around the **unspoken rules** of the American comics market – namely that they should be action or science-fiction genre comics targeted at boys and young adult males and predominantly sold from speciality comics shops, which in themselves were considered to be the domain of boys.

Hence many of the titles being shipped over from Japan were shōnen and seinen series, with plenty of junk as well as a few gems. They were packaged like any other comic book, with graphic novel collections coming out rarely, if at all; the frames would read left-to-right instead of the native right-to-left; and new chapters would be released monthly (although Viz initially tried marketing some of its manga as weekly comics, the experiment soon ended). They might also be colourized – a slow and costly process, but one thought necessary if a series was to compete with, say, the headline-grabbing *Death of Superman* story arc being released by DC Comics around the time manga was gaining a foothold in the early 1990s.

Starting in 1997 and lasting through to the present, a string of series and events helped English-language manga expand from its roots in the "boys' club" comic book stores into the mass-market phenomenon it is today. The first big break was the realization by US publishers that girls – half of the potential market for manga – were being all but ignored and could very profitably be exploited. The continued rise of Japanese pop culture via the success of anime, videogames and merchandising spin-offs such as collectable cards and toys was also fuel that would stoke manga demand.

The Sailor Moon effect

Until the mid-1990s, there were few translated series aimed at **female readers**. The crossover appeal of Rumiko Takahashi's stories, including *Ranma ½* in 1990, *Maison Ikkoku* in 1993 and the various *Rumic World* stories appearing in *Manga Vizion* from 1995 helped Viz, while *Oh My Goddess!*, first published in 1994, was and continues to be a steady seller for Dark Horse (see pp.175, 156 and 164 for more on these).

Once they had studied the female market in Japan via the work of shōjo manga scholar Matt Thorn, Viz began to target this audience in the US. Short stories by Moto Hagio, Keiko Nishi and Shio Seto made their way into pretty much every available format that Viz was publishing at the time – monthly comic books, inserts in *Animerica*, serialization in *Manga Vizion* and graphic novel collections. When Viz started its *Pulp* monthly anthology for older audiences in 1997, there was a shōjo component to that as well, with *Banana Fish* (see p.87).

Popular as these early girls' manga were with American readers, it was the arrival of the *Sailor Moon* anime via syndication on US TV stations in 1995 that really sparked the shōjo boom. *Sailor Moon* may not have crossed over the Pacific under optimal conditions (licensor DIC eliminated some episodes from the original anime and changed character names and some situations to make it more suitable for the younger audiences traditionally targeted by US cartoon series; it was also often placed in early morning time slots) and only 65 episodes were aired before it was cancelled in 1996, but it was enough to give female audiences a taste of a unique shōjo-style story, one that depicted empowered female characters and had an element of romance built in as well.

It would take a new player to capitalize on the opportunity provided by *Sailor Moon*, shaking up the industry in the process: **Mixx Entertainment**, co-founded by Victor Chin, Stuart Levy and Ron Scovil Jr, picked up the licence for the manga by Naoko Takeuchi on which the anime was based and made it the centrepiece of their new manga anthology, *Mixxzine*, in 1997. Mixx Entertainment would evolve into Tokyopop (see p.235), one of the biggest publishers of manga outside of Japan.

Complementing *Sailor Moon* as anchor series of *Mixxzine* was another shōjo title, *Magic Knight Rayearth* by CLAMP, and two seinen series, *Ice Blade* and *Parasyte*. This mix of material appealing to male and female readers wasn't the only thing that made *Mixxzine* stand out. While other publishers aimed for cautious growth, introducing what they thought the market and existing fans could bear, *Mixxzine* simply tried to get itself into as many hands as possible, appearing in comic book racks at newsstands and in bookstores as well as in speciality comics shops.

Believing that few people knew what manga was and that "comics" brought to mind traditional boys' culture, Levy chose to promote *Mixxzine* as "motionless picture entertainment". *Sailor Moon* videos sold at Toys "R" Us included a card offering a free issue of the magazine. More clever marketing ensured that as the first issue of *Mixxzine* hit the streets, the *Sailor Moon* anime was enjoying a second run on the cable USA Network.

People who were aware of the series and its previous syndicated incarnation, as well as an entirely **new audience of girls** that probably would not have gone to comic book stores, picked up *Mixxzine* to see the manga version of the story. Mixx would continue to push its advantage with the female market, first by offering cheaply priced graphic-novel collections of *Sailor Moon* and *Magic Knight Rayearth*, then announcing the creation of a dedicated magazine, *Smile*, to house *Sailor Moon* and other articles and features aimed at girls.

Viz countered in 1998 by launching *Animerica Extra*, a sister publication to the already established *Animerica*. This manga anthology aimed directly at the growing US market for shōjo material debuted with Yuu Watase's *Fushigi Yugi* (see p.126) as well as the continuation of CLAMP's *X/1999*.

Pokémania

At the same time *Sailor Moon* was helping blaze a trail for shōjo manga titles in the US, 151 collectible creatures available on two videogame cartridges for the Nintendo Game Boy were about to extend the market wide open in another direction. The launch of the *Pokémon* game in the US in 1998 spawned a generation of children-turned-*Pokémon*-trainers who simply had to catch all of those creatures, regardless of the format in which they were packaged – the videogames, the trading card game, the Saturday morning cartoon, the weekday morning cartoon, the weekday afternoon cartoon, the videotapes of all those cartoons, and mounds upon mounds of toys, trinkets and other character-stamped doodads.

Launched on the wave of Pokémania was Viz's four-part manga *The Electric Tale of Pikachu*. The story was predictable – *Pokémon* trainer who wants to become the best in the world meets other trainers with the same goal, battles ensue, lessons are learned, people get helped, epic adventures are embarked upon – but narrative complexity never was a defining trait of the franchise. Big sales were, however: not only was the first issue of *The Electric Tale of Pikachu*, released in comic-book format, 1998's top-selling manga, it was also the bestselling comic of that year in any category.

The "100 percent authentic" gamble

While manga series with TV show or videogame tie-ins were garnering respectable sales, there was still a considerable obstacle to getting more manga on store shelves: the time and cost involved in adapting titles for Western markets. Publishers had to either redraw the panels entirely or photographically flip them to accommodate the Western left-to-right reading style, then alter the word balloons so that they could hold horizontal text.

This approach, known as "**flopping**", had several drawbacks. It was costly to hire people to do all of the artistic retouching and the flopped art introduced cultural inaccuracies: the samurai hero of *Lone Wolf and Cub*, for instance, now wielded his sword with his right hand and carried it on his left side, a detail that made anyone familiar with traditional samurai culture cringe. Perhaps most importantly, the original manga creators were not happy that the integrity of their artwork was being compromised.

While translated manga that appeared as it did in Japan was not unheard of in the US, it was rare because most publishers believed that the public would not want to read a magazine or story produced in this unfamiliar format. By the early twenty-first century only Viz had produced unflopped titles: *Dragon Ball*, due to pressure from Shueisha to keep the art intact, and *Neon Genesis Evangelion*, which artist Yoshiyuki Sadamoto would not allow to be licensed unless it was printed in its original orientation. Over in France, Editions Glénat, one of the first publishers to sell compact paperback volumes of manga, starting in 1993, also published in 1995 Akira Toriyama's *Dr. Slump* in its original Japanese format.

In 2002, Tokyopop (formerly Mixx) was ready to take the gamble to go fully Japanese in its presentation of manga. In an initiative they dubbed "100%

Authentic Manga", Tokyopop left the art untouched in its original Japanese orientation with the visual sound effects untranslated. All their manga titles were also published in compact paperback format. The company made huge cost savings by bypassing all of the previous localization hoops, allowing them not only to churn out translated manga at a faster than ever rate but also to sell at a previously unheard of $9.99 per volume.

Fans, for their part, ate it up. It also helped that Tokyopop's launch of its "100% Authentic Manga" line catered to a diverse array of readers with titles such as *Love Hina* (see p.150), *Great Teacher Onizuka* (see p.139) and *Initial D* for male readers and *Marmalade Boy*, *Planet Ladder* and *Paradise Kiss* (see p.167) for female readers. There were crossover hits as well, with CLAMP's *Chobits* and *Angelic Layer* leading the way. And, as with their ground-breaking *Mixxzine* magazine, Tokyopop manga was available everywhere books were sold, as well as in music and DVD stores, which were beginning to stock print titles where there were tie-ins with their traditional inventory.

US publishers strike it rich

Tokyopop's move broke the market wide open with first printings of its unflopped books selling out immediately. Nearly 200,000 books were shipped in April 2002 alone. Manga's visibility grew exponentially as Tokyopop rolled out volumes of ongoing series and added new series to its line-up, with Korean manhwa and domestically produced global manga eventually joining the Japanese properties.

Viz accordingly kept pace, adding several big-selling shōjo titles to its line-up between 2000 and 2003. It also had another ace up its sleeve: a partnership with Shueisha gave it access to the titles the leading Japanese manga publisher released in its *Weekly Shōnen Jump* anthology back in Japan. Accordingly Viz launched an American version of the magazine entitled **Shonen Jump** in late 2002, which ran translated but unflopped stories. That didn't stop the first 300-page issue selling more than 300,000 copies, a figure that trounced the next highest comic on the Diamond Comics sales chart by at least three to one. In 2008, *Shonen Jump* still had a monthly circulation of 215,000.

Part of *Shonen Jump*'s success can be ascribed to the fact that many of the series that are carried in the anthology come with ready-made brand recognition. *Yu-Gi-Oh!* is familiar to all of the *Pokémon* fans now old enough to appreciate the slightly more mature collectible card game. (The magazine's first issue, in fact, came packaged with a rare card for the game.) *Dragon Ball* (see p.116) also had a large following from repeated airings of the anime on cable TV, as did the current reigning champion of manga sales in the Western world, *Naruto* (see p.159).

Translating into failure: Manganovel's story

Draw-it-yourself manga has been a vibrant component of manga fandom, as the ever-increasing numbers of global manga and books on drawing manga have shown. Translate-it-yourself manga, on the other hand, has been a task limited to Japanese-language scholars hired by legitimate publishers or hardcore groups of fans in the nooks and crannies of the Internet engaged in **scanlation** (the unauthorized scanning, translation and distribution of foreign-language comics) – the last group operating on the thinnest of copyright-law margins.

In 2007, Toshiba Corp., in conjunction with Manganovel Corp., tried to tap into the shadowy community of scanlators and turn them into legitimate manga translators by launching Manganovel. The service offered untranslated manga online, with chapters selling for as low as $1.15 and complete volumes for $4–5 (along with a few free samples), with the intent that people fluent in Japanese and another language would take whatever was posted online, translate it into their language of choice, and in turn offer their translated versions online, either for free or for two percent of the original manga's price. Other site visitors could then buy the original Japanese manga packaged with the translation, and the original translator would receive fifty percent of the sale price as a royalty. All of this was accomplished through the MQbit MangaReader, a downloadable program provided by Toshiba on the website.

In theory, the service offered manga at a cost lower than the cheapest manga available in print at the time. In practice, few people bought into the concept of buying manga and either translating it themselves or waiting for someone else to do it for them. The 24 titles the site hosted had little to no reader buzz outside of the site, and marketing appears to have been limited to a couple of press releases. While a modest community did form around the site, translating manga into 23 languages ranging from English to Portuguese to Esperanto, it wasn't enough to sustain the business, which shut down in 2009.

Soon, more publishers, seeing the profits being made by Viz, Tokyopop and Dark Horse, wanted in as well. In 2003, less than a year after both Viz and Tokyopop registered their respective record high sales numbers, two more publishers started releasing manga: **Broccoli Books**, the US branch of a Japanese anime- and manga-merchandise chain of stores, and **ADV Manga**, a subsidiary of the US anime company. The year after, DC Comics and Random

House started their own manga labels, **CMX** and **Del Rey**, respectively, the latter partnering up with the titan of the Japanese publishing scene Kodansha. ADV competitor **Bandai Entertainment** opened a manga branch; and the independent **Seven Seas Entertainment** launched its first global manga titles. For a complete look at the companies who were actively publishing translated manga as of 2009, see Chapter 6.

European and Australian opportunities

By 2007 over 1200 manga titles were available for US fans to buy from some 15 different publishers, generating sales of around $210 million, according to research firm ICv2. However, two years later ICv2 was reporting a **seventeen percent drop in sales** to about $175 million – a sign that the US market for manga may have reached its limit. Milton Griepp, ICv2's president, suggested four reasons for this decline: the overall economic recession in the US; the drop in the number of anime screened on TV; the change in graphic novel buying policy by US bookstore Borders; and the impact that the *Twilight* series of teenage novels was having in siphoning off potential female readers of manga.

There are worries that this drop in sales could signal more fundamental problems for the American manga industry. The recent financial struggles of ADV, Central Park Media and DramaQueen and the shutdown of Broccoli Books in 2009 indicate that not all of the publishers entering the market are seeing financial success. Tokyopop also showed some sign of weakness in 2008 when it split into two entities – one unit to publish books, the other to focus on other multimedia projects – and reduced its planned annual output by half, to two hundred or so titles a year from more than five hundred titles. The company's UK arm also slashed the number of titles it planned to publish in that market by twenty percent.

Despite this it would appear that as far as the potential for **future growth** is concerned, the greatest hope lies with the emerging English-language markets of the UK, Australia and New Zealand, as well as increasing penetration in the more mature manga markets of France, Germany, Italy and Spain. In the UK, top book publishers have thrown considerable weight into establishing lists of manga titles to feed off a growing demand for graphic novels and Japanese pop culture that has blossomed particularly in the last few years off the back of anime hits such as *Naruto*.

Similarly in **Australia**, Tokyopop partnered with children's books supplier Funtastic in 2006 to bring 24 of its titles, including the global manga *Princess Ai*, *Warcraft* and *Peach Fuzz*, to the market, while Viz teamed up with Madman Entertainment, Australia's largest distributor of anime and manga titles, in

2008 to bring their titles in as well. Fan conventions are held in all the Australian states and one of the stars of OEL manga, Queenie Chan, is a Sydney resident.

It is telling, though, that Viz Media's European arm is based in Paris, not London. This reflects the fact that according to JETRO, Japan's External Trade Organization, German and French sales of manga for 2006 totalled $212.6 million, making Europe the largest market for manga outside of Japan; almost two-thirds of those sales were in France. France's comic book market, one of the most diverse in the world, is one that manga can do better in all the same, since it accounts for less than a quarter of the total market and for none of the top-selling titles overall. There is clearly much room for expansion and one way that US, European and Japanese publishers are all seeking to achieve this is by blurring the definition of what exactly might or might not be manga.

The international manga debate

The question of whether manga can truly be called "manga" if it's produced outside of Japan has long been a matter of bitter contention among fans. Purists insist that manga must be created in Japan to be considered as such. Anything else is simply black-and-white comic books done in the style of manga, with foreign artists paying tribute to the artistic methods and techniques used by the original creators. However, such debates become moot when one takes into account how manga developed in the first place (see p.5) and how it is still developing (see p.55).

It can be argued that the earliest examples of so-called "**international manga**" (the preferred term of the Japanese government – it's also been termed **original English-language (OEL)** manga and **global** manga) were the comics created from scratch that were based on such Japanese animated properties as *Astro Boy* in the 1960s, *Shogun Warriors* in the 1970s and *Robotech* in the 1980s (see box on p.39). The trend continued into the 1990s as anime made inroads into the public consciousness, with Adam Warren and Toren Smith's take on *Dirty Pair* being the most successful of these adaptations.

It wasn't until the mid-1980s that Antarctic Press first started producing comics with original stories that had a manga-influenced style to them, first with the anthology comic book *Magazine* in 1985, then with the longest-running global manga still being published today, Ben Dunn's *Ninja High School* in 1987.

While Antarctic Press continues to publish titles that have a manga-esque flair (but without actually coming out and saying the word "manga" prominently on its website), perhaps the most prolific global manga publisher of the moment is Tokyopop. Since 2002, the publisher has offered the most opportunities for creators to publish their works through its Rising Stars of Manga contests. Aspiring manga authors submit a fifteen- to twenty-page short story in one of eight different categories – comedy, action, mystery, romance, drama, science fiction, fantasy and horror – and Tokyopop editors pick the best works in each category to publish in a single-volume anthology. The winners also receive a contract to create an original series. Runners-up also have been known to parlay their exposure with other global manga and comic book publishers.

The seemingly insatiable market for manga in the last decade has spurred traditional American comic publishers to grab a slice of the action, especially as sales of their own core products were slumping. Marvel, who had first explored this avenue back in 1979 with *Shogun Warriors*, gave it another try from 2000 to 2002 with its *Marvel Mangaverse* series of comic books and the sequel *New Mangaverse* in 2005, both of which depict famous Marvel identities drawn in manga style. Under a deal with Del Rey, Marvel is also planning to release in 2009 a shōnen-ized version of *Wolverine* and a shōjo-infused version of *X-Men*.

Ninja High School

Ben Dunn; *pub* Antarctic Press (US, 1987–); ongoing

Jeremy Feeple is just an average high school student caught up in a love triangle, albeit one with alien princesses and ninjas. The alien princess, Asrial, came to the planet to marry Jeremy and

© 2007 Madeleine Rosca

Global manga's take on the high-school genre: *Hollow Fields* was a runner-up at Japan's inaugural International Manga Awards in 2007.

International manga rocks out

It's become increasingly common for noted authors such as Dean Koontz and James Patterson to team up with international manga creators such as Queenie Chan and NaRae Lee to release manga versions of their iconic characters. Now musicians are also making the jump from the stage to manga page, most successfully **Courtney Love** and **Avril Lavigne**, who've been instrumental in developing their respective projects.

Love's *Princess Ai* is arguably the more star-studded of the two. Created out of an idea that Love brought to Tokyopop about a girl searching for her place in the world, the project soon involved *Paradise Kiss* and *Nana* artist Ai Yazawa, with Stuart Levy handling the writing duties himself under his alter ego, DJ Milky. "Ai" is the Japanese word for "love" and the story itself loosely references Love's life… albeit in a setting based more on fantasy than reality. Having said that, a sensitive blond guitarist becomes Ai's main love interest, and her most treasured item is a heart-shaped box.

Lavigne plays a more direct role in the story of *Make 5 Wishes*. In the story written by Joshua Dysart and drawn by Camilla D'Errico, the singer appears as herself, albeit as the imaginary friend of one of her fans, Hana. As such, Lavigne can act as Hana's conscience as the girl struggles through life feeling lonely and unwanted. The story has a bit of an edge to it, though, as a desperate Hana eventually abandons Lavigne in favour of a strange creature that grants her five wishes to improve her life… not quite in the way she expects, of course.

ensure that other alien forces don't lay claim to Earth. The ninja, Ichi, wants to marry Jeremy so she can become the leader of her clan. Recently, the story's focus has shifted more toward Jeremy's younger brother Ricky's encounters with ninja princesses, alien girls and other phenomena.

Hollow Fields

Madeleine Rosca; *pub* Seven Seas (US, UK, Aus, 2007–); *vols* ongoing

The creation of Australian artist Rosca, this reads like a manga version of *Harry Potter* with a more average lead character and much more whimsical evil. Lucy Snow's decision to take a short cut

on the way to boarding school sees her instead ending up enrolled at Miss Weaver's Academy for the Scientifically Gifted and Ethically Unfettered. That's *Hollow Fields*, an academy of the forbidden sciences where "transplantation", "live taxidermy" and "bio-steam grafting" are all core curriculum classes. Now studying to get the best grades is essential to Lucy's very survival.

International competitions

In 2007 two separate efforts to recognize international manga creators were launched: the Japanese government sponsored **International Manga Award** (mofa.go.jp/policy/culture/manga), and the **Morning International Manga Contest** (MIMC; e-morning.jp/mimc), sponsored by Kodansha and its weekly manga magazine *Morning*.

Kodansha first announced its international manga competition as a way of celebrating the 25th anniversary of *Morning*, in late 2006, accepting entries until May 2007. The winner of the inaugural contest, the US team of writer Bikkuri and artist rem, had their short story, *Kage no Matsuri* (*Festival of Shadows*), published in *Morning 2* magazine. The runners-up – *Nigiri Supahero*, a sushi-themed superhero action tale by Liou Ming Law of the UK, and *Vefurrin*, a fantasy story by Hwei-Lin Lim of Malaysia – each received $2000 for their efforts.

In May 2007, manga-loving Tarō Asō, as of 2009 Japan's prime minister but then its foreign minister, announced the creation of the International Manga Award, which was designed, as he said at a press conference, "to enhance the voice of Japanese pop culture and subculture". Asō added that he wanted to make the award "like the Nobel Prize of manga".

Chinese creator Lee Chi Ching won the inaugural award for *Sun Zi's Tactics*, with the runners-up being *1520* by Kai of Hong Kong, *Le Gardenie* by Benny Wong Thong Hou of Malaysia, and *Hollow Fields* by Australia's Madeleine Rosca. All the award winners spent ten days in Japan, meeting with manga artists and publishers; so far though only Lee's work has found a Japanese publisher.

In 2008, the top winner of the International Manga Award again hailed from Hong Kong – Lau Wan Kit for *Feel 100%*, with runner-up awards going to Chinese artist Yin Chuan for *Elapse*, Russian Chezhina Svetlana Igorevna for *Portrait* and Alice Picard from France for *Okhéania 1*.

Hybrid manga

Apart from drumming up further interest in and a wider understanding of the rich variety of manga in overseas markets, one of the main reasons for these awards has been to find and foster **non-Japanese talents**. It is hoped that their sometimes distinctively different drawing styles and stories will reinvigorate Japan's declining market for comics, in the process creating what some may call a hybrid product.

The seeds of such a movement already seem to be sprouting. Alternative American comic book artist Paul Pope, author of *THB*, a sci-fi story set on Mars, worked for Kodansha for five years, during which time he developed the manga *Supertrouble*. Kodansha have also commissioned Felipe Smith, creator of Tokyopop's OEL manga *MBQ* to draw a monthly series for its *Morning 2* anthology, and picked up for publication the successful webcomic *Megatokyo*

(megatokyo.com) for its Kodansha Box line. Interestingly, the Japanese version of *Megatokyo* is being presented exactly the same way it is in English, not flopped to conform with Japanese reading habits.

Writing about Houston-based artist rem's success in the 2008 MIMC contest, Japanese journalist Kanta Ishida noted how this was "further evidence of a growing population of talented mangaka outside Japan" and how reading her dialogue-free story *Kage no Matsuri*, "one wouldn't imagine that it was created by an American artist".

The term **nouvelle manga** has also been coined. It was first used to describe the realistic works of French artist Frédéric Boilet, who lives in Japan and who has been published in such mainstream manga compendiums as *Big Comics*.

At the same time, Japanese artists continue to soak up ideas from overseas and adapt them into their own works – just as they have done since the days of manga pioneer Rakuten Kitazawa (see p.7). Jirō Taniguchi acknowledges the influence of French comics or *bandes dessinées* on his manga style. Taniguchi was the first Japanese to win the highest award at the Angoulême Festival, France's top comics event. And current reigning star of Japan's manga scene Naoki Urasawa is also playing around with American comic book conventions in his 2009 series *Billy Bat*, the first couple of episodes being drawn in the 1930s style of *Dick Tracy* and printed in full colour – highly unusual for series in Japan's weekly manga magazines.

Dramacon

Svetlana Chmakova; *pub* Tokyopop (US, 2005–07); *vols* 3

Amateur writer Christie is attending her first anime convention with her artist boyfriend, setting up a table in the Artists Alley to co-promote their new manga together. But things aren't going well for the couple… and a mysterious, rather charming cosplayer that Christie sees could very well change her life. There's a playful style to Russian-Canadian Chmakova's art and her world is populated with an energy (not to mention chibified cuteness) that shows she has a firm grasp on the shōjo storytelling style.

Megatokyo

Fred Gallagher (and Rodney Caston, vols 1 & 2); *pub* Dark Horse (US, vols 1–4, 2002), CMX (US, ongoing)

This English-language webcomic has broken out of the Internet to become a bestselling print product. Visiting Japan is the dream of many anime, manga and videogame fans. Getting stuck there? Not so much. That's what happens to Piro and Largo… and while a fair amount of hand-wringing takes place, they soon settle in to their new lives – Piro as a worker at a small bookstore, Largo as a somewhat paranoid teacher convinced that "3v1l" lurks everywhere and must be "pwned". It's a story packed with sad-looking girls and parodies of Japanese dating-simulation games and is above all a tribute to the manga that Gallagher enjoys reading.

3

A Manga primer

decoding styles and genres

Ask a fan to define manga and you'll get a range of answers. One person might describe Osamu Tezuka's work in its purest form, each frame seemingly pulled straight from a film reel. Another might argue that manga isn't manga unless the characters sport huge eyes and gravity-defying spikes of hair. There's a camp that believes manga has to be edgy, with plenty of action sequences – on the battleground and in the bedroom. And of course there are the science fiction fans for whom manga means giant robots battling it out for the future of the planet.

The truth is that manga encompasses all these genres and more. It can tell stories ranging from the conventional (girl has crush on boy) to the wildly unconventional (girl has crush on boy… who wants to be the greatest curry chef of all time); elevate stories of office work into compelling drama; and even educate about topics as diverse as statistics or wine. Some genres are common in the West; others are uniquely Japanese. But no matter where it's published, manga tends to fall into the broad age and gender categories used by the Japanese market.

Decoding manga

Manga covers a bewildering range of subjects, aimed at every type of reader imaginable, but it's still readily identifiable as manga, thanks to a number of elements found nowhere else, which together form a kind of **common language**. Although there are exceptions, it's these unique artistic and narrative conventions, sometimes the result of traditional production processes, that distinguish manga from other types of sequential art, such as Western comic strips and comic books.

Manga are comics rendered in black and white – that much is obvious from a first glance. But there have been plenty of Western comics in black and white too, from newspaper comic strips to independent comics, including prominent series like Jeff Smith's *Bone* and Dave Sim's 300-issue *Cerebus*. What makes manga fundamentally different from these examples are the circumstances under which it's produced – and consumed. Many series in Japan are created for weekly magazines, meaning the artist has to churn out an entire chapter of thirty to forty pages of art every week. Such short turnaround times mean that artists must often choose which parts of the page will get an extra layer of artistic detail and which parts will be rendered in a form of artistic shorthand. (For more on how

manga are created, see p.62.) For readers too, the way manga is produced makes for a different experience. Rather than lingering over a full-colour 36-page monthly, avid manga readers in Japan have to whip through many more pages to keep up with their favourite stories.

Readers who immerse themselves in manga quickly notice certain **visual elements** cropping up across different series, elements that can easily bewilder the neophyte – why, for instance, do backgrounds turn sparkly in one section, flowery in another and become filled with lightning bolts in a third section? Why do cherry blossom petals start swirling through the air? How come that character's standing upright in one frame and only his upside-down legs are showing in the next? And what's the deal with those eyes, anyway? It all makes more sense when you realize that over the years, visual and storytelling techniques have developed to the point where certain icons, expressions and events are recognizable shorthand for manga artists to quickly express what they want to say. For instance, instead of showing a girl thinking to herself, "Oh, no! The boy I've loved in secret for so long has just confessed that he likes me! What am I going to say?" by means of a thought bubble, they're more likely to simply show her with squiggles under her eyes, which in manga denotes a shy, embarrassed, "I totally love you too!" feeling.

Once a reader becomes familiar with the visual code and iconography detailed below, understanding manga is no more difficult than understanding a Western comic.

Long-running stories

While there are a few exceptions in which a series has lasted for several decades – *Golgo 13*, *Doraemon* and the tongue-twisting *Kochira Katsushika-ku Kameari Ko-en Mae Hashutsujo* (see pp.138, 112 and 21) among them – or instances where an artist has died before the story could be completed, manga are finite entities with a distinct beginning and end. For the most part, manga readers go into a series knowing that it will end someday, although it may not be in the neat and tidy way that Western audiences expect in their pop culture media. Manga conclusions have a tendency to be open-ended, empowering readers to continue the story as they see fit. It's as if the author is telling readers, "Okay, this is the end of one part of these characters' lives and I'm done telling this story, but from this point forward life in general goes on."

Big eyes, bigger hair

Manga's focus on emotions and the interaction between characters is achieved in part through simpler, more iconic-looking characters, without any superfluous detail to distract from what's important. A side benefit is that they're quicker to draw. Hence, the most prominent physical attributes are eyes and hair. Osamu Tezuka pioneered the "**big eyes**" look associated with manga characters to this day, influenced by popular characters from Western animation like Betty Boop and the Disney stable. The larger and rounder the eyes are, the more innocent and pure the character is supposed to be, and females are often drawn with bigger eyes than males. At the opposite end of the spectrum, characters with shifty, squinty eyes are often the story's villains. Eyes in between these extremes can indicate a loss of innocence, perhaps some sort of shady past that's hidden at the time the story begins.

Artists from Tezuka onwards have embraced the idea that eyes can express and emphasize emotions in different ways. For instance, the eyes of an ecstatic character can be represented simply by a pair of upward-curving arcs. Eyes can turn white and lose their irises to show extreme shock, or they can narrow into half-circles to denote anger. Particularly furious characters have their eyes reduced even further to four-point stars, with the tops of their faces shrouded in shadow, a sign that other characters in the vicinity might want to run for cover. Sadness, on the other hand, can be represented by little trickles of tears or what appear to be waterfalls – even geysers – jetting out from a character's eyes, the irises reduced to wavy blobs.

As for those often wild **hairstyles**, artists have come to rely on them as a way of distinguishing between the different characters depicted in black and white. While the styles may sometimes appear outrageous, they're kept simple enough so that characters can be drawn and identified in a flash. Thus, long hair, bob cuts, cowlicks and pony tails are common, while elaborate curly styles are not. Hair colour can also be used as a distinguishing trait.

Emotional shorthand

Eyes and hair aren't the only forms of nonverbal expression for manga characters. In fact, an entire iconography of emotional expression has developed around characters' heads alone.

When **blood** gushes from (often male) characters' noses, it's an indication that the character is sexually aroused by what they're seeing, often an attractive member of the opposite sex. This notion is based in traditional Japanese folklore. On the other hand, a large **snot** bubble sometimes appears attached to the nose of a character who's fast asleep.

An **open-ended cross** formed by four little V-shapes can appear on the temple or over the head of an angry character, implying that the character's veins are bulging.

Embarrassment (or in the proper context, a shy display of love for someone) can appear as a series of diagonal lines on the cheekbones, to give the impression of **blushing**, with progressively deeper embarrassment displayed by deeper, darker shading.

Another way of displaying embarrassment, exasperation or confusion over a situation is through the use of a single giant **sweat drop** or multiple, smaller drops, seen on the front or the back of the head or hovering over it.

In comedy manga, characters' bodies are sometimes depicted in the simplest of forms while their heads remain large – this style of artwork, known as **chibi**, or super-deformed, is often used to illustrate the most extreme emotions.

Layout, lines and tones

Environmental details – including the choice of screen tones, lines and the arrangement and shape of **panels** on a page – also help establish the mood of a story. When first learning how to draw manga, artists are encouraged to vary panel sizes and to always keep one frame larger than the others to capture the reader's attention. This dominant panel often depicts a moment key to that particular episode – the introduction of a new character or setting, a scene shift, a climax to showcase a special technique, a sudden change of heart, or an expression of shock and surprise, for example.

The **lines** surrounding a character can portray motion in different ways: horizontal lines starting off thick and slowly tapering into a thinner line emphasize the character and the direction in which he or she is .; curved lines emphasize instead the speed at which the character is moving. When lines are drawn vertically in the background, they imply a mood of sadness and gloom – once again, the heavier the lines, the more intense the emotion being portrayed.

Artists also use **screen tones** to save time in creating different textures on their pages, sometimes to give more depth or add a specific style to backgrounds, other times to give characters' clothing added dimension. The traditional method, one that's still widely used today, employs transparent sheets of film with various patterns printed on them in black ink, backed with a special adhesive. To get the desired effect, artists apply the tone to the paper then use a thin-bladed knife to cut the shape that they wish to use, and then rub it onto the surface. A second knife is sometimes used to scrape or blur sections of tone to vary the texture portrayed. The modern alternative is to use image-editing software like Photoshop, whose screen tone libraries accomplish the same effect. There are hundreds of different tone styles and patterns available, whether in transparent sheets or on computers, measured by lines per inch

and density of colour, from 0% (white) to 100% (black).

Sound effects and speech

Ambient sounds and the onomatopoeic representation of particular actions or events are just as much a part of the art as the people, places and things depicted in manga, with the size of the sound effects and their position on the page determining the strength and direction of the sound. Consider them as being like the "zap!" or "kapow!" of Western comics, but on a more frequently used scale. In what is known as **giseigo**, all the ambient noise in a particular scene, from the quietest "doki doki" (representing a heart beating) to the "BUGOOOOOO" of a loud explosion, is given in simple Japanese kana characters. A less familiar concept are the sound effects that are in reality silent, but used symbolically – for example, the "shiiiiiiiiiiin" that appears behind a character's head at awkward moments, or the "hyoi hyoi" and "choi choi" of a dog's paw waving and tail wagging, respectively. This type of sound effect, known as **gitaigo**, is drawn in both the simple alphabet of kana and more complex kanji, and often denotes a certain mood or condition. Harsh, violent sounds can be drawn with sharp angles to the characters, while softer, gentler sounds are drawn with more rounded characters.

Anatomy of a Bloodbath: the artist-editor relationship

Manga publishers have since the 1940s used talent competitions as a way to find new artists from among their readership. From the 1960s it became an established method of submitting work for publication, with professional manga creators judging the competitions. These days, however, publishers can no longer rely on that method alone to grab the best up-and-coming talent, and so publishers scout artists who are already working, whether as a self-published creator of dōjinshi (see p.26) or as an apprentice under a professional mangaka.

Once an artist is taken on by a publisher, the next step is to assign an **editor**, who performs a critical role in bringing out the best in the artist and ensuring his or her work is consistent with the editorial philosophy of the publication while keeping them on track to produce enough content for the particular magazine's cycle. Communication between artist and editor has become even more crucial since the larger publishers created new divisions of labour in the 1960s, to speed up the processes for weekly production of magazines. It's the editor who carries out many of the key steps in this process: checking rough sketches; ordering, supervising and editing lettering and typesetting; and taking responsibility for the manga creators meeting their deadlines with publishers and printers. Editors are also responsible for determining the mix of stories in a particular issue, how many pages of each story to run, and which artists will be used to accomplish that mix. That responsibility can be overwhelming at times. In extreme cases, an artist may sometimes have to produce upwards of eighty pages weekly, to meet the demands of an audience eager to see the next instalments of their favourite series. Editors have been known to confine an artist in a room with nothing but food or to keep him or her "hostage" until the work is finished. And adding to the pressure is the small matter of producing content that meets audience approval. *Shōnen Jump*, for instance, regularly runs an audience approval poll; if a new series doesn't show signs of improving its standing within a ten-week period, it's cancelled.

Many a manga carries **omake** (extra content) about the relationship between editors and artists, with artists showing signs of going crazy as deadlines approach and the "mean" editor breathes down their necks. With all of this work thrust upon them, artists rarely generate series by themselves, often employing assistants to help them create the art. These assistants could be associates, friends... or even parents. For instance, Mihona Fujii, the author of *GALS!*, enlisted the help of her mother on that series... and then proceeded to gently skewer her in a series of cartoons she called "Anatomy of a Bloodbath".

Western publishers take several different approaches in translating sound effects. Some replace the Japanese effects with their English counterparts. Others offer small translations above or below the sound effect or provide a translation key in the back of the book. Still others forego translations altogether, leaving those who have no Japanese-reading experience to appreciate the effects solely for their artistic value.

Speech bubbles aren't too dissimilar to those in Western comics. For instance, it's easy to interpret the mood in which certain lines of dialogue are spoken by looking at the shapes: normal speech and thoughts are rendered in conventional round balloons; fluffy cloud balloons are used for euphoric states; and wavy, sometimes pointy balloons are used when a character is shocked or upset, with increasingly sharp angles representing deeper degrees of aggravation. When bubbles disappear completely, the words left behind can signify either an outer narrative or an internal monologue. Any confusion for Western readers stems from how manga speech balloons have small tails or no tails at all, making it sometimes difficult to determine exactly who is speaking. Confusing though it may be, speech balloons are positioned to work in concert with the other elements on the page to create a natural flow, moving your eyes through the panels on the page.

Categories and genres: sorting it all out

When it comes to categorizing manga, there are plenty of familiar **genres** you can apply, from romances to action-adventures, comedies to horror stories, sports stories and science fiction, plus the less usual cooking, *pachinko* and stories about day-to-day office work… any genre that can be conceived, there's likely to be at least one series that covers it. Mangaka are aware of the challenges of each genre and adjust their styles accordingly: what constitutes high drama in a love story aimed at teen girls, for instance, is different from the drama in a high-stakes mah-jongg match. But with manga embracing all kinds of readership, genre is only part of the story: the Japanese categorize manga by first dividing series into those targeted at either **male or female** audiences, then splitting these into two or three different **age groups**.

That's not to say these categories are set in stone. Many of the categories covered in this section, and especially the main four – **shōjo** (for young girls and teens), **shōnen** (for young boys and teens), **seinen** (older males) and **josei** (older females) – offer series with a broader-ranging appeal. Readers often pick and choose manga from various categories, being quite comfortable reading manga other than those that specifically target them.

Shōnen manga

The target audience for shōnen manga may be boys from early elementary school to their late teens, but its appeal is probably the widest reaching, attracting female as well as older fans. It's also manga's oldest genre, with representative works ranging from Osamu Tezuka's earliest successes to modern-day hits like *Naruto*, *Fullmetal Alchemist* and *One Piece*. The most successful properties can generate considerable spin-off profits, from anime adaptations, toys, videogames and various collectible trinkets. Shōnen properties are, in fact, the most likely to be animated. At over 38 percent of the market, it's the largest category of manga in Japan, where the bestselling shōnen magazines, Shueisha's *Weekly Shōnen Jump* and Kodansha's *Weekly Shōnen Magazine*, regularly shift more than 2 million copies a week each. In English-speaking markets, it's shōnen, along with shōjo manga, that's drawn in the majority of fans over the past decade.

Exactly what gives shōnen its universal appeal can be summed up by the results of a survey conducted by *Weekly Shōnen Jump* soon after it began publishing in 1968. Young readers were asked for the word that most warmed their hearts, what they placed as the first priority in their lives, and what made

them happiest. Their answers – friendship, perseverance and victory – guided *Shōnen Jump*'s story selection from that point forward, not to mention countless other shōnen stories too. It's the reason shōnen heroes are so easy to relate to: outcasts, the clumsy, the shy, the brash, the bold, the skilled and the emotionally flawed – all have been represented in some form in shōnen manga. There's an element of dream fulfillment, too, and no matter what the genre – sports, romance, comedy, fantasy, science fiction, the "harem manga" concept of being caught in a situation with plenty of cute girls around – it's possible to put oneself in the shoes of the characters and empathize with what they're going through. With the action based around friendship and great deeds, there's little, if any, romantic tension in shōnen series, with girls accepted more as peers than as love interests.

Shōnen manga is all about fast-paced action, about great people accomplishing great things, whether in sports or on some historic, fantastic or futuristic battleground. Yet the main characters usually remain humble, modest about their abilities or unaware they're anything special until some key early moment in the series. Should they be overconfident in any situation, they'll get knocked down a few pegs and learn the value of humility in the process. But if it seems like the character will be a middle-of-the-road type of person, the odds are high that something will happen to make him extraordinary. Maybe he'll get hit with a curse, stumble upon a giant robot or become the owner of some sort of magical creature.

Exceptional skills alone won't carry the shōnen hero through a series, though. Around the corner, there lurks an adversary who will stretch him to the limits of his abilities (and beyond) so that he can survive and advance in the story. In fact, many by-the-numbers shōnen manga are structured not unlike a videogame, with regular "boss" characters to defeat as the hero constantly improves his skills in preparation for facing the ultimate evil, his journeys filled with mischief and mayhem. No matter how dark situations may become, there's always a feeling of optimism lurking around the corner.

Bleach

Tite Kubo; *pub* Shueisha (Jp), Viz (US, UK), Madman (Aus); *ser* Weekly Shōnen Jump (2001–); *vols* ongoing; *age* 13+

Tite Kubo, influenced by the supernatural creatures in Shigeru Mizuki's *GeGeGe no Kitarō* and the weaponry and battle sequences in *Knights of the Zodiac/Saint Seiya* (see p.146), created an action-packed tale of souls and swords that has become one of the most popular shōnen titles worldwide and earned a Shogakukan Manga Award in 2005. Ichigo Kurosaki is a newly inducted Soul Reaper who must guard those he loves, help good wandering spirits find eternal peace and defend against Hollows, evil spirits that prey upon the psychic energy of humans. Kubo's strengths are in developing characters whose outer appearances often mask their true

natures and adding absurd touches to otherwise conventional situations.

Captain Tsubasa

Yoichi Takahashi; *pub* Shueisha (Jp); *ser* Weekly Shōnen Jump (1981–88); *vols* 37

A story that embraces many key shōnen manga elements – the power of friendship and teamwork, characters with fantastic special abilities, hard work and a determination to succeed paying off in the long run – within the framework of one of the world's most popular sports, football (soccer). When just over a year old, Tsubasa Ozora was saved from an oncoming bus by clutching onto a football. Now an elementary school student, he dreams of one day winning the FIFA World Cup with the Japanese team. He gets help from the friends he meets along the way and a mentor in Brazilian football star Roberto Hongo. While the series has never appeared in English, there have been successful Italian and Spanish translations.

Rurouni Kenshin

Nobuhiro Watsuki; *pub* Shueisha (Jp), Viz (US, UK), Madman (Aus); *ser* Weekly Shōnen Jump (1994–99); *vols* 28; *age* 16+

This series, set in the midst of Japan's Meiji period in 1878, follows a former government assassin, Hitokiri Battōsai, who has foresworn violence and changed his name to Himura Kenshin. All he wants to do is retire in peace, but when there are old enemies, corrupt revolutionaries and a dirty past to confront, the battles seem unlikely to end. Unlike other tales of wandering swordsmen such as *Blade of the Immortal*, *Lone Wolf and Cub* and *Vagabond* (see pp. 94, 147 and 188), Watsuki has domestic squabbles between Kenshin and kendo instructor Kamiya Kaoru providing light-hearted moments amongst the battles. Watsuki's art mixes stylish sword-fighting sequences with exaggerated character designs.

Yakitate!! Japan

Takashi Hashiguchi; *pub* Shogakukan (Jp), Viz (US, UK); *ser* Shōnen Sunday (2002–); *vols* ongoing; *age* 16+

What *Iron Wok Jan* (see p.142) does for cooking in general, *Yakitate!! Japan* does specifically for breadmaking, transforming the simple act of food preparation into flashy high-drama competition. Earnest young hero Kazuma Azuma possesses the "Hands of the Sun", which help him produce perfect loaves of bread. His goal in life is to make a bread that will put Japan on the map… never mind that getting people to eat bread instead of rice is a challenge in itself. The manga is packed with puns (the Japanese word for bread is "pan", hence Kazuma's goal is to make "Japan", or Japanese bread) and memorable characters, such as Kazuma's former swordsman-turned-baker rival.

Seinen manga

To borrow a term from Ed Chavez at Mangacast, seinen manga is "manly manga for manly men". If shōnen manga is all about action, then seinen manga is where characters take action to the extreme. Older males are the target audience, after all, demanding a more mature style of story, the equivalent of an R-rated movie, with more frank depictions of violence and sex. Moral conundrums are no longer "good versus evil" affairs, but rendered in many shades of grey. The stories are grounded more in reality, whether it's a historical drama,

a raunchy sex comedy or a tale of life at work, and delve into more complex issues and themes than simple friendship, perseverance and victory. Even fantasy elements retain a subtlety that makes them more believable.

Some seinen works have a pulp fiction quality to them, gritty and raw, like the historical dramas *Blade of the Immortal* and *Vagabond* (see pp.94 and 188) or the violent assassins' tales *Crying Freeman* and *Golgo 13* (see pp.103 and 138). Heroes in these series tend to be world-weary individuals who've seen far too much pain in their lifetime and are often flawed emotionally and ethically – unlike the typical shōnen hero. Other series become extended ruminations on pertinent issues: apocalyptic works inspired by the 1945 atomic bombings of Hiroshima and Nagasaki or the earthquakes that have ravaged parts of Japan, like *Akira* and *Ghost in the Shell* (see pp.78 and 136), or cautionary environmental tales like *Drifting Classroom* (see p.118).

Seinen manga shifts closer to shōjo manga than shōnen with its more overt romantic elements, as seen in *Love Roma*, *Maison Ikkoku* (see pp.152 and 156) and CLAMP's *Chobits*. But where shōjo romances take the straightforward "loves me/loves me not" approach, seinen manga tend to examine a relationship in more depth – why we love who we love and how the consequences of our actions affect those around us. Seinen manga don't shy away from depicting sex either, whether the one-night stands of *Lupin III* or *Love Roma*'s culmination of a long-developing relationship.

Seinen series make up an estimated 38 percent of the Japanese market. But while they represented a significant portion of manga translated for the US market in the 1990s, those percentages have since fallen, with shōnen and shōjo manga getting a disproportionate share of Western marketing pushes as manga is positioned as entertainment for teens and young adults. Seinen manga may never be a market leader in the West, but as younger fans mature and begin to explore titles beyond the mainstream, seinen is the category likely to benefit the most.

Chobits

CLAMP; *pub* Kodansha (Jp), Tokyopop (US, UK, Aus); *ser* Weekly Young Magazine (2000–02); *vols* 8; *age* 16+

In the hands of a lesser artist, the story of a student struggling to get into college who adopts a cute female android with a blank-slate memory as his own would be the setup for a cheap romantic comedy. CLAMP (see p.98) takes this concept in a different direction, contemplating the role of technology in society today and exploring the fundamental concept of love and whether it will eventually be possible for humans and androids to share romantic feelings. The story follows Hideki Motosuwa and his life with a discarded working Persocom unit, whom he names "Chii" for her inability to say anything but that when she was first powered up. But Chii may well be a discarded Chobit, some of the most

CLAMP

◄ 1 ►

ちょびっツ
Chobits

Courtesy of Kodansha Ltd

The front cover of the original Japanese edition of *Chobits* volume 1 showcases CLAMP's gorgeous character artwork.

powerful Persocoms of all. And Hideki's falling in love with her… and she with him.

Initial D

Shuichi Shigeno; *pub* Kodansha (Jp), Tokyopop (US, UK, Aus); *ser* Weekly Young Magazine (1995–); *vols* ongoing; *age* 13+

The *Initial D* manga and its subsequent anime adaptation accomplished in Japan what *The Fast and the Furious* film franchise accomplished in the West: a glorification of the adrenaline-pumping, high-stakes underground street-racing culture with enough hardcore racing detail to satisfy aficionados. The series appears at first glance to be a standard shōnen story complete with escalating battle structure: Takumi "Tak" Fujiwara, a teen with natural race-driving talent, rises from humble tofu delivery boy to street-racing legend in the mountain passes of Japan. But there's a realistic edge to the racing sequences, and the occasional focus on Takumi's relationships has a sensitive touch.

20th Century Boys

Naoki Urasawa; *pub* Shogakukan (Jp), Viz (US, UK); *ser* Big Comic Spirits (2000–06); *vols* 22; *age* 16+

In 1969, a boy named Kenji and his friends formed a secret society with a special symbol and a vow to defend the world against villains who would try to destroy it. The vow was largely forgotten by 1997, but when an apocalyptic cult leader known only as "Friend" rises to prominence with the boys' symbol as his group's logo, boyhood fantasies start becoming part of an eerie reality. Naoki Urasawa crafts a deft psychological thriller that plays out slowly and meticulously, with constant cuts between the events of 1969 and 1997, and in the process reveals how childhood innocence often gives way to cynicism in the face of harsh reality.

Shōjo manga

Shōjo manga, aimed squarely at teenage girls, is often stereotyped as the home of unabashedly sappy romances featuring invariably beautiful characters. Countless heroines – usually spunky, independent high school girls (high school begins at age fifteen in Japan) – manage either by accident or through some convoluted scheme to manoeuvre themselves straight into the arms of the hottest guy in school. If the girl is extremely lucky (or unlucky), she'll be at the centre of a whole group of hot guys, with a love triangle or larger love polygon the inevitable result. Chances are good that she'll end up with the guy of her dreams, and his identity is often blatantly telegraphed by less experienced artists. Often these stories have a "fashion show" sensibility, too, with characters showing off the artist's clothing design through frequent close-ups.

Finding true love is by no means all that shōjo manga is about, though, as it offers many of the same genres as shōnen manga. Science fiction? While not as common today, many early shōjo artists tackled such stories, with such examples as Moto Hagio's *They Were Eleven* (see box opposite) and Keiko Takemiya's *To Terra* (see p.186) among them. Sports? There's Mitsuba Takanashi's *Crimson Hero*, about a girl who shuns the traditional Japanese lifestyle at her parents' restaurant, opting

Lost in translation: Four Shojo Stories

In the nascent days of translated manga in the US, books would come and go without so much as a blink from what was then a much smaller audience. One of those books, published in 1996, was a treasure trove of shōjo manga from Viz, titled, appropriately enough, *Four Shojo Stories*. "Japanese comics from a uniquely female perspective", the cover trumpeted. "It's not just girl's stuff anymore." Contained within were stories by three women considered today to be shōjo manga legends.

In **Keiko Nishi**'s "Promise", a mysterious, good-looking boy helps a girl find peace within herself and come to terms with her mother's remarriage. The same author's "Since You've Been Gone" has a married chemistry professor run off with one of his students under the guise of a business trip, but an earthquake figuratively and literally jolts his senses and helps him realize who he truly loves.

Moto Hagio's "They Were Eleven" is a sci-fi classic in which an eleventh person infiltrates what should be a team of ten people placed on board an orbiting spaceship and called upon to survive for 53 days as the final stage of the Galactic University entrance exam. The team must figure out a way to survive, work together with different alien-race team members and, most importantly, trust one another.

"The Changeling" is another sci-fi tale, by **Shio Sato**, featuring a space traveller who discovers a flourishing alien civilization that purged the "noble race" of humans from Earth that preceded it. Yet there is something about aliens that makes them want to embrace humans as much as they want to reject them.

It's an eclectic mix that showcases the diversity of stories in shōjo manga. Shōjo expert Matt Thorn provided a foreword for the book, which would make an excellent starting point for anyone wanting to learn more about shōjo manga. Unfortunately, the book is no longer in print – in fact, it was never supposed to exist at all. As Thorn told MangaBlog, Viz only held the rights to publish *Four Shojo Stories* as individual stories in separate comic books, not as a paperback anthology. "When they asked me to write the intro, I asked, in surprise, 'They gave you permission to collect these stories?'" said Thorn. "The editor (now retired) said, 'If we ask them, they'll say no, but if we go ahead and do it, they may complain, but what can they do about it? Pull the book off the shelves?' Well, that's exactly what they (Shogakukan) did." If you're lucky, copies can occasionally be found in used bookstores.

instead to start up her own volleyball team at school. Shizuru Seino's *Girl Got Game* follows a girl who poses as a boy so she can play basketball at an all-boys school. For horror, there are series like Narumi Kakinouchi's *Vampire Princess Miyu*, about a vampire who banishes god-demons (with the help of a masked pretty boy, of course). Heroic quests are just as much a presence in shōjo manga as in its male counterpart, in series like CLAMP's *Cardcaptor Sakura* and Naoko Takeuchi's *Sailor Moon* (see pp.96 and 180). Even the idea of the shōnen harem manga, where a boy gets plopped into a situation where he's surrounded by a bevy of beautiful girls, gets turned on its head with a manga like Bisco Hatori's *Ouran High School Host Club*, where a girl gets to hobnob with her school's resident group of elite pretty boys.

There's a common thread linking all of these diverse genres, however. Whereas shōnen manga is all about physical action, shōjo focuses more on psychology, relationships and emotions, whether they're displayed in the large, expressive eyes of the main characters or the sparkly or flowery backgrounds that appear when certain characters are in some dreamy emotional state. These tones are rarely found outside of shōjo manga. Some of the more experimental artists take things further, rejecting the conventional grid-based layout, letting the images flow organically across the page, with beauty and serenity expressed by evenly spaced, orderly laid-out images, whereas more

chaotic scenes feature harsher edges and more jarring styles.

Guru Guru Pon-chan

Satomi Ikezawa; *pub* Kodansha (Jp), Del Rey (US, UK); *ser* Bessatsu Friend (1997–2000); *vols* 9

When romance comes into play in shōjo manga, nothing can get in the way of bringing a destined couple together – not even, as in the case of *Guru Guru Pon-chan*, the fact that one partner is a dog and the other is a human. Satomi Ikezawa's story hook is the Guru Guru bone, a special bone that transforms a Labrador, Ponta, into an attractive human girl. But it takes some convincing for Ponta's neighbour Mirai, the boy she loves, to buy into the idea; he knows her secret and is worried that starting a relationship with her will make him a pervert. Even when Ponta is in her human form, she retains all the innocent thoughts and mannerisms of a dog, a tribute to Ikezawa's engaging art.

Kodocha

Miho Obana; *pub* Kodansha (Jp), Tokyopop (US, UK); *ser* Ribon (1994–98); *vols* 10; *age* 13+

Following a well-worn shōjo premise, initial animosity between two characters fades over time as they get to know each other better, eventually giving way to friendship and romance. The players here are Sana, an ever-cheerful eleven-year-old TV star, and Akito, a sullen boy who often causes trouble in her class. Obana's attention to detail on a visual and emotional level makes her series stand out, however. Take Sana's mother, who wears elaborate headdresses, miniature playgrounds in which the chipmunk that lives in her hair can play. Emotionally, here's a world in which nothing can be taken at face value, from Akito's behaviour to Sana's relationship with her manager.

Josei manga

Just as seinen manga is the more mature, realistic relation to shōnen manga, so josei manga is to shōjo. Josei is a much smaller category, though, comprising under seven percent of the Japanese market. It's also a relative newcomer, establishing itself in the late 1970s and early 80s with the creation of such anthologies as Shueisha's *You*, Kodansha's *Be Love* and Shogakukan's *Big Comic for Lady*, designed to appeal to female office assistants in their twenties and thirties – the first women to have grown up with manga and entered the workforce, and a new audience for manga publishers to tap.

As with seinen, josei are grounded in more realistic situations. Out, too, go the sparkly eyes and dream-like wispy backgrounds of shōjo, in favour of less idealized characters and more expressive artistic styles. Meanwhile, the romantic relationships portrayed in josei manga tend to go beyond shy, giggly high school crushes and delve right into the sexual realm. The heroines of josei are determined women who know exactly what they want in life, after all, even if they have to go on some sort of spiritual or physical journey to find their true calling. These women also regularly confront issues ranging from overbearing mothers-in-law to sexual harassment. Unlike their male manga counterparts, though, otherworldly elements of fantasy rarely, if ever, come into play: josei manga is strictly about the real world.

With the focus in English-speaking markets on the teenage demographic, few josei manga have reached the US and fewer still have been marketed as such. The two most popular series, Ai Yazawa's *Paradise Kiss* and *Nana* (see pp.167 and overleaf), were promoted as shōjo series, but for older readers, due to their depictions and discussion of sex. Tokyopop launched one of the more prominent josei efforts in 2005 with its Passion Fruit line, which promised "an innovative, edgy line of manga which reflects the emotional condition of humanity in its moment of creation and procreation" – a marketing slogan that presumably was meant to highlight the manga's mature stories but instead came off making no sense whatsoever. Just two single-volume short story anthologies were released under the imprint before it was retired a year later due to low sales. Various other publishers still dabble in the category but only Aurora Publishing (see Chapter 6) still has a line devoted to josei.

Dolis

Maki Kusumoto; *pub* Shodensha (Jp), Tokyopop (US, UK, Aus); *ser* Feel Young (1998); *vols* 1; *age* 16+

The first thing that grabs you about *Dolis* is its appearance: simply drawn characters, sparse layouts with words often floating through large areas of white space, and little else, with each chapter rendered in a different-coloured ink. Kusumoto's focus is on her characters and the psychology behind their actions. Mitsu, an art history student, and Kishi, a clerk at the bookstore Mitsu frequents, meet and end up falling in love. But in the span of a few chapters, Kishi slowly comes to the realization that the woman whose beauty captivated him actually has multiple personalities, corresponding to a series of paintings for which she modelled. It's an unsettling love story that raises the question of whether two emotionally damaged souls can find a way to heal each other.

Happy Mania

Moyoco Anno; *pub* Shodensha (Jp), Tokyo-pop (US, UK); *ser* Feel Young (1995–2001); *vols* 11; *age* 18+

As a heroine, 24-year-old Shigeta is far from perfect. She drifts from job to job, sleeps with the wrong men, and never seems to get any further in her quest for love and happiness. But in this complex, contemporary romance, there are no easy answers. Even her best friend Fuku, a steadying presence and voice of reason, has relationship problems in the form of an unfaithful partner. And then there's poor Takahashi, who's in love with Shigeta but always gets passed over in favour of her crush of the moment.

Nana

Ai Yazawa; *pub* Shogakukan (Jp), Viz (US, UK), Madman (Aus); *ser* Cookie (2–); *vols* ongoing; *age* 18+

Despite both being twenty years old and having the same name, Nana Komatsu and Nana Osaki couldn't be more different. Komatsu is a naïve, middle-class girl, Osaki a world-weary rocker who was abandoned by her parents and expelled from high school. Their lives come together as they move to Tokyo and share an apartment, but each Nana has her own issues and struggles to deal with, and actions can have sobering consequences. One of them must even deal with an unexpected pregnancy and a marriage for convenience. This shift to a more mature theme around volume 8 prompted Viz to raise the age rating from 16+.

Boys' love, yaoi and shōnen-ai

Manga stories in which pretty boys find love with one another are extremely popular in both Japan and the US. What surprises newcomers to manga, though, is that they're generally not aimed at gay men, but written by and for straight women.

Japanese fans have referred to these stories over the years as shōnen-ai, yaoi and "boys' love" stories. In Japan, **shōnen-ai** was a key evolutionary step for shōjo manga in the late 1970s, as mangaka experimented with stories that featured platonic, sometimes romantic relationships between pubescent boys or young men. Keiko Takemiya's untranslated *Kaze to Ki no Uta* (*Song of the Wind and Trees*), which ran from 1976 to 1984 in the pages of *Shōjo Comic*, is widely considered to be the flagship shōnen-ai series for its depiction of forbidden passion between two young men at a European academy and the subsequent tragedy of love lost. Takemiya later explained in an interview that shōnen-ai was the only way for mangaka like her to address sexuality at a time when such discussions were still taboo for women.

Shōnen-ai manga didn't fade until the early 1980s, around the same time the **yaoi** dōjinshi movement emerged: amateur artists taking the brotherly bonds seen in popular shōnen manga such as *Captain Tsubasa* and *Knights of the Zodiac*, and transforming them into explicitly romantic relationships. The term "**yaoi**" combined the first syllables in the Japanese phrase "*yamanashi, ochinashi, iminashi*" ("no peak, no point, no meaning") and that's what these dōjinshi contained: suggestive sequences and explicit sex with no real attempt at telling a story. The movement rekindled an interest in telling original stories, and professional publications returned to the genre in the late 1980s under the new label of **boys' love** manga – which in Japan today describes both manga and dōjinshi.

Regardless of the terminology, these stories have remained popular in Japan. It's thought that part of the appeal is the freedom given the mangaka to play with relationship roles. Traditionally, the Japanese man assumes the dominant role in a relationship, with a woman submissive to his needs, but in boys' love manga, the roles can be fluid and changeable.

Western readers and publishers have adopted **yaoi** as their catch-all term, but whatever you call it, it's clear the genre has stirred the most fervent, vocal fandom among female readers. Mainly older teens, they spend much time online debating which heterosexual male characters in their favourite series would go well together in a romantic relationship, writing fan fiction and drawing dōjinshi that bring these relationships to life. Online fandom has been one of the primary avenues through which yaoi has grown in popularity worldwide.

J-Boy by Biblos

various; *pub* Biblos (Jp), Digital Manga Publishing (US); *ser* n/a; *vols* 1; *age* 18+

This anthology featuring nineteen short stories by eighteen yaoi creators is perfect for readers who want to get a sampling of what yaoi is all about without having to commit to a single series. Stories range from the fairly innocent (two boyfriends break up and then spend the rest of the story figuring out that they probably shouldn't have broken up) to the somewhat obscene (a roving samurai teaches a dojo how to embarrass an opponent through kinky sex) to the downright kinky.

Yuri manga

The word "yuri" is short for "yurizoku", a term coined in 1971 by the editor of a gay men's magazine who reasoned that if gay men are *barazoku*, or "the rose tribe", then lesbians are "the lily tribe". Lesbians eventually dropped the term in favour of "rezubian", but the word stuck to describe any popular works, including manga, that contain girl-loving-girl content, whether the target audience is lesbians or straight women or men.

The same experimentation by mangaka in shōjo manga in the 1970s that eventually spawned boys' love also produced the first yuri manga, Ryoko Yamagishi's *Shiroi Heya no Futari* (*Our White Room*) in 1971. This short story, published under Shueisha's Ribon Comics imprint, was a tale of two friends-turned-lovers at a boarding school that carried a common theme of early yuri manga: love ending in tragedy because of cultural taboos.

While there have been other stories with yuri overtones since the 1970s, it wasn't until the 1990s that yuri really came into its own. Even then, there was (and still are) a fair number of series in which lesbianism is treated as an adolescent, experimental phase, often for straight male consumption. Hardcore lesbian manga has sold less well, but several lesbian magazines have published yuri as special features in their pages, with one quarterly, *Yuri Hime*, experimenting with an all-yuri format. Yuri manga is flourishing in the US, though, with translated dōjinshi and manga available from a couple of companies – ALC Publishing's all-yuri line-up being the most stable of the ventures.

Maria-sama ga Miteru

Oyuki Konno (text), Satoru Nagasawa (art); *pub* Shueisha (Jp); *ser* Margaret; *vols* ongoing

Based on a series of Japanese light novels (popular fiction for young adults), focusing on a group of girls attending Lillian Girls' Academy, a Catholic school where it is tradition for a

Strawberry Panic! knowingly makes use of the conventions of yuri manga in a school-based romantic comedy.

© 2006 Sakurako Kimino / Media Works

second- or third-year student to give her rosary to a first-year student and promise to look after her and guide her. While the relationships are born out of the values of friendship and respect, some develop into deeper feelings of love. Tying together these largely unrelated stories is the school's student council and the relationships among the student leaders elected to it.

Rica'tte Kanji!?

Rica Takashima; *pub* Michi Publishing/Terra Publications (Jp), ALC Publishing (US, UK, Aus); *ser* Phryne/Anise (1995–2004); *vols* 1

Written as a response to all of those tragic yuri series in science-fiction settings, this story ends up being quite refreshing in its frank, cheerful, depiction of the lesbian community in Tokyo. Rica is a college student who's out of the closet but remains shy and inexperienced, while Miho is an art school student. When the two meet in Nichome, the gay and lesbian district of Tokyo, they hit it off and, with a bit of shy uncertainty throughout, make the transition into becoming a full-fledged, rather cute couple.

Strawberry Panic!

Sakurako Kimino (story), Namuchi Takumi (art); *pub* MediaWorks (Jp), Seven Seas (US); *ser* Dengeki G's Magazine (2005–07); *vols* 2; *age* 16+

Take *Maria-sama ga Miteru* and infuse it with a heavy dose of yuri-based parody (which likely went over the heads of the audience to which the manga was targeted). What emerges is an over-the-top romp through many yuri conventions, revolving around the premise of a group of girls attending one of three schools and the lesbian love interests that develop around their interactions.

Hentai manga

Every pop culture outlet has some little corner where sex reigns supreme. In manga, that place is called **hentai**, the category that brings to mind tentacle monsters, fairies having sex with mutant insects and alien rape. Japan's more relaxed attitude towards sex in the mainstream media, coupled with these stereotypes, has led to the misperception in some quarters that manga equals porn. But while it's true that seinen and josei titles deal with sex quite openly (see previous sections in this chapter), they shouldn't be confused with hentai or ero manga.

Hentai manga in Japan is more like hardcore pornography, in that it's widely consumed but rarely spoken about, and encompasses all sorts of festishistic and niche interests. That said, you can blame the bizarre depictions of sexual acts mentioned above on the inventiveness of artists in evading censorship. Article 175 of the Japanese penal code, originating in 1907, mandates imprisonment for distributors and consumers of "obscene" writings and artwork, a term that was subsequently taken to mean "stimulating sexual desire". In the decades since, the ruling has been interpreted to mean that depicting sex was okay, but depicting realistic sexual acts between two people – and specifically pubic hair and genitalia – was not. And so from the publication of the first adult manga magazine, *Manga Erotopia* in 1973, mangaka have stopped short of showing the offending detail. Publishers have got around the regulation through artistic ingenuity, replacing genitals with suggestively shaped flowers, seashells, snakes, fruit and vegetables, or have chosen to simply blur or block them out. Tentacle monsters and other phallic aliens sidestepped the restriction on showing penetration. As a result, obscenity trials in Japan have been almost nonexistent.

Most of the hentai content being translated and released in Western markets comes from Fantagraphics' Eros MangErotica line and Icarus Publishing (see Chapter 6). The offending appendages are usually retouched back in from the Japanese original.

4

The Canon

fifty essential manga

Choosing just fifty of the best manga is a challenge worthy of *Dragon Ball Z*-era Goku and, inevitably, a subjective exercise. In putting together a list that represents the highlights of manga over the last fifty-odd years, we've chosen titles that have stood – or that will stand – the test of time: the greatest stories in any genre, the most evocative artwork, the most original writing. Most of them are accessible to anyone with a local bookstore or an Internet connection, but not all. Some series are well-known and have appeared on bestseller lists numerous times; others are more obscure; and one series is not even available in English. In amongst this selection of the best manga has to offer, we've also included features on some of our favourite creators, with thumbnail reviews of their other works.

Akira

Katsuhiro Ōtomo; *pub* Kodansha (Jp), Dark Horse (US, UK, Aus); *ser* Young Magazine (1982–90); *vols* 6; *age* 16+

t's hard to overstate the importance of *Akira* in the late 1980s. For many Western fans, Katsuhiro Ōtomo's classic franchise was the gateway to discovering anime and manga. The anime in particular was heralded as revolutionary, its gritty story of two friends turned rivals in a post-apocalyptic Tokyo proving the medium wasn't just for children, but could tell mature and complex stories too.

Equally as important – and predating the film's arrival in the US by a year – was the English translation of Ōtomo's manga, in which readers first appreciated Ōtomo's stylish eye for detail in an epic that eventually would span eight years and more than two thousand pages. It was released in traditional monthly comic book format by Marvel Comics under its Epic Comics imprint from 1988 to 1995, with a frustrating gap of two years before the last five issues, due to Epic folding. As well as the monthly format, other changes were made so as not to alienate Western readers. Based on Ōtomo's recommendation, Marvel hired renowned colourist Steve Oliff to make the manga resemble a traditional American comic – and look more like the anime – while narrative boxes were added to previously wordless introductory panels. It wouldn't be until 2000 that the English-speaking world got to see Ōtomo's original, black-and-white vision largely unaltered, when Dark Horse released the first of six oversized trade paperbacks. The only change to be retained was the flopped pages.

Akira's themes and concerns were solidly rooted in Japan's recent history, but that knowledge wasn't necessary to enjoy the manga: what so many readers (and viewers) responded to was a stylish, dystopian science fiction tale, one that chimed with a burgeoning cyberpunk genre. *Akira* opens with the annihilation of Tokyo in World War III, showing how thirty years later, the new metropolis of Neo-Tokyo built upon its ruins is already in decay. Now it's a city where biker gangs rove the streets, the government is a puppet of the military and there's a growing resistance movement. All of which is just the setting for much violence and chaos to come, the catalyst being a bunch of genetically modified children, the subject of covert government experiments in the 1960s and 70s. The most powerful of them is subject number 28, Akira.

But as usually happens with covert scientific experiments, something goes horribly wrong: Akira's power went off the charts… and blew up the scientists working on the project, Tokyo, and all but three of his fellow guinea pigs. Akira himself was cryogenically frozen and kept under close guard by the military, particularly the man known as the Colonel, who wants to protect Neo-Tokyo from a second assault. And so it's another experiment subject that upsets this uneasy peace and sets in motion the multiple tragedies of Neo-Tokyo. Out riding late at night, biker gang member Tetsuo comes across one of the surviving children from the experiment, now an old man but with his powers intact. Tetsuo swerves to avoid him and ends up injured; a military team arrives and whisks him away.

When Tetsuo emerges, he is subject number 41, a drug-fuelled maniac who wields unspeakable psychokinetic power. The first task he takes upon himself is to free Akira from the cryogenic chamber. Just how powerful Akira is doesn't become apparent until a sequence late in the third volume. The boy, having seen one of his friends gunned down before his eyes, unleashes a fury that leaves Neo-Tokyo ruined in much the same way that his powers destroyed the original Tokyo. As drawn by Ōtomo, the wordless sequence shows page after page of buildings bending, then shattering with the concussive force that Akira sends forth.

Their power undeniable, Akira and Tetsuo are adopted as gods by a new religious group, while a number of factions arise to fight the pair. Chief among them is Shotaro Kaneda, leader of the gang Tetsuo was in, who gains a number of valuable allies along the way, including Kei, a member of a terrorist resistance movement, the Colonel, and Lady Miyako, leader of her own religious sect and one of the children on whom the early experiments were conducted.

Akira would turn out to be the pinnacle of Ōtomo's career as a manga artist. It would also be the last major manga series he would work on; following its completion, he focused more on his film work. But if there was any manga series with which an artist could choose to go out on top, *Akira* would be it.

Cover of the original Japanese edition; *Akira* would soon be Westernized for an English-speaking audience.

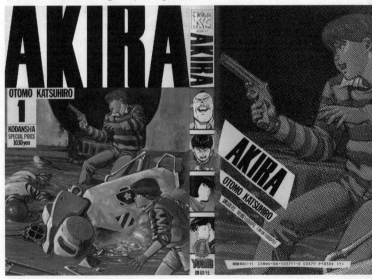

Courtesy of Kodansha Ltd

Ashita no Jō

Tetsuya Chiba; *pub* Kodansha (Jp), no English translation; *ser* Shōnen Magazine (1968–73); *vols* 20

One day in March 1970, more than seven hundred people turned up at Kodansha's offices to mourn the death of professional boxer Toru Rikiishi following a gruelling battle with Joe Yabuki. A full-scale boxing ring was set up, a Buddhist priest conducted the funeral service, and mourners dressed in black brought flowers and incense. What made the funeral unorthodox was that Toru was a fictional character, the greatest rival of the hero of *Ashita no Jō* (*Tomorrow's Joe*) until the tragic climax of the series' first story arc. That climax resonated so much with poet Shuji Terayama that he called for a funeral soon after it was published, resulting in the public memorial described above.

That any character would be mourned in such a manner is remarkable, but that it should be an opponent of Joe was entirely fitting. Toru's challenge served a key purpose in transforming a wild child into a responsible young adult, giving Joe an avenue to channel his rage as a premier professional boxer. It was a story that appealed to the student revolutionaries of the late 1960s – if Joe could battle his way from the depths of humanity to its heights as a boxing champion, they could wage a successful battle against the government establishment as well. *Ashita no Jō* thus was emblematic of manga in the late 1960s – while Tetsuya Chiba's artwork retained a cartoony feel reminiscent of what Osamu Tezuka and Shōtarō Ishinomori were producing, the mature theme and relatively high level of violence were aimed squarely at the maturing manga audience. Chiba wrote sports manga before and after *Ashita no Jō*, but no series would resonate quite as strongly in Japanese society as his boxing series did.

When readers first meet Joe, he is a fifteen-year-old orphan and an incorrigible delinquent wandering the back streets of Tokyo, picking fights with whoever gets in his way. The only person who believes in Joe is the town lunatic and drunk, Danpei Tange. Danpei, a former boxing trainer who has fallen on hard times, sees a certain fighting spirit in Joe that he hopes to harness so he can return to his own glory days of training. To that end, he tries to get Joe to embark on a strict boxing regimen, insisting that he wants to be his trainer. He even takes on two part-time construction jobs so that he can pay for a new boxing gym in which Joe can train. Joe's response? First, he dismisses him outright as a crazy old drunk guy. Then, once he realizes that Danpei is serious, he decides to play along and uses the small allowance the trainer gives him to pay for *pachinko* schemes and assorted other scams.

Danpei's instincts are of course correct – Joe has a fury within him that makes him a passionate fighter. He can dispatch entire gangs with his raw skills, and children from the street loyally follow him wherever he goes. But Joe looks out for himself and his own best interests, and is not the type of person to take advice from anyone.

It takes someone with the dogged persistence of Danpei to slowly break through this exterior. When Joe gets caught and sent to jail, Danpei sends him postcards containing suggested training routines, and Joe eventually begins to take heed. The techniques come in handy for dealing with the other inmates, but Joe's first encounter with the rising boxing star Toru, who knocks him out in front of the other inmates, is embarrassing enough that Joe decides to use his incarceration to train as a boxer, so that he can finally face Toru on his own terms and beat him.

By the time Joe faces off with Toru in the boxing ring in a match set up at the prison, you've begun to respect Joe for his tenacity rather than rail against his delinquency, and his beating by Toru evokes a sympathetic response. Joe repeatedly getting up after being knocked down doesn't symbolize the brash rebellion and stupidity that it would have at the beginning of the series, but rather his persistent courage.

As Joe changes and matures, so too do the other characters in the story. Danpei becomes a respected boxing manager once more, the inmates that Joe meets undergo similar transformations once they take up boxing as well, and Joe even picks up a few new friends along the way (as well as a love interest, Saeko, heir to a businessman's fortune).

Joe's career in boxing would be a long and fruitful one. For five years, readers followed along faithfully as he made his way out of prison, captured the bantamweight championship and continued to rise through the ranks. He even retired from boxing – soon after Toru's death, chronicled in the eighth volume – but later made a successful comeback. The end of the series was alternately celebrated and mourned as Joe passed into history as a champion in readers' hearts.

Astro Boy

Osamu Tezuka; *pub* Kobunsha(Jp), Dark Horse (US, UK); *ser* Shōnen (1952–68); *vols* 23

The mechanical boy known as Tetsuwan Atomu (Mighty Atom) in Japan and Astro Boy in English-speaking countries was the first – and the earliest internationally recognizable – symbol of manga. Much of his fame came from the animated series, which debuted in 1963 as Japan's first weekly animated TV series and went on to thrill audiences worldwide with stories steeped in science and technology. If Osamu Tezuka was Japan's answer to Walt Disney, Astro was its answer to Mickey Mouse – an iconic character living in a vibrant, energetic world designed to engage children's minds. At a time when Japan was healing from the wounds inflicted during World War II, the *Astro Boy* manga offered readers hope for the future… as well as some precautionary tales in the interest of achieving that future.

The early life story of Astro is one of rejection followed by redemption. Dr Tenma, director of the Ministry of Science, built the robot after his son Tobio died in an accident, harnessing the knowledge of the experts at the ministry to meticulously craft a machine that resembled Tobio in every way. The procedure was a success… to a certain extent. For while the robot became a perfect emulation of Tobio at the time of his death, it was fundamentally still a mechanical construction, unable to advance beyond a certain point and lacking the human ability to grow. Tenma, disgusted by the shortcomings of his glorified doll, sold him to a robot merchant. Some time later, one Professor Ochanomizu went to the circus and saw the "Mighty Atom" perform. Recognizing Astro's potential, Ochanomizu convinced the circus to give him up and promptly set about improving on the design. It was at this point that the character was given many of the powers for which he is known today: the ability to fly through the air like a space rocket, to speak sixty languages fluently, the judgement to determine whether people are morally good or bad, strength equal to 100,000 horsepower, hearing that can be amplified a thousand times, eyes that can double as searchlights, and machine guns planted in his rear (always a favourite among the kids). Ochanomizu also builds him a robotic family, with a mother and father, sister Uran and brother Cobalt.

Yet despite having all the trappings of a human life, he remains an anomaly. Like Pinocchio, he is a boy who is not really a boy. His heart may be close to that of a human but it isn't entirely human, so the human world doesn't trust him. Neither does the robot world embrace him, because to them he's too human, and the humans are the world's oppressors, having imposed on robots strict segregation policies as well as the Laws of Robotics governing their operation. As a result, Astro often serves as the bridge between two cultures, to lessen the prejudice between them, while at the same time suffering from prejudice himself.

In a sense, this is the timeless theme of the *Astro Boy* world. It's not that Astro embarks on fantastic journeys, meeting strange alien races and encountering technologies that, drawn from the perspective of the 1950s and 60s, still seem futuristic today. (The time in which the manga is set, of course, is no longer in the future, with Astro's creation occurring in the once far-off year of 2003.) It's that even in Tezuka's vision of a future world, society continues to struggle with issues such as segregation and warfare. While Astro is dispatched to solve problems like this, clear-cut victories are rarely achieved; more usually Astro gets damaged or simply runs out of energy, often in heroic acts of self-sacrifice to protect whichever party he felt to be right. He may be a champion for justice... but sometimes the "justice" that humans ask him to enforce is not straightforward good versus evil.

Take the story "Blue Knight", serialized from October 1965 to March 1966.

Astro Boy rescues Professor Ochanomizu, the man responsible for transforming the little robot boy into a powerful champion of justice.

Naoki Urasawa's Pluto-nic homage

One of the most popular *Astro Boy* stories was "The Greatest Robot on Earth", published between June 1964 and January 1965, in which a wealthy sultan builds a robot named Pluto that's designed to rule over all of Earth's robots. To that end, Pluto goes around the world on a mission to defeat the seven most powerful robots… which naturally includes the pride of Japan, Astro. The only way that Astro feels he can defeat Pluto is through an increase in horsepower from 100,000 to 1 million, an upgrade that Professor Ochanomizu is reluctant to grant. And as the inevitable showdown between Pluto and Astro approaches, readers confront the question of why humanity creates such advanced technology simply to destroy or be destroyed. In the end, the sultan realizes how pointless it is to build such technology, and Astro hopes for a day when all robots will be friends and never have to fight one another again.

It was from the framework of that original story that Naoki Urasawa created *Pluto*, which ran from 2004 to 2009 in Japan and won the Osamu Tezuka Cultural Award and the Japanese Media Arts Festival Manga Division Excellence Prize. Yet while *Astro Boy* provided the foundation, the mood and themes of the series are far more mature than in the original story, being aimed at a seinen audience.

The central character in *Pluto* is the German investigator Gesicht, who in the original *Astro Boy* story was one of the seven powerful robots targeted by Pluto. All of the robots' backgrounds are fleshed out in Urasawa's version: families are created, and the author examines the dynamic that exists within those families and in the broader, robot/human society. Atom and Professor Ochanomizu make appearances, though they're transformed by Urasawa's more realistic art style.

Manga were adopting darker, more mature themes around the time "Blue Knight" was released, and Tezuka was asked to give Astro a new edginess, making him a "bad kid" rather than the "goody two-shoes" that readers were used to seeing. In the resulting story, a robot named Blue Bon has rebelled against his creator and, calling himself the Blue Knight, has resolved to defend robots against their human oppressors. During one of the Blue Knight's duels with Astro, he leaves behind a sword that doles out electrical shocks to some robots that wield it but not others. The humans, convinced that the sword is a tool through which they can determine which robots are "safe" and which robots could end up like the Blue Knight, thus kick off an ethnic cleansing programme, sending the "dangerous" robots to what amounts to robot concentration camps. When Astro's parents end up on the "unsafe" list, Astro rebels against humans for the first time in his life, rescues his parents... and allies himself with the Blue Knight's cause. Yet once the ensuing war between humans and robots ends with the robots coming out on the winning side, Astro can't bring himself to follow the Blue Knight's order to kill the humans. Robots can be repaired and brought back to life, Astro reasons, but humans can't. At the climax of the story, Astro throws himself in front of an energy lance that

the Blue Knight hurls in an attempt to kill his creator, and is destroyed in the process. Of course, Astro gets repaired in a subsequent installment, but that's another story.

In spite of the character's popularity worldwide, Tezuka was never truly happy with his creation. He felt creatively stifled by the short, episodic nature of the stories, preferring the long serialized story arcs that he pursued in *Phoenix* (see p.171), the manga he considered his life's work. Yet *Astro Boy* was the right manga for the right time, a series that embraced hopes for the future as much as it raised stimulating questions of the present.

Azumanga Daioh

Kiyohiko Azuma; *pub* MediaWorks (Jp), Yen Press (US, UK); *ser* Comics Dengeki Daioh (1999–2002); *vols* 4; *age* 13+

*A*zumanga Daioh is the best English-translated example of the 4-koma, or four-panel, manga style, a format similar to comic strips in Western newspapers. Like those strips, 4-koma manga feature a setup and punch line within four panels; in *Azumanga Daioh*'s case, Kiyohiko Azuma's four-panel sequences combine with several short stories told in a more traditional, multipanel manga format to build a comprehensive

story about a group of girls attending a Japanese high school.

Only the loosest of plots serves to connect this series of as the foundation for this interweaving of character portraits. Child genius Chiyo enrols in high school and meets a bunch of new friends; together they share the usual high school experiences like sports and cultural festivals, cramming for exams, and going on class trips and other outings together; and then they graduate. Rather simple when you think about it, but like the TV series *Seinfeld*, it's an everyday setting that's ripe with opportunities for humour.

But this bald description can't convey the depth of character development that takes place throughout the series. Each character has her own fans, from cute little pigtailed Chiyo, to Sakaki, the most beautiful and athletically gifted of the group. Sakaki loves animals and one of the series' running gags involves her unsuccessful attempts to get one of the neighbourhood cats to like her. Thrown into the mix are Tomo, a crackling ball of energy, always looking for a chance to compete, and her best friend Yomi, the straight girl in Tomo's nonstop comedy routine. Kagura, on the other hand, is a talented all-round athlete and swim team star but less enthusiastic about her studies.

And then there's Osaka, who provides some of the most memorable moments in the series. Her real name is Ayumu Kasuga, but she's a transfer student from Osaka, a city whose people are stereotypically considered more culturally backward than most of the rest of Japan. While she tries her best to dispel the stereotype, the truth is that Osaka is a tad spacey, prone to daydreaming and non sequitur observations.

Nominally overseeing this madness is teacher Yukari Tanizaki, a woman who resembles an older version of Tomo with her impulsive ways. She's more a friend to her students than a teacher, often sharing more about herself than her students really wanted to know. She has an ongoing rivalry/friendship with gym teacher Minamo "Nyamo" Kurosawa, who is on a much more even keel than Yukari… that is, if one doesn't put too much alcohol in her.

There are times when this series takes a turn toward the truly bizarre – any scenes featuring Chiyo's "dad", imagined by both Sakaki and Osaka as an oval-shaped floating cat with creepy saucer-like eyes, offer a few head-scratching moments. Every stereotype about manga in a school setting also shows up sooner or later, although boys are rarely ever shown. (The one occasional male character is the older, somewhat creepy Kimura.) All things considered, though, don't be surprised if you find yourself thoroughly involved in the lives of the characters, perhaps even shedding a few tears like Chiyo does as the series comes to an end.

Banana Fish

Akimi Yoshida; *pub* Shogakukan (Jp), Viz (UK, US); *ser* Bessatsu Shōjo Comic (1985–91); *vols* 19; *age* 16+

Gritty, inner-city gang warfare is not usually the subject of shōjo manga; then again Akimi Yoshida's *Banana Fish* isn't a typical shōjo. A down and dirty crime story, it's one with a literary sensibility, to boot – the title is a reference to J.D. Salinger's short story, "A Perfect Day for Bananafish". When Viz first published the series as part of its mature-audience manga anthology *Pulp* in the late 1990s, Yoshida's take on American life in the 1980s already looked dated, but its complex plot and atypical artwork more than made up for it in entertainment value.

There's quite a bit going on in this take on 1980s New York City, a sleazy metropolis that to the Japanese embodied the individual freedom and energy lacking in Japan. Ash, whose character design was inspired by a combination of tennis star Stefan Edberg and actor River Phoenix, is a seventeen-year-old gang leader trying to break away from a sordid past of child abuse, male prostitution and general servitude under homosexual Mafia boss "Papa" Dino Golzine. While he's endured this life for nine years and has become one of Dino's enforcers with his own gang to command, his struggle to break away from Dino's control takes shape just as the manga begins. Ash is more than a stereotypical street thug – he's charismatic and intelligent, and even the police respect him for using these qualities to unite seemingly disparate youth gangs under one umbrella group. But while Dino is preparing Ash to be his successor, all Ash wants to do is to figure out the mystery behind "Banana Fish", the only words Ash's brother has uttered since he returned from the Vietnam War in a vegetative state, following an incident where he gunned down several of his comrades.

A conspiratorial web of secrets, lies and double-crossings, connected by the desire to control the Banana Fish drug, slowly but surely reveals itself. Through all of this, Ash places his complete trust in Eiji Okumura, a nineteen-year-old assistant to journalist Shunichi Ibe from Japan who is helping write a story about youth gangs in the US. While Eiji and Shunichi start out as observers, Eiji's naïveté eventually ends up pulling him into the gangland warfare.

Up to this point, the story would be perfectly at home in a seinen manga. The shōjo sensibility of this series, however, begins to emerge as the relationship between Ash and Eiji evolves. There's a sort of unspoken trust that reveals itself in their first meeting, when Ash hands over his gun to Eiji, something Ash has never done before. Later, when Ash gets injured, it's Eiji who helps treat his wounds and keeps watch over him. It soon becomes clear – very subtly at first – that Eiji and Ash are forming a close bond with each other, eventually becoming lovers.

Akimi Yoshida's artwork was a clear signal that this wasn't a typical shōjo manga, rejecting the soft-edged, sparkle-filled screentones in favour of the artistic conventions of shōnen and seinen manga. The style emphasized the realism of both the characters and a setting that takes in the complex politics within the US justice system at the time. The effect of all this was that guys who normally wouldn't have read shōjo manga were picking it up and following the story in equally large numbers as the girls it was originally aimed at.

Barefoot Gen

Keiji Nakazawa; *pub* Shueisha (Jp), Last Gasp of San Francisco (US, UK, Aus); *ser* Weekly Shōnen Jump (1973–74); *vols* 10

Keiji Nakazawa was only six years old when the US dropped a nuclear bomb on his hometown of Hiroshima on 6 August 1945, leaving his father, older sister and younger brother among the eighty thousand dead and he, his mother and infant sister to fend for themselves. The sister died several weeks later, but his mother lived until 1966, her body slowly ravaged by the effects of radiation to the point where no bone fragments were left in her cremated remains.

While Nakazawa had largely repressed his memories of the bombing, the frustration and anger over seeing his mother's remains spurred him to write a series of anti-war novels and manga based on his experience. In 1972, when Shueisha's *Monthly Shōnen Jump* published his 45-page autobiographical manga *Ore wa Mita* (*I Saw It*), editor Tadasu Nagano was so impressed he encouraged Nakazawa to write an expanded version for serialization: the semi-autobiographical *Barefoot Gen*.

Following *Barefoot Gen* proved to be tricky during its initial serialization. Nagano edited the series in Shueisha's *Weekly Shōnen Jump* for a year and a half before leaving the post, then the new editor wanted to take the magazine in a different direction and promptly cancelled the series. It would take eight years and three different magazines – two of which went out of business – for *Barefoot Gen* to complete its run.

Despite these setbacks, a moving story would emerge, one that vividly depicted the horror inflicted on the Japanese and the struggles of coming of age in the aftermath of war. To the Japanese, it was an eye-opening account of how bombing victims were marginalized in society, and copies of the series are now housed in primary and middle-school libraries across Japan. To the rest of the world, including Japan's wartime enemies, the translated series revealed the impact of the war on Japanese civilian life.

Lead character Gen Nakaoka is a year older than Nakazawa was in 1945, but otherwise Gen's family reflects Nakazawa's, even down to Gen's father Daikichi being an outspoken critic of the war who believes Japan should strive for peace with the Allied powers. It is pointless, he argues, for people to sacrifice themselves for a nation run by a military controlled by the wealthy, a view that was at odds with the prevailing feeling at the time.

As the proverb goes, "the nail that sticks up gets hammered down", and so Gen's father, and by extension the entire Nakaoka family, gets hammered down with extreme prejudice by their neighbours and the authorities alike. But the family's faith and support of one another keeps them going. Even when older brother Koji goes against his father's wishes and enlists in the Imperial Army,

as the train is pulling away from the station, Daikichi shows up to shout his enthusiastic encouragement of his son. Family ties end up trumping politics every time.

Looming in the background during this first volume or so of the manga is an inexorable sense of impending disaster: we know what will happen on 6 August. Nakazawa juxtaposes images of the approaching US bomber Enola Gay with scenes of the Nakaoka family going about their daily life, and the actual bombing sequence happens over a span of just four pages, a single flash in time represented by the blinding flash Gen sees after the Enola Gay drops its load.

The bomb's impact may last only an instant in Nakazawa's narrative, but its aftereffects linger through the rest of the series. The initial impact is depicted with flesh melting off bodies, corpses littering the streets and buildings reduced to rubble. Then the horror becomes personal when Gen and his mother find the rest of their family trapped under their house. They try to save them, but in the end can only watch helplessly as fire sweeps through the wreckage of the building.

Despite the suffering of the survivors, they're still subject to the same old prejudices. Gen and his mother head inland with his newborn baby sister, but the first family they stay with harbours a grudge against them for sucking up already limited resources. And so Gen is forced to grow up before his time in a

89

Japan that is obsessed first with war, then with survival and the shame of defeat. Through it all, though, there remains a sense of hope, mostly down to Gen's determination in the face of whatever insults and prejudices are thrown his way.

An account of the story through the eyes of an adult would be gruelling enough to read. The perspective of a child – and one who sees most of his family die before his eyes, at that – makes for a devastating read, and one that's more easily identifiable for younger readers. Yet Nakazawa's message is also one of dogged determination, of persevering and surviving through the hard times to ensure the mistakes of the past are never repeated.

Battle Royale

Koushun Takami (text), Masayuki Taguchi (art); *pub* Akita Publishing (Jp), Tokyopop (UK, US); *ser* Young Champion (2000–05); *vols* 15; *age* 18+

Before the *Battle Royale* novel and manga were licensed for release in the US, the series was already notorious for the live-action Japanese film, directed by Kinji Fukusaku, which featured a class of fifteen-year-olds slaughtering one another in order to survive. To this day the movie has never been formally released in the US, and fans continue to speculate about the reasons, whether it's sensitivity following the Columbine High School massacre in 1999, or unreasonable expectations from the studio, Toei.

Still, curiosity over what all the fuss was about surely helped drive fans to the novel and manga when they first hit the shelves in 2003, without any of the hassles that the movie encountered. The original novel, translated and released by Viz, had the advantage of having no pictures, leaving readers to imagine for themselves what was going on. As for the manga, a glimpse at Masayuki Taguchi's grotesquely exaggerated human figures elicits a different reaction from watching real-life teenagers battle it out on the screen, and one more easily viewed as escapist entertainment.

Battle Royale takes the concept of William Golding's classic novel *Lord of the Flies*, in which the destructive savagery of human nature is demonstrated when a group of boys is left to fend for itself on a remote island, and moves it further into the darkness, imagining a scenario where the children didn't end up on the island by accident. *The Program*, a state-run reality TV show central to *Battle Royale*'s dystopian future, takes its unknowing participants, straps onto them collars designed to explode should they think of escaping, gives each of them a weapon and instructs them to survive until only one remains. It's a showcase of the best and worst of human nature, taken to extremes through its cast of 42 students.

Caught in the middle of the survival-of-the-fittest carnage is Shuuya Nanahara, an orphan and aspiring rock star who ended up in the wrong class at the wrong time. The stakes become tragically clear to him when his best friend from the orphanage, Yoshitoki Kuninobu, is shot in the face at point-blank range and killed by their new, not-so-gracious host, Yonemi Kanon, the teacher assigned to the class by *The Program*. Shuuya ends up joining forces with Noriko Nakagawa, the girl Yoshitoki had a secret crush on, vowing to protect her in his friend's memory, and with Shogo Kawada, the survivor of a previous installment of *The Program* who transferred into Shuuya's school and now must try to live through a second round. Trust is key for these classmates-turned-rivals; any alliances are tenuous at best, due to the constant awareness that anyone could turn in an instant and blow everyone else away. It's this dynamic that keeps the core alliance of Shuuya, Noriko and Shogo so fascinating to follow.

Even with the benefit of past experience or close friendship, though, survival is by no means assured. Not when others have a win-at-all-costs attitude, such as Kazuo Kiriyama, a boy

A demonstration of the explosive collars designed to keep the students trapped on the island in *Battle Royale*.

so scarred by earlier life experiences that he has become a soulless, eerily efficient killing machine. Another damaged soul is Mitsuko Souma, whose own ruthlessly effective strategy for survival is to seduce the boys before killing them.

Takami focuses on a handful of central characters, but the rest of the class members aren't necessarily faceless individuals. Well, sometimes they do become faceless – the killing scenes are rendered in unrelenting detail by Taguchi, with blood and fragmented body parts flying – but every student has a distinguishing trait, regardless of how briefly they might survive. Such attention to individual detail both visually and in characterization heightens your sympathy with the characters, and several

story arcs are heart-rending to read. One couple decides to take their own lives and jump, hand in hand, off a cliff to the rocky shore below. Another pair of friends make their way to a hilltop gazebo and use a megaphone to appeal to the others to put down their weapons and join them in peace, only to be gunned down where they stand by Kazuo.

Right from the start, you know there's no possibility of a happy ending. The society depicted is in a state of irreparable moral decline. And yet there are positives and even occasional joy to be found even in these most horrific of circumstances, as well as a dire warning for the future. However disturbing it can be to watch *Survivor*, be thankful this is still only the stuff of nightmares.

Black Jack

Osamu Tezuka; *pub* Akita Shoten (Jp), Vertical (US); *ser* Shōnen Champion (1973–83); *vols* 17

The first half of Osamu Tezuka's manga career from 1946 to 1967 was characterized by series targeted towards children, *Astro Boy* being the defining work. From 1967 until Tezuka's death in 1989, though, his series took on more experimental, mature themes and an increasingly realistic art style. With 243 chapters serialized in a boys'

magazine over a ten-year span from 1973, *Black Jack* would be to the later stage of his career what *Astro Boy* was earlier: a series that was and remains to this day immensely popular with Japanese audiences. But where *Astro Boy* was quickly adopted by the West thanks to the anime that first aired in the 1960s, *Black Jack* has had a tougher time breaking into Western awareness.

The anime went straight to video, while the manga translations have had a spotty history, Viz publishing two volumes in the 1990s, and Vertical taking it up with a new translation almost a decade later.

Black Jack is rooted in the medical training Tezuka underwent before pursuing a career in manga, though it's safe to say that the medical techniques employed by the eponymous doctor go beyond anything Tezuka might have learned in real life. Black Jack is a maverick, operating outside the established medical system as an unlicensed doctor, alternately scorned and respected by his peers. His unorthodox personality is embodied by his appearance: wild black hair with a white streak and a scar running down his face. He's an angel of life and death, a judge, jury and executioner all in one… and he's the doctor who makes house calls when no one else is willing to do so. Ready though he is to heal and help people, it's always on his own terms… and those terms often involve a high price.

Some of the doctor's methods were deemed so controversial that a number of chapters have been purged from the series since they were first published. Three chapters, "Finger" (chapter 28), "Vegetable" (chapter 41) and "Seat of Pleasure" (chapter 58), only ran in *Shōnen Champion* and were never published in subsequent reprints; and there has been just one reprint in Japan of "The Wall" (chapter 171) and "Falling Object" (chapter 209). Even the official Osamu

© Tezuka Productions and Vertical, Inc.

The unorthodox Black Jack, taking on the patients no other doctor will touch, though always on his own terms.

Tezuka website gives only the original publication dates and no further detail.

Black Jack is already renowned for saving three hundred lives by the time we meet him, when he's called upon by a rich man to save his arrogant son, critically wounded after some reckless driving. The doctor says he can only do it by sacrificing someone else's body, to which the man agrees, sending hired thugs to grab a witness from the crash scene. After a quick trial and conviction, the innocent witness is sent off supposedly to be executed, much to the dismay of his grieving mother. Black Jack then conducts the surgery and gets his money… or so it would seem. In fact, he judged the rich man's son wasn't worth saving and instead reconstructed the witness's face to look like the son, giving him the fee so that he and his mother could start a new life elsewhere.

A softer side to Black Jack is brought out by his assistant – the only other major recurring character throughout the series – Pinoko. A little girl meticulously reconstructed out of a fetus/tumour removed from an eighteen-year-old woman, she nonetheless insists she's nineteen and believes herself to be Black Jack's wife, adding a bit of comic relief to the series.

The huge popularity of these tales, featuring ethical and moral questions, told via often graphic anatomical illustrations complete with blood, illustrates the diverging paths of comics in Japan and the US in the 1970s and early 1980s. It's a different story today, though, when plastic surgery is televised and operation videogames like *Trauma Center* top the charts, allowing an appreciation of one of Tezuka's best and most influential works on its own terms.

Blade of the Immortal

Hiroaki Samura; *pub* Kodansha (Jp), Dark Horse (US); *ser* Afternoon (1994–); *vols* ongoing; *age* 18+

Many of the series covered in this book feature artwork some-where on a scale between Disney-influenced cartoon fantasy and grotesquely exaggerated human figures. *Blade of the Immortal*, on the other hand, offers a gorgeously detailed realism that ranks Hiroaki Samura as one of the finest artists working in manga today. The story, too, is the essence of refined elegance, a tightly plotted tale of swords and samurai and one man's quest for vengeance and redemption. It's no surprise that the series has earned worldwide recognition, winning an Excellence Prize at the Japan Media Arts Festival in 1998, an Eisner Award in 2000, and the UK's Eagle Award for manga in 2004, 2005 and 2006.

For that one man in question, the swordsman Manji, immortality grants the opportunity to atone for his past, a mission that requires him to kill ten evil men for every good man he killed earlier in life. This task is a hundred times harder than it sounds, thanks to an earlier rampage where he killed his former lord and 99 other men sent to capture him, including the husband of his younger sister. The shock of seeing her husband's death was so great that she mentally regressed to the point where she acted like a child. Manji took up the responsibility of caring for her, but her subsequent death at the hands of a rogue gang prompts him to make the deal that will afford him immortality with Yaobikuni, an 800-year-old nun. She feeds him *kessen-cho*, bloodworms that live in his bloodstream and heal all his wounds. When he has killed one thousand evil men, she'll remove the *kessen-cho* and allow him to die in peace.

The series easily could have developed into a wandering swordsman epic, with Manji cursing his lot in life while cutting down vast numbers of opponents. Samura, however, charts a different path, surrounding Manji with a cast of characters who are just as morally conflicted, if not more so, than he is. Not long after

Manji begins his quest for redemption, he takes on a travelling companion: Rin, a sixteen-year-old girl who is pursuing her own quest for vengeance. She sees Manji as a sword for hire who can help her exact her vengeance; he sees her as his surrogate sister, someone he can protect to atone for his sister's death. Together they hunt down Anotsu Kagehisa, the man responsible for annihilating Rin's family and destroying her father's martial arts school.

Typically for this series, nothing is black and white. Rin's determination to avenge her parents' deaths wavers as she struggles over whether her actions are justified, while Anotsu himself clouds the issue early in the series, telling her that her spirit is more in tune with his own school than her father's. Both Manji and Rin balance on the precarious line between maintaining and upholding their honour and descending into the blind rage of revenge. It's a line that often gets blurred, and where each one stands in relationship to that balance causes the two to separate and reunite several times throughout the series.

With such emotionally conflicted protagonists, it stands to reason that other enemies and allies are depicted in a similarly blurred fashion. While you might question Anotsu's "ends justify the means" attitude, you can't help but admire his aim to battle the endemic corruption and create a stronger Japanese society.

Samura's attention to detail extended to the English-language publication of

Blade of the Immortal, too, making it unique in an era when manga publishers routinely flopped pages and translated sound effects to give the artwork a Western comic-book feel. In contrast, Samura requested that Dark Horse publish his artwork unflopped, to which end they cut up the individual panels and pasted them back in a left-to-right orientation, a process that was acknowledged to create some continuity flaws. Sound effects were left untranslated wherever possible, but when translation was crucial to understanding the story, Samura would redraw the panel to ensure a harmonious blend of effect and art.

Cardcaptor Sakura

CLAMP; *pub* Kodansha (Jp), Tokyopop (UK, US), Madman (Aus); *ser* Nakayoshi (1996–2000); *vols* 12

So-called "magical girl" manga, where an otherwise unremarkable girl gains the power to accomplish extraordinary deeds with the help of a magic wand and a cute companion, existed before *Cardcaptor Sakura* debuted in 1996. CLAMP's take on the genre made it their own, though. It was the first time the four-artist collective had ever worked on a series for younger girls – their previous efforts were targeted towards teens and older audiences, mostly either tragic romantic fantasies or parodies of some of their favourite genres. *Cardcaptor Sakura*'s dress-up doll mentality, which sticks heroine Sakura Kinomoto in a new costume every time she transforms, no doubt contributed to the shōjo manga's massive success, together with the anime opening up countless merchandising opportunities.

Appealing directly to the younger audience is main character Sakura, a typical ten-year-old fourth grader who hates maths, loves physical education classes and is considered to be the most cheerful girl at school. Now, thanks to Kerberos the Magnificent (at least that's what he calls himself; Sakura promptly shortens it to Kero-chan, which she feels is more suitable for such a cute little creature), she's been tasked with hunting down a series of magical cards that have gone missing from a book that she inadvertently opened in her father's study. The book was supposed to have been guarded night and day by Kero-chan in his role as the Creature of the Seal, but he fell asleep and the

Mahō shōjo at its most inviting on the cover of CLAMP's *Cardcaptor Sakura* volume 1.

classmate Tomoyo Daidoji. Tomoyo not only knows about Sakura's secret but is usually right beside her and Kero-chan, videotaping their exploits and designing every costume Sakura wears. If Tomoyo existed in the real world, she'd snap up every last piece of *Cardcaptor Sakura* merchandise, too. She can certainly afford to do all of this, being the daughter of the president of the Daidoji Toy Company with bodyguards and the latest technological wizardry available to her. But her first love is always Sakura.

In the first half of the series, Sakura and Tomoyo's devoted friendship serves as a backdrop to the action-packed sequences of Sakura rounding up the Clow Cards one by one. Meanwhile, the mythology behind the series is developed through the tarot-like quality of the cards and the depiction of the cards' spirits.

But what the series really hinges upon – particularly in the second half, after Sakura becomes a Master of the Clow and transforms the cards with her own magic into Sakura Cards – are the relationships among the characters. Sakura and her family share a close bond, strengthened by memories of their late mother, who died when Sakura was three and her older brother Touya was ten. The siblings' relationship can be strained at times, as Sakura feels Touya gets in the way between her and his hot-looking friend, Yukito, whom it later turns out he too has a crush on. There is, though, a more serious love interest for Sakura, in the form of Syaoran Li, a distant

nineteen Clow Cards escaped into the real world. Each card has a special power or element associated with it; wielding the Sword card, for instance, makes the bearer an instant sword expert. With her latent magical ability and a special magic staff Sakura gains the powers of the Cardcaptor to capture the cards and return them to the Book of the Clow.

Serving as Sakura's supportive morale booster in this task is a friend so close that they'd be in a romantic relationship were it not for her naïveté: her

CLAMP

Manga artist collective: Satsuki Igarashi (1969–), Nanase Ohkawa (1967–), Tsubaki Nekoi (1969–), Mokona (1968–)

CLAMP – which means "a pile of potatoes", according to the artists – is manga's equivalent of a rock band that started off playing in the garage and ended up churning out chart-topping global hits. Fans rattle off their names as easily as an earlier generation would those of John, Paul, George and Ringo; and about six thousand fans waited hours at Anime Expo 2006 in California to see them make their US anime convention debut.

So it wasn't altogether unexpected when the core four of the all-female collective did the rock-star thing of changing their names for their fifteenth anniversary celebration in 2004. As de facto group spokeswoman Ohkawa explained, the group simply wanted to try out new names. So Mokona Apapa dropped half of her name because it sounded too immature for her liking; Mick Nekoi changed her first name to Tsubaki because she was tired of having people comment that her name was similar to that of Mick Jagger; Ohkawa changed her name to Ageha to go along with the others, but has since returned to her original Nanase; and Satsuki Igarashi changed her name by using different Japanese characters to write it.

While their breakthrough mainstream hit was *RG Veda* in 1989, the group's working relationship began earlier as an artists' circle producing amateur manga, or dōjinshi, at Japan's premier showcase for amateur manga talent, Comic Market (aka Comiket). The group was bigger back then, with as many as eleven women filling their ranks at one point. Of those who have left, the only ex-CLAMP member to have made an impact on the Western market is Tamayo Akiyama, whom Tokyopop marketed as an ex-CLAMP member with the hope that it would boost sales of her books. The group's signature works in those days were the "CLAMP Presents" dōjinshi, in which they parodied popular series like *Captain Tsubasa* and *Knights of the Zodiac*, as well as lesser-known series and even live-action movies.

It's their ability to produce work catering to a wide range of different audiences that has continued to make CLAMP so successful. Popular works have included such disparate series as *Angelic Layer* (shōnen), *Chobits* (seinen), *Cardcaptor Sakura* and *Magic Knight Rayearth* (both shōjo for younger age groups), *X/1999* (shōjo for older teens) and *Legal Drug* (shōnen-ai). Each series features an art style tailored for its audience; the art in *Angelic Layer*, for instance, emphasizes action sequences and speed lines, while *X/1999* is filled with images of beautiful boys, elegant girls and backgrounds of feathers flying everywhere. This willingness to adapt has granted them a good deal of creative flexibility; as Ohkawa told Timothy R. Lehmann in *MANGA: Masters of the Art*, publishers often meet with them, lay out the basic target audience for the series, and then let CLAMP take it from there. Ohkawa is the one who determines the rough story, while the others flesh out the ideas and design the characters and settings.

Several US publishers have benefited from the sales bump that a CLAMP series has provided, including Tokyopop (which received the lion's share of CLAMP work during the manga boom of the early 2000s, Viz (*X/1999*), ADV (*Kobato*), and Del Rey (*Tsubasa Reservoir Chronicle* and *xxxHolic*). Dark Horse is the latest publisher hoping to benefit from the CLAMP cachet, with a series of "mangettes" that were unnamed at the time of writing.

Clover

pub Kodansha (Jp), Dark Horse (US); *ser* Amie (1997–99); *vols* Jp 4 (suspended), US 1; *age* 16+

Coming off the success of *Cardcaptor Sakura*, *Clover* was a visually rather simple, spare work by comparison. Yet if anything, CLAMP approached this series with an even greater attention to detail, distilling the artwork to elements cast in black and white and arranging those elements on the page in a cinematic style that often breaks away from the traditional panel-grid format. What results is a story that is at turns starkly beautiful and violent, a cyberpunk tale with similarities to *Akira* but with an edgy shōjo sensibility.

In a country ruled by powerful psychics known as Wizards, the Clover Leaf Project rates and segregates children based on their latent powers. The most powerful, Three-Leaf and Four-Leaf Clovers, are promptly isolated from the rest of society until such time that they are deemed ready to lead. Now one of the Four-Leaf Clovers, Su, is about to enter the outside world for the first time… The magazine in which it was serialized folded in 1999, leaving *Clover* unfinished, and with CLAMP currently juggling *Tsubasa Reservoir Chronicle*, *xxxHolic*, *Kobato* and work for Dark Horse, a return to the series in the short term seems unlikely.

Man of Many Faces / Duklyon: CLAMP School Defenders / CLAMP School Detectives

pub Kodansha (Jp), Tokyopop (US); *ser* various (1989–93); *vols* 2 / 2 / 3

CLAMP's first major crossover project was one of their professional works that most closely echoed the spirit of the group's gag dōjinshi days. All three series are set at the CLAMP

CLAMP cont.

School, a sprawling, five-point campus built by the Imonoyama business conglomerate that incorporates every level from kindergarten to high school. (It's also a convenient common setting in which CLAMP allowed many of their dōjinshi-era characters to play.) The first series, *Man of Many Faces*, featured Akira, a boy who leads a double life as the youngest in a long family line of mysterious thieves, and how he falls in love with Utako after he escapes into her room while fleeing the scene of one of his thefts. *Duklyon*, CLAMP's spoof of the *tokusatsu* (transforming costumed super-hero) genre, features Kentaro and Takeshi as costumed superheroes that battle a line-up of bad guys that get progressively wackier as the series progresses. The final series in the trilogy, *CLAMP School Detectives*, is CLAMP's take on the mystery genre. It brings back Akira as the class treasurer together with two other characters to solve mysteries: Nokoru, the smartest student in school, and Suou, a martial arts master.

The One I Love

pub Tsunokawa Books (Jp), Tokyopop (US); *ser* Young Rose (1993–95); *vols* 1; *age* 13+

CLAMP tackles the subject of love in these twelve short stories, from the nervousness of confessing a crush on Valentine's Day, to a woman spurned by her lover in favour of a younger woman, to a woman who feels stressed out at the altar about her prospects after getting married, and other key romantic points in life in between. Published in a magazine targeted at young women in Japan, this was lighter fare than the other two series CLAMP was working on at the time: *RG Veda* and *X/1999*.

Tsubasa Reservoir Chronicle

pub Kodansha (Jp); Del Rey (US, UK); *ser* Weekly Shōnen Magazine (2004–); *vols* ongoing; *age* 13+

relative of Clow Card creator Clow Reed, introduced as a rival who believes his lineage entitles him to the cards more than Sakura. While he's initially drawn to Yukito for his magical energies, he eventually falls for Sakura as well.

The appeal of these characters – and especially the growing relationship

The group's longest-running series to date (ignoring the on-hiatus *X/1999*), *Tsubasa* is the first CLAMP series to be serialized in a weekly shōnen magazine. It's also the fulfilment of many hardcore CLAMP fans' dreams to see characters from the group's various series interact with one another in a common universe. These characters aren't simply pasted into a new story, though: updated and refined character designs show how CLAMP's art has developed, while the characters themselves take on new roles and personalities more befitting of the series' teen-targeted action-adventure focus. Sakura and Syaoran of *Cardcaptor Sakura* are the stars here, but this time Syaoran takes centre-stage as Sakura's would-be saviour. The reason she needs saving is because her memories, represented by feathers, have been scattered across multiple dimensions. It's up to Syaoran and friends – the banished ninja Kurogane and Fay, a magician on the run – to recover those feathers and restore her memories.

xxxHolic

pub Kodansha (Jp), Del Rey (US, UK); *ser* Weekly Young Magazine (2003–); *vols* ongoing; *age* 13+

While *Tsubasa Reservoir Chronicle* takes a visceral, action-adventure approach to its story, its current crossover partner, *xxxHolic*, takes a more emotional, ephemeral approach, spotlighting CLAMP's most complex and elegant artwork to date. High school student Kimihiro can see demons and spirits, and it's driving him crazy. For help, he goes to a shop that grants wishes, but in exchange the customer must surrender something of equal value. The owner, the mysterious witch Yuko, grants him his wish in exchange for him becoming her assistant and helping to grant other people's wishes; joining him on some of his tasks are Domeki, Kimihiro's calm, sarcastic classmate whom Kimihiro considers to be a rival (although Domeki couldn't care either way), and Kunogi, Kimihiro's love interest who inadvertently brings bad luck to everyone except for her parents and Domeki.

between Sakura and Syaoran – was such that CLAMP didn't leave them behind in the final volume of *Cardcaptor Sakura*. Instead, the couple were brought back as central characters in the parallel universe setting of one of their ongoing series, *Tsubasa Reservoir Chronicle* (see box above).

Case Closed / Detective Conan

Gosho Aoyama; *pub* Shogakukan (Jp), Viz (UK, US); *ser* Shōnen Sunday (1994–); *vols* ongoing; *age* 16+

The premise and art style of *Detective Conan* – renamed *Case Closed* in English-language markets due to the potential for legal conflict with the owners of the *Conan the Barbarian* franchise – would suggest that it's a detective series aimed at children. It features a cute bespectacled boy who runs around solving mysteries, whose friends chip in and get involved in his adventures, and then the adults get all the credit in the end. Closer examination reveals that it's anything but a children's series: the murder scenes are rendered in grotesque detail, with victims shown hanged, shot, stabbed with knives, blood pooling from gaping wounds. This sense of darkness encased within a shell of innocence permeates the series.

By all appearances, Conan Edogawa should be the greatest detective in all of mangadom. Gosho Aoyama has showcased his skill in cracking cases for more than a decade now, which should position Conan among an elite of fictional detectives – Sherlock Holmes, Hercule Poirot, Miss Marple – whose exploits inspired his author. His name is even an amalgamation of two notable detective novelists – Sir Arthur Conan Doyle and Edogawa Rampo, whose mysteries starring detective Kogoro Akechi are bestsellers in Japan. The only problem is that Conan appears to be a six-year-old child – granted, one who solves all of bumbling private eye Richard Moore's cases, but a child nonetheless.

It wasn't always like this. Conan is actually Jimmy Kudo, a teen investigator highly valued by the police force for his brilliant insights into open cases. After following several mysterious men in black, he was drugged with an experimental poison and left for dead. When he awoke, his mental abilities were intact, but he'd reverted to the physical form of a young boy. The only person aware of his secret is next-door neighbour Dr. Hiroshi Agasa, a self-proclaimed genius inventor who acts much like James Bond's Q, providing Conan with various gadgets to help him overcome his physical limitations and boost his crime-fighting skills. Thus Conan gets a voice-altering bow tie, with which he can imitate the voices of adults around him; sneakers that increase his strength; and braces that act as a set of instant handcuffs.

Naturally there are mysteries to solve, although the biggest mystery in the series remains unsolved – the identity of the syndicate controlling those men in black. Details have trickled out every now and then, but it's been left to readers to piece together a sense of how the group works. In other respects *Detective Conan* is a typical whodunnit series – a crime is committed, clues are gathered, and a suspect is caught. It's in the characterization and the story woven around the core plots that this series shines.

Since Conan is now six years old again, he has to go through the first grade all over again, meeting a group of charming buddies with whom he shares adventures. Meanwhile, Jimmy's closest friend was the private eye's daughter, Rachel, and now that Jimmy is Conan, he has to come up with excuses for his older persona going missing and have Rachel confide to him her crush on Jimmy.

Aoyama knows how he plans to end his long-running series, which had sold more than 120 million volumes in Japan alone as of 2007, but is making his readers wait. Interestingly, the Viz manga, which began in 2004, retained the anglicized names used by the Funimation anime that screened in the US as part of the Cartoon Network's Adult Swim line-up. The characters' original names and their meanings are discussed in the included glossaries.

Crying Freeman

Kazuo Koike (text), Ryoichi Ikegami (art); *pub* Shogakukan(Jp), Dark Horse (US); *ser* Weekly Big Comic Spirits (1986–88); *vols* 9 (Jp), 5 (US); *age* 18+

Before *Crying Freeman* came along to rock readers with its blend of sensual beauty and gritty gangland violence, Kazuo Koike and Ryoichi Ikegami had collaborated on 1973's *AIUEO Boy* (also known as *The Starving Man*), a story of revenge set in 1970s America that captured the rebellious attitudes of Japanese student protesters at the time. Then their career paths went in separate directions, with Koike becoming known as a premier writer of historical samurai dramas – *Lone Wolf and Cub* (see p.147), but also titles like *Lady Snowblood*, *Samurai Executioner* and *Path of the Assassin*. Ikegami, in turn, was building a reputation as a collaborative artist on works like *Mai the Psychic Girl*, becoming known

Courtesy of Dark Horse Comics

Ikegami's uncompromisingly brutal artwork is paired with Koike's complex story of a conflicted assassin in *Crying Freeman*.

for his detailed scenery and realistic drawings of people who radiated energy – the men exuding power, the women oozing sexuality.

When Koike and Ikegami reunited in 1986, the storytelling experience they had gained since their first collaborative effort was evident. *Crying Freeman* retained the rebellious, resilient spirit of *AIUEO Boy* and refined it, pairing the elegance of Koike's story with the brutality of Ikegami's artwork. It's apparent even from the title: conventional macho wisdom would have you believe that real men don't cry. But Yo Hinomura is just as hardcore an assassin as any other in seinen manga, despite shedding rather a lot of tears. And he makes lovely pottery, too.

That one of the world's up-and-coming ceramic artists would live a double life as an assassin so ruthless that the police and the yakuza have to team up to try to take him down makes for a rich, intriguing back story. Yo's inadvertent brush with the criminal underworld during an exhibition – he saw someone stashing money in one of the displays – put him in the cross hairs of the 108 Dragons clan of the Chinese Mafia, which promptly kidnapped him and brainwashed him to carry out their assassination orders. But while their command over him is absolute, it has a side effect: whenever he eliminates his targets, his soul is momentarily freed to act as it once did, and he sheds tears of regret for his victims.

Suffice it to say that Yo has his vulnerable, sensitive side, which is further drawn out by his relationship with Emu Hino, an aspiring artist who witnessed Yo killing a syndicate boss. Resigned to the fact that he would return to kill her, she begged him to take her virginity first, because she had fallen in love with him the moment she saw him crying after he killed his target. Yo complies with the first part, but can't bring himself to kill her as he's fallen in love with her too.

On the run from the police, they are given new identities by the Chinese Mafia – he becomes Long Tai Yan ("Sun Dragon"), she becomes Hu Qing Lan ("Tiger Orchid"). They are also groomed to take over leadership of the clan from the elderly Mother Tiger and Father Dragon… without anyone in the organization suspecting that they might be planning to take it down from the inside.

With the complex background explained, the series kicks into a higher gear, as Yo hones his leadership skills and eliminates foes outside the organization as well as other traitors within. One would-be traitor, Bai-Ya Shan, the granddaughter of Mother Tiger and Father Dragon, initially plots a coup d'état against Yo. Once she's defeated, though, she becomes an ally to the couple… and the primary comic relief in the series, for her insistence on being "little sister" (though her height and girth suggest anything but "little") and bodyguard for them, which means often running into missions stark naked.

As is fitting for a series centred on neverending warfare between rival syndicates, the body count rises steadily from the first page and doesn't let up until a few thousand pages later. Unlike in shōnen manga, there's no escalation in the powers of the rivals that Yo faces, but rather constant violent action throughout, broken up by frequent bouts of passionate sex. It's unbridled 1980s pulp action at its finest, establishing a standard for manly romances that has yet to be surpassed.

Cyborg 009

Shōtarō Ishinomori; *pub* various (Jp), Tokyopop (US); *ser* various (1964–98); *vols* Jp 36, US 10; *age* 13+

"From the dawn of man, humankind has entangled itself in conflict and struggle", Ishinomori muses at one point in *Cyborg 009*. "It's as if humanity thrives on a culture of conflict, clashes and bloodshed." And while the desire for world peace may be a noble one, there's profit to be made from warfare, in this case by the group known as Black Ghost, which is working on a project to convert humans into battle-ready cyborgs. These cyborgs are intended to take global conflicts into space, safely removed from Earth's fragile resources. Nine people are plucked from around the world – a baby from Russia, a New York street punk, a Native American, a Chinese pauper, a German smuggler, a French woman, a washed-up English actor, an African tribesman and a Japanese delinquent – and subjected to experiments, giving them various cybernetic enhancements and powers in the process. For example, one gets the ability to morph into various objects; another can fly at up to Mach 5 speeds; while the baby becomes a genius who can telepathically communicate with his teammates.

But it's the last person brought in – Joe Shimamura, soon to be Cyborg 009 – who becomes the crowning jewel of the cybernetic programme. With his super speed, superhuman strength, an ability to travel underwater, night vision and a computer-like brain, he's a combination of the other cyborgs' powers and then some. And he also happens to be the Japanese guy: an inspiring anti-war hero for Ishinomori's original audience.

The results of the experiments are exactly as Black Ghost expected. What they didn't anticipate was that the 00-Team, under lead scientist Dr Isaac Gilmore, would turn rogue and make a run for it. From the second half of the first volume onward, Gilmore's team battles to retain its freedom and halt Black Ghost's plans to profit from the next world war. Ishinomori's theme of a group of superheroes battling against an evil organization, gaining more power by working as a team, would be influential (see box on p.108).

In spite of all of the technological gadgetry installed within these humans-turned-cyborgs, all of them possess the trademark Ishinomori Flaw, an element of humanity that stains otherwise flawless mechanized beings. The Black Ghost group persists with the human-to-cyborg project even after the original team rebels, and when these new creations are sent to attack the rebels, Joe often appeals to that spark of humanity, trying to turn their attackers into allies.

Like Tezuka's *Astro Boy*, which Ishinomori assisted on, *Cyborg 009*'s cartoony, Disney-esque appearance hides a serious message at its core, calling for peace as the world spirals time and again towards war. Nowhere is this more apparent than in a story arc from 1965, in which the 00-Team finds itself in the middle of the Vietnam War, trying to stop Black Ghost as it supplies its war machines to the Viet Cong and dispatches its latest agents of destruction, the Cyborgmen, to the battlefield. Amid a backdrop of indiscriminate death and destruction, the 00-Team comes upon a

girl looking for her brother, from whom she was separated after they fled from a firefight in which their parents were killed. While she believes he joined the Viet Cong, it turns out that he was kidnapped by Black Ghost and reconstructed in the form of one of the Cyborgmen.

When the two are finally reunited, the brother, ashamed of what he has become, frees the captured 00-Team members and commits suicide. "They built me for war, death and destruction," he tells his sister. "I'm no longer capable of a peaceful life, especially here." The machinations of war make little sense, and members of the 00-Team end up sacrificing themselves in the interests of peace on numerous occasions. They never stayed dead permanently, though; Ishinomori resurrected the series several times due to reader demand.

Shōtarō Ishinomori

Manga artist and anime/tokusatsu creator, 1938–98

Shōtarō Ishinomori may not be nearly as well known as Osamu Tezuka in the Western world, but the contributions he made to the early development of manga and Japanese pop culture conventions are undeniable. As one of the first of the new breed of manga artists to emerge in the post-World War II Japanese manga market, the career of Ishinomori (born Shōtarō Onodera in 1938; "Ishinomori" is a reference to his home town) followed the same pattern as most other successful creators at the time. His first published work was *Nikyuu Tenshi* in 1954, a short story that caught the attention of Osamu Tezuka, who invited Ishinomori to assist him with *Astro Boy*. On graduating from high school in 1956, Ishinomori did just that, contributing to what would later become Astro Boy's "Electro" story arc. His work would show the influence of Tezuka's style.

Where Ishinomori would make his own mark and establish himself as the "King of Manga" would be in developing superhero and supergroup archetypes, first in manga and eventually gravitating towards anime and *tokusatsu* (live-action superhero) series. His characterization of the superpowered hero with an emotional flaw, first seen in *Cyborg 009* (see p.106), would manifest itself in adapted *tokusatsu* series such as *Kamen Rider* and *Kikaider*. With their elaborate costumes and transformations, these series in turn fuelled interest in Ishinomori's manga properties, which were often turned over to other artists to maximize production.

Ishinomori died from heart failure a few days after his sixtieth birthday. Shortly afterwards, the *Guinness Book of World Records* posthumously recognized him as the comics creator who had generated the most output in his lifetime, with more than 128,000 pages produced. About 10,000 of those pages were devoted to an informational manga, *Manga Nihon no Rekishi* (*A Manga History of Japan*), which has never been translated.

108

Kamen Rider

pub Sun Comics (Jp); *vols* 4

The first of Ishinomori's manga to go the *tokusatsu* route, Kamen Rider is the story of Takeshi Hongo, a human altered by the evil secret society Shocker but who managed to escape before he could be brainwashed. Now with the ability to transform into Kamen Rider, Takeshi must turn on his evil creators and save the world. Ishinomori's manga diverged from the live-action series in that Hongo actually was killed by twelve Shocker Riders, but the blow suffered by one of the Riders knocked some sense back into him, and he took over the Kamen Rider mantle.

Japan Inc.

pub Nihon Keizai Shimbun (Jp), University of California Press (US); *vols* 1

Back in the heady days of the Japanese bubble economy, American businesspeople wanted insight into just what was making this successful economy tick. And so this manga was created, to cover the main economic issues – from rising oil prices to banking globalization – in an entertaining style. The bubble may have burst three years after this manga saw print in late 1986, but it's still a neat glimpse into the prevailing attitudes of the time.

Skull Man

Kazuhiko Shimamoto; *pub* Media Factory (Jp), Tokyopop (US); *vols* 7

In the original, hundred-page story published in 1970, Skull Man was one of manga's first antiheroes, a man willing to sacrifice innocent people's lives if it meant taking a step towards his own goals. Kazuhiko Shimamoto resurrected the character in 1997 at the behest of an increasingly ill Ishinomori, receiving copies of the proposed story and plot notes. This story follows Tatsuro Kagura, an adopted son seeking revenge against the people who killed his birth parents. Little does Tatsuro realize that the person who killed them was his grandfather – and that for the past few years, said grandfather has been raising his younger sister as well. All the while, he must also fight off shape-shifting creatures created by scientific experiments gone horribly wrong. The completed modern series, while criticized for having an unsatisfying ending, successfully expands on Ishinomori's original story while keeping its essence intact.

Death Note

Tsugumi Ohba (text), Takeshi Obata (art); *pub* Shueisha (Jp), Viz (UK, US), Madman (Aus); *ser* Shōnen Jump (2003–06); *vols* 12; *age* 16+

Good-versus-evil morality tales quickly get dull. Besides, the world doesn't usually operate in black and white: innumerable, subtle shades of grey is more like it. It's in this grey area that *Death Note* dwells, a series whose ambiguous morality is embodied by its main character, seventeen-year-old Light Yagami. One of the top high-school students in the country, Light is feeling bored when he spots a notebook on the ground and takes it home with him. As it turns out, the notebook is a Death Note, used by the shinigami, or death gods, to determine the time and circumstances of people's death (see box opposite). This particular notebook was the property of the mischievous shinigami Ryuk; just as bored as Light, he's curious to see what will happen to the book when it falls into human hands. Light is permitted to use the Death Note to kill people, but there's a catch: when his own name is written in the book, he is fated to suffer an eternity of terror and torment in a limbo that is neither in heaven nor hell.

In spite of that warning, Light takes up the challenge. For his first, tentative step, he targets a criminal he sees on TV, who has taken several people hostage in a nursery school, and lets him die via the default method of a heart attack. A few criminals later, Light's confidence has grown, and before long what began as an experiment has turned into a one-man crusade to create a utopia without evil. As word spreads of his exploits, a cult springs up on the Internet worshipping the deeds of Kira (derived from the Japanese pronunciation of the word "killer"), "the messenger from hell who will not suffer the presence of evil in this world".

This premise alone wouldn't be worthy of a twelve-volume manga. Indeed, Light's reign of unfettered vigilante justice lasts for all of 46 pages before it attracts the attention of Interpol and the mysterious crime investigator known only as L. L is rather eccentric: he rarely speaks face to face with other people, and only his closest associates know what he looks like. But his crime-fighting skills are unparalleled, making him the perfect foil to Light's clever manoeuvrings.

A complex chess game of extraordinary wit emerges. Light knows that L is after him, so he works to find out the true identity of L so he can murder him and thus have free licence to continue his killing spree. L, in turn, suspects

Rule to a kill

To list all of the rules and regulations involved in the proper use of a Death Note requires a book in itself: licensed Death Note replicas contain forty pages worth of rules gathered from throughout the manga as well as the anime series. These, then, are the first four rules, governing principles upon which the rest build:

✦ The human whose name is written in a note will die.

✦ A note will not take effect unless the writer has the person's face in their mind when writing his/her name. Therefore, people sharing the same name will not be affected.

✦ If the cause of death is written within forty seconds of writing the person's name, it will happen.

✦ If the cause of death is not specified, the person will simply die of a heart attack.

✦ After writing the cause of death, details of the death should be written in the next six months and forty seconds.

Light is Kira and tries to catch Light in some kind of slip-up so he can deliver swift justice. It's a constant game of one-upmanship between the two characters, and it's a thrill to watch as L plies his craft and an increasingly paranoid Light begins to target members of the team investigating him. Writer Tsugumi Ohba plants several "gotcha" moments in his story where one person gains a distinct advantage and the other is forced to adjust his strategy to recover.

This two-header can't go on forever, though, and the plot takes a different turn halfway through the series, a turn that has caused a rift amongst *Death Note* fans. Some believe the series gains an added dimension from this point onwards; others feel let down and manipulated, perhaps unfairly so as the shocking twist was part of Ohba's plan right from the start, along with the decision to finish on the 108th chapter (representing the number of earthly desires in Buddhism). But with blurring boundaries of right and wrong, whether justice is delivered is always going to be a matter of individual judgement.

Dr. Slump

Akira Toriyama; *pub* Shueisha (Jp), Viz (UK, US, Aus); *ser* Shōnen Jump (1980–84); *vols* 18; *age* 13+

Any English-speaking manga fan will be familiar with *Dragon Ball*; they're less likely to have come across Akira Toriyama's previous series, *Dr. Slump*, a showcase for the artist's comedic skills that's been slower to reach a Western audience.

When a mangaka names two of his core characters after different types of Japanese rice cakes, it's likely a sign that he's crossing over into zany shōnen territory. In this case, Dr. Senbei Norimaki and his robot girl Arale were set up to deliver a classic comedy series.

Toriyama never makes clear why Senbei, an otherwise brilliant inventor who goes by the nickname of "Dr. Slump" because he hasn't created anything of note lately, was inspired to create Arale. Maybe he just wanted company around the house; maybe it was to satisfy his continual craving to invent stuff. Or maybe it's because he needed a tool to spy on buxom junior high school teacher Ms Yamabuki. In any case, what he ends up creating is a humanoid robot... who, when fully assembled, immediately starts pointing out all of her maker's design flaws, like giving her a flat chest, blurry vision that requires glasses to correct, and leaving out the ability to fly and launch missiles from her stomach.

While Arale appears to be human to those around her, her mechanical nature manifests itself in several ways. She's blissfully unaware of her superhuman abilities, tossing giant boulders and cars into the air like they were tennis balls and running off at super speeds screaming "KIIIIIIII-IIIN". She unscrews her head and pops it off for fun. Her hobbies include poking at piles of poo with a stick, then using the stick to pick it up and carry it around like a lollipop. All of this drives Senbei crazy as he tries to pass off Arale as his younger sister, his daughter, or whichever relative suits the situation at hand.

Not that anyone in his home town would really notice she's a robot, as in Penguin Village everything – from the sun, moon and sky to a tube of toothpaste – can talk. Gamera, the famed giant mutant turtle of Japanese cinema and "friend to all children", stops by regularly to chat, while residents can ride around in hippopotamus-drawn carriages. Surely a girl who can stand in the middle of the road, get hit by a car and walk away without a scratch while the car lies in a mangled heap wouldn't make anyone blink.

Adding to the surreal flavour, characters regularly break the fourth wall and talk to the audience, for instance promoting earlier volumes of the manga and commenting on how ridiculous some of the situations get. One character notes how Toriyama's female character designs are so similar that she can successfully impersonate her teacher. Even Toriyama gets in on the fun, immortalizing himself and his editor, Kazuhiko Torishima, in the series. The artist himself is portrayed as a slightly inept bird ("tori" means "bird" in Japanese), while Torishima is less flatteringly represented by the comically inept foil to Senbei, Dr. Mashirito ("Torishima" spelled out backwards in Japanese).

Other characters are parodies inspired by Japanese and American pop culture. Suppaman is a parody of Superman, adding Japanese flair to the character (he eats pickled plums for his strength) while comically playing off his weaknesses (he really has no super-powers, often getting around by stealing some poor child's skateboard). The full name of another character, Arale's and Senbei's flying companion Gatchan, is Gajira – an amalgamation of the names "Gamera" and "Gojira" (or "Godzilla" in Western translations). References to *Star Wars* and *Star Trek* also abound.

Is there a point to all of this insanity? Not really, although there are a few central story arcs, such as when Senbei and Mashirito face off or when Senbei gets married to Ms Yamabuki. Meanwhile, Arale unwittingly defends the planet from outside threats time and time again, simply by terrifying the aliens when they glimpse her power.

Arale and the gang eventually turned up for three chapters of *Dragon Ball* (see p.116), helping Goku defeat General Blue. It has been suggested that this crossover places Penguin Village squarely within the *Dragon Ball* universe. By the time the cast makes this cameo in *Dragon Ball* volume 7, though, Toriyama was already moving away from the nonstop gags of *Dr. Slump* and starting to develop *Dragon Ball* into a more action-oriented series. The sequence seems to be Toriyama's way of telling readers that while he was taking *Dragon Ball* in a different direction, the madcap world of *Dr. Slump* would never be altogether lost.

Doraemon

Fujiko F. Fujio; *pub* Shogakukan (Jp), Shogakukan English (UK, US, Aus); *ser* various magazines (1969–96); *vols* Jp 45+, US, UK, Aus 10

When Japan sought an ambassador to promote its animation worldwide, it turned not to a real person, but a nearly forty-year-old Japanese pop culture icon: Doraemon, the robot cat from the future. And for good reason: generations have enjoyed the animated series, an annual animated movie and piles of merchandise, since the work of "Fujiko F. Fujio" – actually the pen name used by artists Hiroshi Fujimoto and Motoo Abiko – first appeared in December 1969 in six educational magazines published by Shogakukan targeting children from nursery school to fourth grade. From there, the manga expanded into more magazines; got its own flagship title, *CoroCoro Comic*, in 1977; and earned Shogakukan's first manga award for children's manga in 1982.

The Fujio partnership dissolved in 1987, and Fujimoto died in 1996. Yet Doraemon continues to thrive, and is to Japan much as Mickey Mouse is to the US, a character with a simple, easily identifiable look – in the case of Doraemon, a round head, giant eyes, whiskers and a rounded body – whose adventures appeal to audiences of all ages worldwide. It's a shame that English-language publishers have yet to formally license the series – the material holds up remarkably well in the only official English translation to date, a bilingual edition released under the Shogakukan English imprint.

The first chapter establishes the framework for what would be a successful formula for years to come, introducing Nobita Nobi, a rather unexceptional child. He's below average in sports, a bit low on the intelligence scale, often the butt of jokes played by other children in the neighbourhood, though he does have a love of nature and respect for all living creatures.

Enter Doraemon, a mechanical marvel created on 3 September 2112, and sent back by time machine to what was then present-day Japan by Nobita's great-great-grandson, Sewashi. Sewashi wants Doraemon to help improve Nobita's standing to ensure a happier, more prosperous future for his descendants. Doraemon and Nobita don't start off on the best of terms – when Doraemon first shows up in Nobita's desk drawer, he warns that Nobita will hang himself and burn himself in short order, then eats all of Nobita's rice cakes and disappears again. When Nobita subsequently does hang himself (accidentally off a tree branch, while getting his friends' shuttlecock off the roof) and burn himself with hot water in his bath, he begins to take the robot cat more seriously.

Doraemon's secret weapon in helping Nobita is a four-dimensional pouch, from which he can pull out any conceivable device. Unfortunately, these don't always work as expected, landing the pair in an even deeper, often more comedic predicament than before. Doraemon isn't exactly the pinnacle of twenty-second-century technology, either. He has no ears because a robot mouse bit them off, and he's turquoise because he felt embarrassed after his robo-girlfriend laughed at him.

"To the Beach by Submarine", featured in the second volume of the Shogakukan English edition, is a typical episode. Nobita is left out of a trip aboard the neighbourhood rich kid Suneo's new boat. To compensate, Doraemon pulls out "the submarine", a vessel that expands and contracts to fit its surroundings when placed in a body of water. However, the submarine can only teleport short distances, so to get to the beach, the pair have to board the craft sitting in the

bathtub and then take a trip into some poor guy's glass of ice water, and then a goldfish bowl, a cup of green tea, a kiddie pool, a toilet and an underground sewer line. They finally end up on the boat – but in Suneo's container of hot tea.

Many of the scenarios play out identically: Nobita has a problem; Doraemon pulls out a gadget; something goes horribly wrong; hilarity ensues. Granted, there are variations to the theme – such as when another character gets their hands on one of these toys and encounters disaster in short order. But this comfortable comedic rhythm is what drives the manga, in much the same way as a Looney Tunes cartoon of the same era.

Doraemon has pulled hundreds of gadgets from his pouch over the years, like the Dokodemo Door (a door that acts as an instant portal between any two points in the universe), the Take-copter (a propeller attached to a suction cup to enable flight) and Memory Bread (bread that, when eaten, helps the consumer remember information from book pages imprinted on the slice beforehand). The sheer depth in variety no doubt has inspired generations of readers in their creative thinking as well.

Dragon Ball

Akira Toriyama; *pub* Shueisha (Jp), Viz (UK, US), Chuang Yi (Aus); *ser* Shōnen Jump (1984–95); *vols* 42 (released as 16-vol *Dragon Ball* and 26-vol *Dragon Ball Z* in US, UK, Aus); *age* 13+

The story of *Dragon Ball* is also the story of Akira Toriyama's storytelling evolution, one that led him away from the gag-filled whimsy of *Dr. Slump* (see p.114) to a more intense world packed with action and suspense, precisely the qualities that have given it mass appeal worldwide. Both Japanese and English-speaking audiences have embraced series hero Goku, albeit in different ways.

Before *Dragon Ball*, Son Goku was best known to Japanese audiences as the hero of *Saiyuki*, the Japanese translation of the sixteenth-century Chinese epic *Journey to the West* – also known as *Monkey*. A mischievous monkey with magical powers, Son Goku formed part of a Buddhist monk's entourage on their journey from China to India in search of sacred scrolls. Similar traits appear in *Dragon Ball*'s Goku, a mischievous boy (with a monkey's tail) who travels as part of an entourage in search of the sacred Dragon Balls, seven spheres which, when gathered together, will summon a wish-granting dragon.

Also in evidence is the influence of *Dr. Slump*, especially in the early chapters,

which play out much like *Saiyuki* with *Dr. Slump*-like humour built in. The first two volumes feature Goku and his cohorts gathering most of the balls, then losing them to a would-be world conqueror named Pilaf. But like Goku's transformation under the full moon into a completely different beast, the series establishes its unique identity after the group disperses – Goku's friends back to town, and Goku himself to the island of renowned martial arts teacher Kame-sen'nin.

It's here that the storyline develops into a series of increasingly difficult challenges that Goku and his friends must face, as the evil forces plotting to gather the Dragon Balls for their own purposes grow progressively stronger. Sure, there's still some humour now and then, but as Goku matures from a naïve kid into a powerful warrior, the series adopts a far more action-packed, sinister tone. The battles grow wilder, taking to the air and employing more spiritual powers, and the bodies start piling up. Toriyama's art changes accordingly, as characters gradually lose the rounded, innocent look that he established in

Dr. Slump and gain sharper angles that leap off the page with their energy and intensity.

Western fans, however, were introduced to a Goku from later in the series, an older character renowned for dishing out and enduring punishing blows in *Dragon Ball Z*, the popular, action-packed animated adaptation of volumes 17 to 42 of the manga. Its appeal lay in epic battles that lasted over multiple episodes, the camaraderie that developed among the heroes, and the emotional impact felt when one of those heroes fell in battle. When those volumes of the manga were translated, they were re-numbered as volumes 1–26 under the *Dragon Ball Z* banner – a distinction unique to Western translations. Goku's origin story would eventually appear in translation, but only after the success of *Dragon Ball Z* proved there was an audience for more of Goku and his gang.

Toriyama's rhythmic storyline formula carries through the entire series. First a search for the Dragon Balls launches. Good and evil groups battle it out for control of the balls, and some characters fall in battle. The balls are gathered, a wish is granted and the balls scatter, hidden for seven years. In the interim, the world's toughest fighters battle it out in the Tenkaichi Budokai tournament. Then a new, greater threat arrives, and the cycle begins anew. This familiar plot structure was repeated for eleven years with progressively stronger enemy forces. Toriyama did at one point want to phase out Goku, but the readers were having none of it. Then he decided to end the manga after the Freeza story arc, which ran from chapter 242 to 329, but his publisher pressed him to continue the series, extensions that forced Toriyama to sharpen his skills at closing up plot holes and providing retroactive explanations – even down to recasting characters as aliens from other planets.

Finally, after 519 chapters, Toriyama declared he would be taking a short rest, one that continues to this day. There have been attempts to continue the story with animated movies, the 64-episode *Dragon Ball GT* anime series and several videogames. Yet none of these has managed to tie together the mayhem and keep the series focused like Toriyama did in his manga.

The Drifting Classroom

Kazuo Umezu; *pub* Shogakukan (Jp), Viz (US); *ser* Shōnen Sunday (1972–74); *vols* 11; *age* 16+

Kazuo Umezu is regarded as one of the masters of horror manga, an artist whose work effortlessly conveys the grotesque over a framework of psychological twists and turns. And while *The Drifting Classroom*'s early 1970s art style can appear rather conservative by today's standards, Umezu's message of planetary preservation remains as fresh and relevant as ever.

The classroom in question doesn't drift so much as it is violently thrust with a single resounding "thwomp" into the future, in an earthquake-like phenomenon, instantly separating 862 students and teachers at Yamato Elementary School, a three-year-old boy and a delivery man from the lives they once knew and plunging them into what appears to be a vast alien wasteland.

In that split second, sixth grader Sho Takamatsu goes from being upset at his mother for throwing away his favourite marbles to wondering if he'll ever see her again. Back in the present day, his mother appears to be going crazy since he disappeared, claiming that she can hear his voice. Thing is, she's telling the truth – there are odd supernatural forces at work here, and Sho seems to be the only person in the school who is able to communicate with the present-day world… and only in times of great stress, at that. Call it the power of love transcending all barriers. It's also a contrivance central to the plot. Take, for instance, the time when Sho comes down with a life-threatening virus, and the only way his mother can get medicine to him in the future is to deposit a vial into the mummified body of a star baseball player… who happens to be very much alive in the present day. How she manages to pull off that feat is testament to how tightly plotted this work is.

Sho and his mother need to rely on that psychic bond, because the school survivors are subjected to a continuous gauntlet of terror from the moment they come to rest in their new world. Buildings, subways and vehicles lie abandoned and covered in sand amid an endless desert landscape. Water has all but disappeared. The only things that appear capable of growing are some rather odd-looking mushrooms, while giant insect-like creatures have evolved to fill the void humanity has left on the planet. The only food available to them is whatever is stored in a single room, leaving them with no other option but to strictly ration what's left and devise other ways of surviving.

The greatest threat to the school survivors, however, comes from within their ranks, as Umezu explores the idea that even the most civilized of people, whatever their age, can transform into ruthless savages when thrust into a crisis situation. Unlike the raw, visceral thrill that *Battle Royale* provides in having its characters decapitate one another, though, Umezu approaches the idea from a more psychological angle. The children are a bit wiser than the adults – most of whom end up squabbling with one another, going crazy or squabbling about going crazy, and are for the most part dead two volumes into the series' eleven-volume run. The exceptions are one teacher, Mr Wakayama, who turns on the students in the interest of survival and doesn't last much longer, and Mr Sekiya, a deliveryman whose drive for self-preservation convinces him that he must manipulate the children into doing his will – finding him food, helping him survive, generally staying out of his way – and eliminating them once they are no longer of any use.

As the situation gets bleaker, the days turn into weeks and hope fades that they will ever return to their old lives, the children begin turning on each other, too, fighting over the leadership roles and sacrificing scapegoats. Any time Sho and his group venture outside the school for some reason – investigating the source of a leaf, fleeing from terrifying giant mutant insects summoned by one person's wild imagination, finding medication for a plague that threatens to kill them all – they return to find the situation worse than before.

Much screaming in terror ensues, and fewer than a hundred children make it through to the end. But there is logic behind the shift to the new world that gradually becomes clearer as the series progresses. Everything from the empty buildings to the giant mutant insects came about as a result of human carelessness back in an earlier time, where people used up resources without any regard to the consequences. Still valid today, it was an early environmental message in a period of excess, sent to a Japanese readership that was increasingly sacrificing natural spaces to feed a growing concrete beast.

Fist of the North Star

Buronson (text), Tetsuo Hara (art); *pub* Shueisha (Jp), Gutsoon! (US); *ser* Weekly Shōnen Jump (1983–88); *vols* Jp 15, US 9 (suspended); *age* 18+

O ver-the-top fighting series were all the rage in *Weekly Shōnen Jump* between 1983 and 1987, with *Dragon Ball*, *Jojo's Bizarre Adventure* and *Knights of the Zodiac* (see pp.116, 144 and 146) all debuting in that period.

The idea that would become *Fist of the North Star* came from a brainstorming session between artist Tetsuo Hara and his *Weekly Shōnen Jump* editor, Nobuhiko Horie. Back in 1983, another of Hara's series, *Iron Don Quixote*, was dying a slow death in *Shōnen Jump* and Horie suggested that the artist try something new. Horie knew that Hara wanted to work on a series centred on Chinese martial arts and was an expert on acupressure points.

One year after the demise of *Iron Don Quixote*, *Fist of the North Star* debuted in *Shōnen Jump* in a self-contained chapter; the concept was popular enough that it was expanded to a series that originally was set to run three years but ended up going five. Hara struggled with the shift to weekly serialization, so writer Sho Fumimura, working under the pen name Buronson – a tribute to action-film star Charles Bronson – was brought in to help script the series. Buronson would add the final element to what would become a beloved series for years to come – while Hara's original story was about rival martial arts schools, Buronson changed the setting to a post-apocalyptic wasteland inspired by the movie *Mad Max*, and incorporating elements from *The Road Warrior* and Bruce Lee films. What resulted was a series that became one of the most celebrated in Japan in the past three decades. It's still one of *Shōnen Jump's* top ten bestselling series of all time, with an estimated circulation of 47 million to 60 million copies in Japan. Replicating its success in English-speaking markets has been a dicey proposition, though, with two publishers trying and failing so far to complete the series.

In the world of *Fist of the North Star*, in the year 199X (sic), food and water may be in short supply, but violent explosions of blood and flying body parts certainly aren't. Which is largely thanks to the most clinically efficient destructive force in all of manga: Kenshiro, master of the deadly techniques of Hokuto Shinken. These legendary techniques utilize acupressure points to tear the body apart from the inside without any visible damage on the surface. This gives rise to the signature moment in Kenshiro's battles: after attacking his opponent with a flurry of fists, he'll stand back. "HA!" the opponent will usually retort. "Your attack did NOTHING!... Now I will KILL YOU!" To which Kenshiro replies simply: "You are already dead". And sure enough, a close-up frame shows the smug opponent register surprise... just before his head and body split open and formerly internal organs become distressingly externalized. It gets quite messy, particularly when he takes on several gang members at once.

Kenshiro, in short, is a god among men, who not only hands down judgement to those who are evil, but protects those he believes are good. And no one embodies good more than the women and children who pop up from time to time as he wanders the desolate landscape. Two of his travelling companions are orphan children he meets at the beginning of the series – Bat, a wandering thief, and Lin, a girl rendered mute when she saw her parents die in the nuclear holocaust that precedes the story. There is no greater sin to Kenshiro than the death of a child; if such a thing happens on his watch, it's

highly likely that his inner spirit will rage, his shirt will be ripped off and reveal the scars of the Big Dipper constellation emblazoned on his chest, and... well, it's time for more heads to explode.

And so the series goes, starting with his first opponent, former best friend Shin, a master of the deadly rival school techniques of Nanto Seiken who stole away Kenshiro's fiancée, leaving him with his trademark scars and killing his master in the process. Once that problem is dealt with, there's his adopted brother, Raoh, the self-proclaimed "Conqueror of the Century's End", merely the first of Kenshiro's increasingly more powerful foes.

When compared to his rivals, Kenshiro may be a bit too powerful, as acknowledged by the Japanese readers who ranked him third behind Goku from *Dragon Ball* and Doraemon in a survey of the most powerful manga characters of all time. His victory is rarely in doubt, but instead of the thrill of life-or-death battles, fans satisfy themselves with seeing good not only triumph over evil, but stomp it into a bloody pulp so that it has no chance of ever rising again.

Fruits Basket

Natsuki Takaya; *pub* Hakusensha (Jp), Tokyopop (US, UK), Madman (Aus); *ser* Hana to Yume (1998–2006); *vols* 23; *age* 13+

*F*ruits Basket is one of the bestselling manga series ever produced, its sales in the West unhindered by a grammatically incorrect title (though fans do call it *Furuba* for short). In many ways it's a traditional shōjo story, with ingredients including high school, boys, family problems – but with a unique twist. More unexpectedly, it's also a lesson on the Chinese zodiac. Author Natsuki Takaya, looking for a starting point for her new series, recalled that the dictionary she used had a zodiac chart in it and proposed using it as the manga's main motif.

Takaya's series originates with a legend in which the animals invited by God to a banquet became the animals of the zodiac. While twelve animals showed up and were immortalized, a thirteenth – the cat – was fooled by the rat into believing that the banquet was a day later, thus ensuring his place outside the pantheon for all eternity. The Sohma family has a curse rooted in this legend, with all its members possessed by spirits of the zodiac. If a member of the opposite sex hugs any one of them, they transform from human form into their particular zodiac animal. It's a secret that has kept them somewhat sequestered and emotionally distant from anyone who would attempt to embrace them and welcome them into the world at large.

But that was before Tohru Honda, quite probably the nicest girl in school, came along. Tohru has fallen on hard times as the series opens, and has chosen to live in a tent, accompanied by a picture of her mother. It's not that she doesn't have a home, but her grandfather, who took her in after her mother was killed in a traffic accident, has asked her to stay with friends while the house is remodelled, and she doesn't want to impose on anyone.

The camping ground she unwittingly picks is the property where Yuki Sohma – her princely classmate – and his older brother/guardian Shigure live, and the two let her stay with them. Cousin Kyo comes crashing in shortly afterward, demanding that Yuki fight him to settle a long-standing feud – as the zodiac's cat and rat, respectively, they're always at odds. Tohru rushes forward to stop the fight, slips, accidentally grabs Kyo and – poof! – she's left holding a clearly agitated cat, and the Sohma animal-transformation secret is revealed. But while other outsiders who discovered this secret have had their memories erased, Shigure allows her to keep her memory intact. Tohru's unconditional acceptance of them touches their hearts somehow… and the fact that her favourite zodiac animal is the cat certainly catches Kyo off guard, as he's used to being the outcast of the family.

Mysteries abound, the biggest concerning the head of the Sohma family, Akito, a polarizing, parental influence who for some reason allows Tohru to stay within the Sohma family circle. Others concern the relationship dynamic amongst the family members, a complex network of love and hate (helpfully illustrated by a two-page flow chart in the *Fruits Basket Fan Book: Cat*).

Tohru's fragility – seen in her need to belong and her fear of losing her friends – lies largely hidden behind her kind, generous nature. In this way her character is symbolic of the series as a whole – sweetness on the surface, with a constant undercurrent of dark secrets and melancholic moods. The whole "transforming animals" gimmick eventually settles into the background, making way for progressively deeper explorations of the curse that binds the Sohmas. Each of the characters is well-rendered, retaining some qualities of their animal counterparts, and they're cute, too. In Takaya's dreamy artwork, huge-eyed Tohru's often surrounded by boys far prettier than she is. But *Fruits Basket* is more than just a collection of pretty faces; it's a progressively complex story that draws you in with its cuteness and keeps you reading with its collection of deepening mysteries.

Fullmetal Alchemist

Hiromu Arakawa; *pub* Square Enix (Jp), Viz (US, UK), Madman (Aus); *ser* Shōnen Gangan (2001–); *vols* ongoing; *age* 13+

If anime and manga fans hadn't heard of *Fullmetal Alchemist* through imported and fan-translated materials before 2004, they certainly were well-informed about it after that year's *FMA* media blitz. Cover stories and extended features ran in all the main anime and manga magazines, heralding the arrival of the anime on the Cartoon Network in November, while the anime's English-language voice actors spread the word at conventions across the US, UK and Australia.

The manga that started it all is the poignant tale of two brothers, Edward and Alphonse Elric, who wanted to be

The brothers Elric still dream of a day when they will be able to recover their flesh and blood bodies.

reunited with their dead mother. What they got instead was a tragic lesson in the principle of equivalent exchange. This fundamental law of the manga's steampunk-style world states that for anything to be created, something of equal value must be destroyed. Alchemy is the advanced scientific practice at the centre of *Fullmetal Alchemist*; those skilled in it are able to manipulate substances from one form to another through special transcriptions known as transmutation circles, in which the alchemist analyses the physical attributes of the object, breaks it down into its fundamental pieces and rebuilds it into the new form.

Where the brothers Elric went wrong was in their desire to bring back their dead mother through a transmutation circle. Not only did the experiment fail – creating a mutant, who thankfully turned out not to be their mother – but they themselves were horribly disfigured in the process. Younger brother Al paid the higher price – his entire body disintegrated in the process, and the only reason he's still alive is that a fast-thinking Ed bound his soul in a suit of armour. At the same time Ed lost his own right arm and left leg and now uses prosthetic automail (mechanical) limbs.

Their alchemy skills did not go unnoticed, however, and they are approached by Col. Roy Mustang, known as the Flame Alchemist, who recruits them as State Alchemists under his command. Only Edward is able to take the exam, though, and upon passing he gains the title of Fullmetal Alchemist. Yet all is not as prestigious as it may seem with the State Alchemists, as they're often called "dogs of the military" for how they're considered to have sold their souls in exchange for special entitlements.

The thing that motivates most of the characters in the series is the idea that inspired Arakawa's tale: the Philosopher's Stone, an item that can bypass the law of equivalent exchange and allow for transmutation without a circle – even the forbidden act of human transmutation. Ed and Al want it to regenerate the lost portions of their bodies, while others seek it for its enormously powerful potential. Unbeknownst to the brothers, the Stone is in fact a military creation based on living human tissue. And there's another organization – comprising test subjects from the experiments that resulted in the Philosopher's Stone – the homunculi of the Ouroboros, who want it just as badly, in order to fulfil their own shady aims.

As the story progresses and the corruption within the system slowly reveals itself, it seems that the only people in whom Ed and Al can safely place their trust are the mechanic Winry Rockbell and her grandmother, Pinako. Winry may pick on Edward every time he stops by to get his automail tuned up or sometimes replaced completely after a battle, but it's no secret that she enjoys his visits as an opportunity to apply the latest knowledge she's picked up on automail technology.

Aside from these two allies, everyone, it seems, has something to hide, some tragedy for which they are trying to atone. Society's ills are never far away either: prejudice, class wars, civil war and secret conspiracies abound, and usually involve the military too. These weighty themes are cleverly woven into the narrative, evidence if any were needed that a successful shōnen manga can be about more than the fights.

Fushigi Yugi: The Mysterious Play

Yuu Watase; *pub* Shogakukan (Jp), Viz (US, UK), Madman (Aus); *ser* Shōjo Comic (1992–96); *vols* 18; *age* 16+

Well-written books have the ability to whisk readers off to fantastic realms… in the virtual sense, anyway. No one expects to be literally sucked into an alternate world, which is exactly what happens to Miaka Yuuki and her friend, Yui Hongo. Both girls are cramming in order to get into Jonan High School, the top-rated school in their city, and while Yui has a good chance, Miaka is more likely to win a competitive eating contest (her seemingly endless appetite is a running joke throughout the series). Then, while they're studying in the local library, an earthquake hits, knocking them into a room with a door clearly marked "DO NOT ENTER" and jostling a book, *The Universe of the Four Gods*, to the floor. "Herein contains the tale of a young lady and her quest to gather the seven constellations of Suzaku together", the introduction reads. "And if you, the esteemed reader, should read to the story's end, the spell contained within this book shall bestow upon you the powers of the heroine, and grant you your wish. For indeed the moment the page is turned, the story will become reality." And so begins Watase's classic romance blended with action-packed adventure – and enough beautiful boys to satisfy the most demanding bishōnen appetite.

Upon turning the page, Miaka and Yui find themselves in a desolate wasteland in a seemingly ancient world. Miaka's first concern is that she'll never see her favourite fast-food restaurants ever again. Just as a group of slave traders arrives to capture them, a hot-looking guy swoops in and rescues them, then asks them for money. And just as suddenly, they're back in their own world, preparing for the high-school entrance exam. But the brief glimpse of her dashing rescuer has left Miaka wanting more. When an argument with her mother over her continued struggles at cram school comes to a head, she goes back to the library, pulls the book off the shelf and jumps back into its alternate world.

She eventually meets up with the handsome rescuer, a guy with the Chinese character for "demon" written on his forehead, Tamahome. And then the emperor's men promptly capture the duo. It turns out that Emperor Hotohori wants to make Miaka the priestess of Suzaku, in accordance with the ancient legend outlined in *The Universe of the Four Gods*. When an empire is on the verge of collapse, the legend goes, a young lady appears seeking the power of the god Suzaku, and when she possesses it, the empire will be led into a new era of glory.

Thus Miaka's true adventure begins, to seek out the seven constellations of Suzaku – seven Celestial Warriors who, once gathered together, will give her the power to have her ultimate wish granted: to get into any school she wants. Since this is a shōjo manga, those seven protectors also happen to be the prettiest boys in the universe; through it all, though, Tamahome remains the guy closest to her heart.

But she's not the only visitor from her home world. Back in the present-day world, Yui feels the pain any time Miaka gets hurt, and as Miaka falls for Tamahome, she begins to share those feelings. When Yui returns to the alternate world, though, she is met by Nakago, the leader of the Seiryu Celestial Warriors, a merciless, cold presence who manipulates people until they've exhausted their usefulness. Yui is soon tapped to be the priestess of Seiryu, a decision that immediately puts her at odds with Miaka… and slowly but surely, their once-solid friendship starts coming apart. How they deal with this conflict, and the way it's eventually resolved, is one of the central threads of the series. And with romantic fantasy and high adventure, as well as subplots crossing between the present world and the alternate world, it all makes for a compelling read.

The fantasy world of *Fushigi Yugi* has an ancient Chinese flavour, though Watase admitted it departed significantly from the historical facts. Still, the Chinese element was important enough for Watase to ask that Viz keep the original Chinese names intact in its translation rather than converting them to their Japanese equivalents.

Yuu Watase

Manga artist and writer, 1970–

Thanks to some heavy marketing by Viz, who picked up on the popularity of *Fushigi Yugi* and ran with it, Yuu Watase – a pen name, written with kanji characters taken from the names of some of her male characters – is one of the more recognizable names in the Western shōjo manga market today. Her popularity was such that she was invited to Anime Expo in Los Angeles in 1998 even before her work was formally published in the US, drawing a sizeable crowd.

Of course, the fact that she also draws what are considered some of the prettiest pretty boys in shōjo manga doesn't hurt, either. It's those boys, along with her penchant for weaving elements of Chinese, Japanese and Western mythology into her stories and an uncanny understanding of just what girls want in their romances, that have kept her readers coming back to her stories time and again.

Manga and drawing have been lifetime loves for Watase, who admitted in an interview published in the first *Fushigi Yugi* art book that she was a "very strange" child, foregoing the usual childhood games and finding friends in favour of coming up with new manga stories. She debuted in 1989 with the sixteen-page short story *Pajama de Ojama (An Intrusion in Pajamas)*, a cute love story based on a legend that if a girl likes a boy, she should take a picture of him, stick it under her pillow at night, and try to wear the same pyjamas he wears when she goes to bed, the result being that she'll get to spend seven minutes after midnight with him. In 1998 she was honoured with the Shogakukan Manga Award for shōjo manga for *Ceres: Celestial Legend*.

Absolute Boyfriend

pub Shogakukan (Jp), Viz (US, UK), Madman (Aus); *ser* Shōjo Comic (2003–05); *vols* 6; *age* 16+

Watase takes the classic love robot romantic comedy and reworks it from the girl's point of view. Riiko has never been lucky with love, so when a Kronos Heaven salesman gives her a card for a website that sells love androids, she takes advantage of the "customize your own boyfriend" feature and orders one. But she forgets to return Night after the three-day trial period, meaning she now owes Kronos Heaven a cool ¥100 million. The salesman allows her to keep Night on the condition that she helps them collect data on how women think, in an effort to perfect future models. Riiko has to deal now with her growing love for Night and his for her.

Ceres: Celestial Legend

pub Shogakukan (Jp), Viz (US, UK); *ser* Shōjo Comic (1996–2000); *vols* 14; *age* 16+

It's easy to see why this series won an award: it checks all the shōjo boxes alongside a dose of Watase's trademark action. On her sixteenth birthday Aya Mikage discovers she's the reincarnation of Ceres, a celestial maiden (*tennyo*) of Japanese folklore, and the psychic powers bubbling within her are the most powerful ever registered in the family line. Unfortunately Aya's family, owners of a global corporation, would prefer to see their daughter dead rather than possessing such an awesome power. Now Aya, on the run from her family, must track down Ceres' celestial robe, opposed by her twin Aki, who's harbouring the manifestation of the ancestral father of the Mikage family.

Imadoki

pub Shogakukan (Jp), Viz (US, UK); *ser* Shōjo Comic (2000–01); *vols* 5; *age* 16+

Tampopo Yamazaki thinks she's fulfilled her lifelong dream by getting into Meio, a prestigious high school in Tokyo. She's brought back to reality, though, when she realizes that she's a nobody there, shut out from the complex network of family connections and wealth that defines the school's social order. Yet Tampopo isn't one to give up easily; she starts a gardening club, and slowly begins attracting the attention of people like Koki Kugyo, a boy who initially shunned her but shares her love for gardening. The question is whether class differences can be set aside for what's turning out to be a budding romance.

Galaxy Express 999

Leiji Matsumoto; *pub* Shogakukan (Jp), Viz (US, UK); *ser* Monthly Big Gold (1996–2000); *vols* 5

Artist Leiji Matsumoto is known as the father of the Leijiverse, a sprawling outer-space setting that encompasses many of his science-fiction works in anime and manga, including *Galaxy Express 999* (pronounced "three-nine"), a train that travels through space. In 1981, *Galaxy Express 999* was one of the first feature-length anime to be translated and released in the US, introducing a fledgling fanbase to Tetsuro Hoshino, a boy who longed for a mechanical body so he could enact revenge on his mother's killer, and Maetel, the enigmatic time-and-space traveller who brings him on-board the *999*.

But while the movie was translated, the 1977–81 manga on which it was based was not; a market for translated manga simply didn't exist at the time. It would take seventeen years before Western audiences got to read *Galaxy Express 999*, and even then it wasn't the original series but a sequel, written by Matsumoto in 1996–2000. While it takes some prior knowledge of what happened in the movie to fully understand what's going on, the manga is well worth reading, especially as it's the sole fully translated example of Matsumoto's manga work set in the Leijiverse.

The concept of a space-travelling train originated in Matsumoto's childhood, when he lived near the railroad tracks. Hearing the rails ringing, he would imagine the train passing by and flying into space. "The story takes place in a time when there's no need to go through qualifications or paperwork to journey through space", Matsumoto said in a 1996 interview with *Animerica* magazine. "You just need to buy a train ticket. And the train takes you to space. That's what I longed for, so that's what I made."

In this new *Galaxy Express 999* story, Maetel returns to Earth a little over a year after Tetsuro and finds a planet that has been stripped of its natural beauty and overrun by artificial constructs. With only a 24-hour stopover scheduled, she follows what she describes as "destiny" and rescues Tetsuro, who has been languishing in solitary confinement thanks to his opposition to Earth's global artificialization policy. After a brief scuffle that sees Tetsuro freed, then captured again, then freed once the *999* barges straight through his holding room and literally picks him up, the two head off on another journey through the Sea of Stars.

Matsumoto weaves commentary and satire on modern-day life into the various planets visited by Maetel and Tetsuro. People who rule with selfish interests in mind govern one planet; another is governed by absolute law regardless of whether circumstances change to make those laws moot. Yet there are some stops that recall positive aspects of Earth as well. A resort planet is home to a single, rarely used hot springs inn, a place that Japanese readers would associate with rest, relaxation and a cleansing of the soul. On the bittersweet Planet of Serene Dreams, the spirits of unborn children play.

But all of these planets are mere pitstops en route to the duo's ultimate destination: a place called Eternity, described by Maetel as the "ultimate existence that supports the centre of the universe". Eternity is governed by Ankoku no Shihaisha, the Ruler of Darkness, whose aim is to destroy all living creatures. Tetsuro is optimistic that Earth will be restored to its past beauty, even when Ankoku no Shihaisha

forces the sun to go supernova, obliterating the entire solar system. Still, there's something within Tetsuro that fascinates Ankoku no Shihaisha, the same youthful determination to keep the memory of Earth alive that soothes Maetel and prompts Captain Harlock, whenever their paths cross, to offer encouragement.

However, Maetel and Tetsuro never do reach Eternity… at least, in the pages of this manga. The final frame is a tight shot of Maetel's eyes, where she tells Tetsuro: "Three-Nine will take you to the great being who controls light and time… Darqueen's eternal opposite! From there, your new journey will begin, taking you beyond light, beyond time… to the very reason you were born!" Perhaps Matsumoto never meant for the epic to end, leaving the reader to decide whether Tetsuro makes it to Eternity or not. And perhaps some manga are never meant to have neatly wrapped up endings, left forever to drift among the stars.

Leiji Matsumoto

Manga artist and anime director, 1938–

While still a teenager, the artist formerly known as Akira Matsumoto won the "best new artist" contest in *Manga Shōnen* in 1953 for his story "Mitsubachi no Bouken" ("Adventures of a Honeybee"). He had decided to skip college in favour of a full-time career as an artist, and worked on a number of shōjo series between 1953 and 1971. It wasn't fulfilling work, though, and these days it's hard to name any of Matsumoto's early shōjo titles.

During these formative years in the industry, he met and married fellow shōjo manga artist Miyako Maki, who would go on to create the Japanese equivalent of the Barbie doll, Licca-chan. But it wouldn't be until 1971 that he would get his second big break with the series *Otoko Oidon* (*I Am a Man*), a slice-of-life story about a student fresh out of high school struggling to get into college. Matsumoto won the Kodansha Culture Award in the children's manga category for that series in 1972.

Matsumoto was already dreaming of bigger worlds, however, and of ways to bring them to life beyond the printed page. For like his contemporaries Osamu Tezuka and Shōtarō Ishinomori, Matsumoto was fascinated by the animation work of Walt Disney and Max Fleischer and longed to become involved himself, joining the production staff of what would become one of the cornerstone anime series of the 1970s and the source for the *Star Blazers* cartoon series in the US: *Uchuu Senkan Yamato* (*Space Battleship Yamato*). The series' success would spark a number of legal battles over its ownership. Matsumoto handled the art design in his own unique style, tossing out many of the original ideas that producer Yoshinobu Nishizaki had proposed. As a result, both men have laid claim to the *Yamato* copyright over the years, and it wasn't until 2003 that the matter was finally settled: Matsumoto got the conceptual art and character and ship design, and Nishizaki got the "Yamato" name and the plot. His artistic style is unmistakeable, featuring pensive, willowy women, masculine heroes and elaborately rendered machinery, whether it's a spaceship or a World War II biplane.

Matsumoto's Leijiverse is filled with recurring characters, including the beloved Captain Harlock. In an interview in 2005, he described the characters as being like his children. "The good characters represent my own belief in what is good," he said. "For example, Captain Harlock. He lives freely under my flag; I am the kind of person who would sacrifice my life to protect my family and friends. For the bad characters, I make them as evil as possible, infuse them with traits that I find loathsome. I don't want to populate my stories with half-baked villains."

Matsumoto has also expanded his influence beyond traditional anime and manga. He is the chairman of the Copyright Board of the Japan Cartoonists Association and the Association of Copyright for Computer Software and has pushed for mechanisms that prevent illegal copying of copyrighted works and campaigns to educate the public. In 2003, Matsumoto collaborated with the French musical group Daft Punk on *Interstella 5555: The 5tory of the 5ecret 5tar 5ystem*, a series of anime music videos that were eventually compiled and released as a feature on DVD. Since then he has also moved into the realm of online comics; his latest project, *Out of Galaxy: Gin no Koshika*, debuted in Japan via Nintendo's WiiWare download service. While English subtitles are available, Nintendo has not announced whether it will make this online manga available to English-language territories as well.

Uchuu Senkan Yamato (Space Battleship Yamato)

pub Akita Shoten (Jp); *ser* Adventure King (1974–75, 1978–79); *vols* 3

Matsumoto worked on the manga at the same time that the anime was in production and the basic framework remains the same: the vessel has one year to pick up a device on the distant planet of Iscandar that can neutralize the radiation poisoning Earth's atmosphere before everyone on Earth dies. Matsumoto ended up getting more of a chance to flesh out the story in his manga after Yamato's TV run was cut to 26 episodes from the planned 39, even though production on the anime outpaced that of the manga.

Senjō (Battlefield)

pub Shogakukan (Jp); *ser* Big Comic (1973–78); *vols* 8

Less well known than his sci-fi stories is Matsumoto's collection of short stories set in World War II. The only one to be formally translated

into English, "Ghost Warrior" (in Frederik Schodt's *Manga! Manga!*) follows two displaced Japanese soldiers on a remote Pacific island Schodt noted that Matsumoto's war stories "are neither pro-war nor anti-war, but a romantic/existentialist view of the human struggle to survive – of the bonds between men and between men and machines in extraordinary situations."

Uchuu Kaizoku Captain Harlock (Space Pirate Captain Harlock)

pub Akita Shoten (Jp); *ser* Play Comic (1977–79); *vols* 5

Captain Harlock is one of Matsumoto's most iconic characters and the one who has appeared in his manga the longest, debuting in "Mitsubachi no Bouken" – which was quite a way from the sci-fi icon he would become. The way Matsumoto depicts Harlock shifts from series to series; here, he and his crew on the *Arcadia* defend a complacent Earth from a race of alien women, the Mazone, who themselves are refugees from a dying planet.

Genshiken

Kio Shimoda; *pub* Kodansha (Jp), Del Rey (US, UK); *ser* Afternoon (2002–05); *vols* 9; *age* 16+

There is a wide range of anime and manga fans out there, from the hardest of the hardcore to those who are just along for the ride because their significant others are into it. Kio Shimoda manages to capture a good cross-section of fandom in *Genshiken*, crafting a marvellous tribute to fans in the process.

The Genshiken of the title, the Society for the Study of Modern Visual Culture, is a group on the very fringes of the Suioh University club caste system. Their official listing consists of a room number, a picture of an anime character and the phrase "Here we are". Yet none of the members really cares about outsider perceptions; as long as they have a videogame loaded up, some art materials, their manga library and the latest installment of their favourite anime and manga series, "Kujibiki Unbalance", to discuss, they're happy.

Stepping into this weird, wonderful world for the first time is freshman Kanji Sasahara, a guy who wants to look at erotic dōjinshi but doesn't know how to go about it. He could join the regular anime and manga clubs, but having a thing for anime characters performing sexual acts isn't exactly the easiest thing to confess to a group of strangers. Yet the Genshiken gang – group leader and dangerously obsessive otaku Harunobu Madarame, costume-making and model-building expert Souichiro Tanaka, skilled videogaming fanatic and fellow freshman Makoto Kousaka and resident artist Mitsunori Kugayama – are more than happy to accommodate his interests. As an initiation prank, they leave him alone in the club room, spy on him as he browses through the bookcases and cabinets and burst in to congratulate him when he finds the group's dōjinshi stash.

Sasahara slowly grows into a full-fledged member from that point forward, and the rest of the group evolves right along with him. Transfer student Kanako Ohno becomes the first female to willingly join the group and instantly becomes a love interest for Tanaka with her fascination with cosplay. Kugayama struggles with his insecurities in producing his own dōjinshi. Many shopping trips are taken to Tokyo's Akihabara, otaku capital of the world, and various anime and manga conventions. In later volumes, closet hardcore yaoi fangirl Chika Ogiue and the brash, tolerance-stretching Manabu Kuchiki also join the group, adding more chaos to the dynamic.

The only person wholeheartedly resistant to the otaku lifestyle is Kousaka's girlfriend, Saki Kasukabe, who longs for an entire day that she can spend with him without geek culture getting in the way. The group gradually erodes her defences, though – particularly Ohno, who gets her to (reluctantly) cosplay with her. And when she indirectly causes a fire that ultimately threatens the group's existence, her guilt over the resulting fallout makes you feel genuinely sorry for her.

The strength of Shimoda's storytelling lies in the fact that he doesn't over-romanticize or condemn the otaku lifestyle. Instead, he shows vignettes that could happen with any gathering of otaku in real life – their conflicts, their romances, their willingness to wait in long lines for hours on end just for the chance to get that limited-edition collectible of their dreams.

A tribute to otaku: the front cover of the original Japanese first volume of *Genshiken*.

Ghost in the Shell

Masamune Shirow; *pub* Kodansha (Jp), Dark Horse (US), Titan Books (UK); *ser* Young Magazine (1989–91); *vols* 1; *age* 18+

host in the Shell was to the mid-1990s what *Akira* was to the early part of the decade: a manga series that came to prominence with the success of its feature-length anime adaptation. Audiences were drawn in by its cyberpunk setting, its early blending of traditional 2D animation with 3D computer animation, and a plot in which cyborg Motoko Kusanagi and Public Security Section Nine battled a hacker known only as the Puppetmaster in a virtual world. The film's style and concept of virtual reality would be a major inspiration for Larry and Andy Wachowski in making *The Matrix*.

But the Puppetmaster conflict was only one part of Shirow's original manga, and a part that was expanded upon and given a slower pace by anime director Mamoru Oshii at that. The locale is also changed: the manga is set in a high-tech metropolis in Japan in 2029, while the anime takes place in a futuristic Hong Kong-like city. Anime aside, the *Ghost in the Shell* manga works on its own terms as a gritty, fast-paced crime-scene investigative drama, with hot babes and some philosophy thrown in for good measure.

Central to the manga is the notion that, in 2029 Japan, the line between humans and technology is blurred. People can connect their brains directly to computer networks, roaming through the virtual realm as "ghosts", while cyborgs are implanted with organic human material and treated as if they're humans. The main character, Motoko, is such a construct, the archetypal version of Shirow's long line of strong-willed, sexy female characters, which appear in *Black Magic* (1983), *Appleseed* (1985–89), *Dominion* (1986) and *Orion* (1991), amongst others. Motoko also has a ghost that she can manoeuvre through the virtual web of information and experiences… as an infamous sequence in which she has three-way sex with two other female cyborgs demonstrates. The sequence showcases Shirow's renowned talent in erotic art – and has attracted plenty of readers over the years.

Wreaking havoc in Motoko's world are cyberterrorists known as "ghost hackers", who can directly access people's minds, overwriting their victim's memories and thoughts and controlling them like puppets. Worse still, it's impossible to know when your own mind is being hacked; only an outside observer can detect the signs.

This is where Section Nine comes in, a group of security observers on the periphery of the Japanese government, led by Aramaki, a gruff elderly man who will do whatever it takes to protect his team. Batou, Motoko's right-hand man, is a light-hearted cyborg and the team's main muscle, and several other members, including the mostly human Ishikawa and Togusa, provide tactical support. But even the specialists of Section Nine have their hands full dealing with the ghost hacker known as the Puppeteer. Their struggles with him continue through the entire series, and even at the end you're not quite sure whether things have been resolved.

That's partly because the action sequences and political intrigue give way to exploring the basic philosophies behind what makes humans human. When the Puppeteer finally infiltrates Motoko's mind towards the second half of the series, her teammates see her start to behave erratically and they try to piece together what is going on. Meanwhile, Motoko and the Puppeteer are engaged in deep conversations about what the Puppeteer represents, and how he feels about becoming a sentient being within the network. He speaks at one point of fragmented information about Motoko existing in her colleagues, genes and memes growing in a genus-1 Toroid, macrocosmic ascension and indeterminate declension. Umm… right. Helpfully,

detailed footnotes are interspersed between frames, with Shirow obsessively explaining the technologies and scientific, cultural and social backgrounds behind his creation. Dark Horse's second translated edition also contains fourteen pages worth of additional author's notes.

The story does have its lighter moments, often provided by the spider-like Fuchikoma helper robots that Section Nine relies on for combat and surveillance backup. The Fuchikoma are rather childlike in their behaviour, for instance throwing a tantrum and demanding a higher grade of oil before they'll carry out a task. One short, four-page chapter is devoted to the robots' plans for a revolution, stalled when Batou promises his Fuchikoma unit some oil "with a new fragrance", and when Motoko manipulates another unit into agreeing to stick with the status quo.

After *Ghost in the Shell*, Shirow would go on to write two sequels, the eleven-chapter *Ghost in the Shell 2: Man-Machine Interface* (serialized in *Young Magazine* in 1997) and *Ghost in the Shell 1.5: Human Error Processor*, four chapters from *Ghost in the Shell 2* that were originally intentionally left out of the tankōbon version by Shirow himself. While both have their share of fans, a good portion of those two works loses the precarious balance between action and philosophizing that the first series maintains, sinking under the weight of what amounts to extended bouts of psychobabble.

Golgo 13

Takao Saito; *pub* Shogakukan (Jp), Viz (US); *ser* Big Comic (1969–); *vols* ongoing; *age* 18+

The adventures of the trained assassin Duke Togo, better known as Golgo 13, number more than four hundred stories, filling thousands of printed pages in Japan. Exposure in Western markets may be more limited, but you don't really need to read it all to get a sense of what this assassin can accomplish. The stories are all self-contained, each with its own complex network of relationships and real-world intrigue, ready to be broken wide open.

In the world of *Golgo 13*, being a target of the famed assassin means you're marked for certain death. His skill is such that sometimes he barely needs to appear in the manga that bears his name; all he has to do is show up in a few frames, pull a trigger and bang – his target has joined the choir invisible.

But when the assassin has been plying his craft for the better part of four decades, making *Golgo 13* one of the oldest manga still in publication in Japan today, all those brief appearances add up to a rather impressive dossier. If there's a conflict or conspiracy in the world sometime in modern history, chances are that the assassin played a

role in it. The 1989 student uprising in Tiananmen Square in China? He was hired to take out a Tibetan activist. The 2000 US presidential election, with the controversy over the vote count? He shot the ballots involved in the Florida recount, causing Al Gore to lose and solidifying George W. Bush's victory. He also helped President Bill Clinton stop Saddam Hussein's would-be weapon of mass destruction, aided South African president Nelson Mandela in halting a terrorist plot, and went up into space at the request of President Gerald Ford to prevent a disabled secret US government spacecraft from interfering with a scheduled rendezvous between the *Apollo* and *Soyuz* spacecraft.

Golgo 13 is in a sense a contemporary version of the rōnin, or masterless, samurai stories of years past. The emotionally detached assassin wanders the land without allegiance to any particular group, cause or nation, taking on jobs when he feels they match his personal code of ethics. In Golgo's case, he makes contact with his employers just once and refuses to shake hands in case it reveals which hand he uses to shoot – rather than a sword, Golgo 13 wields a trusty

M16 rifle, with which he's missed a target only once throughout his career. And this contemporary rōnin also provides women with new heights of pleasure thanks to his skills in the bedroom. He isn't a James Bond playboy type, though – many of his sexual encounters are with prostitutes, and he never exhibits the same signs of pleasure as his partners. Several theories exist as to why he has sex before his missions, including as a means to distract himself from approaching danger; a way of spreading his genes whenever he feels a threat to his own life; or simply in order to fulfil an ambition to have sex with as many women as possible.

The art is thoroughly consistent, thanks to the studio system created by Saito, and has evolved little from its origins in the 1970s, making it look rather dated to more recent manga readers. Viz's definitive thirteen-volume series (published 2006–08) takes advantage of the manga's longevity, each volume pairing a story of contemporary appeal with a "classic" adventure set in the 1970s. The series also benefits from exhaustive notes collectively entitled "File 13: Secrets of the World's Deadliest Assassin", which get readers up to speed on the assassin's career, everything from the torture methods that Golgo 13 has endured to an entire essay on his sexual technique, the last an indication of utter devotion to the source material.

GTO: Great Teacher Onizuka

Tohru Fujisawa; *pub* Kodansha (Jp), Tokyopop (US, UK), Madman (Aus); *ser* Weekly Shōnen (1997–2002); *vols* 25; *age* 16+

A class full of delinquents that has already chased away several teachers is bad enough. But putting in charge of this class a former delinquent who got into teaching because he wanted to bag cute high school girls? A recipe for disaster – and for a lengthy drama series that sees everyone changed for the better by the end. While the concept may be a cliché, Tohru Fujisawa freshens it up with a tough yet sympathetic lead character and a sense of perverted humour that appeals to *GTO*'s older teenage audience.

Fujisawa revisited one of his earlier manga series, *Shonan Junai Gumi*, to find his lead character, Eikichi Onizuka, a guy whose background as a teenage hooligan gives him an aura of toughness and machismo. At the beginning of the series, Onizuka is far from being the "great teacher" promised in the title – his rough-and-tumble appearance and attitude aren't exactly key selling points to would-be employers. His

days are spent lying underneath staircases lamenting his lot in life, smoking cigarettes and peeking up girls' skirts, his nights at home with porn mags in a bachelor-pad hovel.

Far from being the tough womanizer, though, he's a rather sympathetic 22-year-old who hopes to make a decent living and find some purpose in life.

The Onizuka of volume 1 has some way to go before he can claim to be the Great Teacher.

Courtesy of Kodansha Ltd

That purpose, as he figures out when he tries to romance a cute high school girl, only to see her run back into the arms of her ex, a rather homely looking schoolteacher, is to become a teacher himself. Because if that guy could land a girl like her, then imagine what kinds of girls a smooth guy like him could score.

The path Eikichi takes to become that great teacher is fraught with potential pitfalls. It doesn't help that he's assigned to teach the worst students – from his original training class to eventual permanent employment at Holy Forest Private Academy. But his bold naïveté and determination to overcome any obstacle turn out to be exactly the qualities needed to get through these tough times. Call it a mixture of street smarts and sensitivity, in the end he cares too much about the girls to take advantage of them, although he manages to do some utterly stupid things along the way.

One incident has a girl in his class gaining Eikichi's sympathy by telling him her parents don't pay any attention to her. She gets herself invited round to his place and promptly strips down to her underwear, while another student shows up to take the compromising photo.

Eikichi responds in typical fashion, rallying some of the guys in his old gang to scare the living daylights out of the boys responsible for the trick. When the teacher arrives at school the next day, he finds the boys have become model citizens, sweeping up the messes all around the school. As for the girl, after learning more about her story, he heads over to her house with a lead pipe and intimidates her parents into paying more attention to their daughter.

He may appear to be rather thuggish and brutal on the outside, with a tendency to act before thinking, and his methods may be a bit unorthodox. But that's the appeal of the *Great Teacher Onizuka* series: Eikichi is the type of character that audiences can root for, who makes a fool of himself but ultimately comes out on top through sheer determination and a good heart, finding a solution that provides everyone, including the reader, with a happy ending.

Iron Wok Jan

Shinji Saijyo; *pub* Akita Shoten (Jp), DrMaster (US); *ser* Shōnen Champion (1995–2000); *vols* 27; *age* 13+

Iron Wok Jan and its tale of cut-throat cuisine is one of those manga that boggles the minds of comics readers raised on a diet of Marvel and DC superheroes. But while the subject of cooking may seem alien to Western readers, it's not uncommon in Japan, and manga such as *Kitchen Princess*, *Oishinbo* (magazine staff searches for the elements that comprise the Ultimate Menu), *Mixed Vegetables* and *Addicted to Curry* have begun to draw the attention of Western readers

In the world of shōnen manga, heroes like Goku in *Dragon Ball*, Ed and Al in *Fullmetal Alchemist* or Luffy in *One Piece* (see pp.116, 123 and 166) are beloved because they beat overwhelming odds to get to the top, leaving their humbled, defeated opponents with a new sense of awe and respect for them. Jan Akiyama is not one of those heroes. There's no denying he has talent as a sixteen-year-old trainee chef at Gobancho, a highly regarded Chinese restaurant in the heart of Ginza. His pedigree, as grandson of the legendary "Master of Chinese Cuisine" Kaiichiro Akiyama, is unparalleled. But he not only knows that he's the most talented person in a room, he also takes every chance to lord that

superiority over anyone else; he hates it when people dare to question him and his caricatured facial expressions range from a sinister smirk to a determined scowl.

All of which should have readers hating him, but there's a reason they end up sympathizing with him anyway: Kaiichiro spent long hours beating the skills of making fine Chinese cuisine into Jan from a young age. When Kaiichiro got too old to taste what Jan made for him one day, he sent him away with an excuse that he needed more medication, then set his house on fire and committed suicide. It was Kaiichiro's final hope that by sending Jan to work for his bitterest rival, Mutsuju Gobancho, he could carry on their rivalry even after death.

But sending Jan to the restaurant serves to raise up a number of rivals, all determined to defeat him, some of whom have more noble intentions than others. On the "good" side of this equation is Kiriko Gobancho, Mutsuju's granddaughter and a talented up-and-coming Chinese cook in her own right. While Jan's philosophy is that cooking is all about being the best, Kiriko, in contrast, believes that cooking is about devotion and dedication to the craft, and to the customer who will eat the food. She can pick up any cooking technique simply by observing it and then transform it into something even better. Other rivals, like the corrupt food critic Nichido Otani, hate Jan because he exposes some fundamental character flaw in themselves. In Nichido's case, his reputation as Japan's premier food critic is threatened when Jan dares to question the effectiveness of his legendary tastebuds.

Kiriko and Jan find themselves constantly battling with each other for the upper hand at Gobancho. But the two also are called upon to hone their skills in the not-so-friendly confines of tournament competition, where they meet other would-be chefs with their own philosophies on what cooking should be about, from style and substance to tradition to high-innovation technologies.

And God forbid one should get Jan angry during these times. When Jan loses one particular battle because his noodle dish didn't show enough originality, he first goes in back and beats himself up physically and emotionally over the loss, then re-emerges to prepare a unique dessert. Using blood drained from live pigeons – slaughtered right in front of the audience to guarantee freshness – he makes "blood eggs", little eggs with different flavours that manage to enrapture both judges and audience members alike. Not all the dishes are quite so exotic, but virtual feasts can give way to concoctions that make one wonder whether they actually qualify as food. Those who think Chinese cuisine equals chow mein noodles in a cardboard box are in for a shock, with such delights as *gu xue ge ju bu xun* (baked pudding with frog fallopian tubes and papaya) and a custard soup with eggs, chicken broth, fresh milk, vegetable soup and sheep brains on the menu. With recipes like that up for grabs, *Iron Wok Jan* has a different flavour than shōnen manga like *Naruto* or *Dragon Ball*. But despite its less fantastic premise, it's in many ways just as exotic to a Western reader.

JoJo's Bizarre Adventure

Hirohiko Araki; *pub* Shueisha (Jp), Viz (US, UK); *ser* Weekly Shōnen Jump (1987–2004), Ultra Jump (2005–); *vols* ongoing; *age* 16+

When *JoJo's Bizarre Adventure* was first released in Japan in 1987, the series gained a modest audience with story arcs that followed the Joestar family's battles against the immortal vampire Dio. After two years, twelve volumes of manga and two generations' worth of Joestar stories, though, Hirohiko Araki shook up his series by introducing a new element to his third-generation Joestar story: "Stands", telekinetic alter egos of the main characters who battled alongside them and possessed psychic superpowers.

The "Stardust Crusaders" arc, which lasted for close to four years and 151 chapters over fifteen volumes, became the most popular in the series by far and has remained so even as the series has progressed through four subsequent story arcs – the last of which continues to be serialized in Japan today. The audience gained since then has helped make *JoJo* the second longest series currently being serialized in *Weekly Shōnen Jump* (behind *Kochira Katsushika-ku Kameari Kōen-mae Hashutsujo*). The only thing that has stopped *JoJo* sales cold was a controversy that emerged with the anime adaptation in 2008, when it was discovered that a page from the Koran had been inserted into several frames in one of the episodes. In response, publisher Shueisha halted shipments of the manga to ensure that no offensive scenes had been inadvertently inserted there either.

In its English translation, *JoJo*'s success has been more limited. Over the years numerous manga series have entered the Western consciousness through their anime adaptations, but *JoJo's Bizarre Adventure* was first experienced as a fighting arcade game (and subsequent console versions), released by Capcom amid a flood of such games in the wake of *Street Fighter II*'s massive success.

The game was based on the "Stardust Crusaders" arc, so when Viz began publishing *JoJo*, the translation started with a quick summary of the first twelve volumes before launching into the more familiar story. In it, a salvage crew searching for treasure dredges up the casket in which Dio and Jonathan Joestar were sealed earlier in the series and inadvertently unleashes Dio's terror on the rest of the world once more. Dio's resurrection triggers the emergence of the Tarot-inspired Stands, a mystical force that Jotaro Kujo, grandson to second-story-arc-hero Joseph, struggles to understand while he keeps himself locked away in a police cellblock. An emerging Stand also manages to cripple Jotaro's mother, though, and it soon becomes apparent that Jotaro, Joseph and a band of allies they recruit along the way will have to travel to Egypt and defeat Dio... yet again. It should be a simple matter of hopping on a plane, but Dio, with his powers of mind control, summons a whole posse of Stand users to impede their progress by any means necessary. So what ought to be a straight shot from one point to another turns into a transcontinental tour of destruction.

Whether by plane, boat, car, submarine or helicopter, it seems as if team JoJo can't catch a break, not being able to go for more than a few hundred miles before they encounter their next challenge, conveniently located in the most scenic locales that Asia has to offer. Araki even provides opening hours and other tidbits of information about each

site, informed by his own travels. All the while, the Stand users' powers grow more and more exotic. Some Stands shrink themselves down and duke it out in Joseph's brain. At various points the team find themselves under attack from zombies, babies and even dogs, all possessed by Stands.

Through all of this ever-spiralling weirdness, Araki has a gift for making his fight sequences more than just glorified, brutal slugfests; there are elements of strategy and battles of logic involved as well. What emerges are fights with an epic feel that grows throughout the series, so that you can't help investing in the characters' struggle to find an advantage that can swing the fight's outcome while protecting their weak points.

Almost as weird as the enemies are the artist's naming conventions: virtually all of the important characters' names are references to rock bands, musicians or albums. Viz's translation keeps most of the references intact. This campy sensibility, along with the increasingly over-the-top battles, form a combination too delicious to resist for Western readers who have fallen in love with the series.

Knights of the Zodiac / Saint Seiya

Masami Kurumada; *pub* Shueisha (Jp), Viz (US); *ser* Weekly Shōnen Jump (1986–90); *vols* 28; *age* 13+

Knights of the Zodiac was one of the classic series that drove *Weekly Shōnen Jump*'s popularity in the mid- to late 1980s. Like *Dragon Ball* and *Fist of the North Star* before it and *JoJo's Bizarre Adventure* afterward, *Knights* features characters using punches, kicks and myriad special fighting techniques in order to gain the upper hand on their opponents. In this case, Masami Kurumada mixed elements of Greek mythology with the team-fighting concept established in *Cyborg 009* and the escalating battle structure of *Dragon Ball* to create a series that follows its own distinct shōnen path.

Boys were naturally drawn in by the over-the-top violent action sequences and elaborate battle armour that the characters wore: in fact, *Bleach* author Tite Kubo cited the series as influential in plotting his own battle sequences and characters' weaponry. Meanwhile, Kurumada's slightly effeminate-looking male characters helped attract a female readership, too. Most notable among these female fans was CLAMP, whose dōjinshi manga featuring the *Knights* characters helped launch their careers.

The *Knights'* story reaches the heights of melodrama, starting at the personal level with a one-on-one battle, and gradually building into a world-spanning epic. The central character, Bronze Knight Seiya, leads his friends and orphanage brothers Andromeda Shun, Swan (Cygnus) Hyoga, Dragon Shiryu and, on occasion, Phoenix Ikki (named after constellations, hence the manga's title) into countless battles over the course of the series. Typically, the heroes will make grandiose claims, the villains make even more grandiose claims, one side throws a damaging blow that leaves their opponents close to death, and then the struggling side summons a source of inner strength to throw an even more damaging blow that leaves their opponents even closer to death.

The knights first fight one another as part of a tournament organized by Princess Sienna, to prove themselves worthy of assuming the elaborate armoured suits that are the sacred cloths of Athena. The tournament and its related fallout lasts for twenty-four chapters – approximately five and a half volumes, or a fifth of the series – before the focus shifts, when Sienna stands revealed as the modern incarnation of the goddess Athena herself.

While the first story arc is devoted to the protection of Athena and the ultimately successful defence of Sanctuary against its false leader, subsequent story arcs expand into grander territory, to the point where the Knights are taking on the other gods within and outside of the Greek pantheon who challenge Athena. After that, it's on to Hades and the climactic story arc, where the surviving Knights go up against the powerful undead forces of all of the opponents who were killed throughout the series.

The battles start at ridiculously powerful levels and get even crazier as the characters progress. Überpowerful fighters who can crush each other into

the ground is after all part of what made *Dragon Ball* so much fun. Here, though, death is slightly more meaningful, used to nudge certain characters out of the spotlight for a little while and as a rallying point for the surviving characters to regroup. Everyone dies at least once. Seiya kills one of his opponents in the opening tournament with a powerful punch, then uses the same punch to jump-start his heart and bring him back to life. Dragon Shiryu goes blind twice (once by putting out his own eyes) and dies several times. Phoenix Ikki resurrects himself so many times that the other characters eventually stop making a big deal about it and carry on regardless. Trying to inject any logical sense into what's going on is futile. Better just to sit back and enjoy the ride.

Lone Wolf and Cub

Kazuo Koike (text), Goseki Kojima (art); *pub* Futabasha (Jp), Dark Horse (US, UK); *ser* Weekly Manga Action (1970–76); *vols* 28; *age* 18+

Osamu Tezuka and his peers may have established the cinematic method of storytelling in manga, but their character artwork, regardless of the subject matter, retained a certain Disney-esque cartoon quality. *Lone Wolf and Cub*, Kazuo Koike and Goseki Kojima's epic tale of

a wandering rōnin who travels the land, pushing his son around in a small cart, helped manga evolve into a medium for adult audiences, with its deliberate pacing and frames of art that appear to be inspired by live-action films rather than cartoons. In Japan, between eight and nine thousand pages make up the entire story, and more than eight million copies were sold when it was first released in the 1970s.

It was one of the earliest manga to influence Western artists, with comics writer Warren Ellis suggesting that Koike and Kojima were innovators in graphic novel violence, and Frank Miller crediting its influence on *Ronin*. In fact, it's one of the oldest English-translated series in print today, produced by First Comics from 1987 with covers by American comics artists Bill Sienkiewicz and Matt Wagner, as well as Frank Miller, who also wrote an introduction. It ran for 45 issues before the company went bankrupt and was subsequently picked up by Dark Horse.

Itto offers his son Daigoro a stark choice: the road of the assassin or the path to heaven.

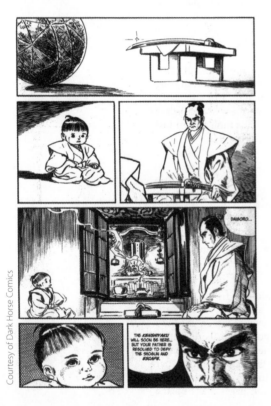

The "lone wolf" of the series is Itto Ogami, a former shogun's executioner who has become a wandering assassin for hire to clear his name of a crime he did not commit and avenge the deaths of his family. While Itto's one-year-old son Daigoro survived the massacre, Itto doesn't automatically give him a free pass; instead, he offers him a choice between a sword and a ball, with his life hinging on the outcome. The symbolic meaning of the choice is clear: a child's carefree life or a future of unrelenting battle and hardship. Had Daigoro chosen the ball, Itto would have slain him immediately. Fortunately, he chooses the way of the sword and the two set off together on what Itto characterizes as the road to *meifumadou*, the Buddhist hell filled with demons and damnation.

The countless self-contained battles the duo undertake are all building towards an eventual clash with none other than Retsudou Yagyu, leader of the Yagyu clan and instigator of the Ogami clan massacre. One by one, Yagyu clan members get their shots at taking out Itto for good, but the ultimate showdown is destined to be between Itto and Retsudou. One of their earliest encounters, in fact, lasts for 178 panels, one of the longest fight scenes ever to be depicted in comics.

The juxtaposition between the grizzled Itto, who has seen more than his share of suffering, and the innocence of Daigoro is stark indeed. Itto's internal conflict is similar to that of the reluctant yet clinically precise assassin Yo Hinomura in Koike's later series *Crying Freeman* (see p.103) – as a samurai Itto knows that his life will always hang in the balance, yet as a father it is his duty to protect his son from that danger. Putting a son – especially one so young – at risk of losing his life is a tactic that many of Itto's opponents question. Kojima's artwork helps bring the conflict to the foreground using scenes of graphic violence interspersed with images of calm landscapes and close-ups of Daigoro either silently observing the bloody battles or off contemplating something else, physically detached from the action.

Ultimately this dynamic humanizes the series, giving it a layer of depth that takes it beyond what could easily have been a revenge bloodfest. Dialogue can be sparse at times, letting the actions on the page tell the story. But an unspoken bond exists here. As Itto says: "A father knows his child's heart, as only a child can know his father's. Father and child walk through life, hand in hand! This is *seikan*, the bond of life. When father and son rely on their bond to do what they must to survive."

Love Hina

Ken Akamatsu; *pub* Kodansha (Jp), Tokyopop (US, UK), Madman (Aus); *ser* Weekly Shōnen Magazine (1998–2001); *vols* 14; *age* 16+

Love Hina was one of the first breakout hits in Tokyopop's "100% Authentic" era in 2001, appealing to both sexes in its targeted older-teen demographic. In many ways a typical harem manga, the genre in which a single, socially awkward male character finds himself surrounded by a cast of cute females, it wasn't the first such story to gain a respectable audience in the West, following in the footsteps of *Oh My Goddess!* (see p.164), which began in 1994, and *No Need for Tenchi!*, the manga spin-off of the anime, starting in 1996. But where *Love Hina* differed, and what made it appeal to so many girls, was its grounding in everyday life, with only the occasional tangent into cartoonish fantasy. In place of *No Need for Tenchi!*'s beautiful alien princesses or the trio of deities in *Oh My Goddess!*, *Love Hina* features appealing characters who could be friends, neighbours and classmates in real life.

Keitaro Urashima is the hero, a student struggling to get into Tokyo University because of a childhood promise he made to a girl he liked. Hoping to get away and relax after his latest entrance exam failure, he goes to the rural hot springs owned by his grandmother. What he doesn't know is that his grandmother converted the inn into a girls' dormitory, so the last thing he expects to see are a bunch of girls clad only in towels and smiles walking in on his escape from reality. What's more, his grandmother has retired, and now the inn-turned-dorm is his to run if he wants it.

Time to parade out a variety of female stereotypes designed to fulfil a wide range of fanboy fetishes, from the outwardly feisty girl with a heart of gold to the shy girl who has trouble expressing her feelings. A typical harem manga story would see the six main girls stick to these roles and have every one of them eventually fall in love with Keitaro to boot. In *Love Hina*, the girls don't automatically fawn over him; he has to earn their respect. The girls grow and mature into more well-rounded people over time, sometimes with the help of Keitaro, sometimes through the lessons they learn on their own. Akamatsu chooses the relationships he wants to focus on, eventually settling on the love triangle that develops by the sixth volume among Keitaro, feisty Naru Narusegawa, and Mutsumi Otohime, a rather absent-minded, frail twenty-year-old whose intentions, like Keitaro's, are often innocently pure.

Keitaro, for his part, is a resilient individual, never giving up on his dream to go to Tokyo University nor his new roommates. Early encounters with Naru, the girl most opposed to his moving in, follow a pattern: Keitaro accidentally bumbles into a situation and catches someone in a compromising position, Naru sees this happening (or is the victim herself), cries out "PERVERT!" and smashes him to kingdom come. Yet somehow he presses on, undaunted, always trying to find the good in a certain situation and helping out wherever he can. This charm eventually wins everyone over to his side, including, predictably, Naru.

It's the equivalent of comfort food in manga form – audiences know what they're getting and they know what likely will come out of the entire exercise. Yet at the same time it offers a message of hope, that even the most hopeless among us can achieve our dreams.

Courtesy of Kodansha Ltd

Love Hina volume 1: which of the bevy of cute girls will find true love with Keitaro?

Love Roma

Minoru Toyoda; *pub* Kodansha (Jp), Del Rey (US); *ser* Afternoon (2002–05); *vols* 5; *age* 16+

When MangaBlog, Brigid Alverson's daily roundup of manga news and reviews, sought recommendations for a reader looking for "slice of life" manga, several people suggested *Love Roma*. And for good reason: Minoru Toyoda's first and only notable manga to date portrays through simple, blocky artwork the story of a humble high school romance, where two students meet, fall in love with each other with the encouragement of their circles of friends, and work out the kinks along the way to develop a solid relationship.

At the series' core is the spirit of *manzai*, a type of Japanese stand-up comedy where a funny man, or *boke*, says something ridiculous and a straight man, or *tsukkomi*, tries (often in vain) to correct him. Whenever Hajime Hoshino and the target of his affection, Yumiko Negishi, are out in public, whether at school or out on a date, their conversations often turn into a virtual comedy routine, with Yumiko often playing the tsukkomi to Hajime's boke pronouncements and the people around them acting like an audience, oohing, aaahing, laughing and clapping at whatever happens between the couple. This is all

to the great embarrassment of Yumiko, of course. But Hajime is someone who wears his emotions on his sleeve and is willing to go out on a limb for Yumiko because he really likes her.

The *manzai* dynamic gives this romantic comedy a different feel from shōjo/josei romances like *Peach Girl* (p.169) or *Paradise Kiss* (p.167), and other seinen romantic comedies like *Love Hina* (p.150) and *Maison Ikkoku* (p.156). Expressions of love aren't treated as momentous, dramatic events – instead, they're portrayed with a touching simplicity and an unflinching honesty that helps drive the story. The first frame of the manga features Hajime saying to Yumiko, "Negishi-san, I like you. Can we go on a date sometime?" There's just one problem: Yumiko has no clue about who the guy is, or why he'd be interested in asking her out on a date.

She eventually agrees to at least walk home with him – a move greeted with applause by the other people in the room, who heard the entire exchange. Even then, love between the two isn't instantaneous lightning-bolt stuff, but a gradual process that develops over the course of the five-volume series. As Yumiko tells him on their first date, while riding a Ferris wheel: "When I'm with you … I feel happy … I don't know why … Sometimes what I say is too honest … My friends say I always find fault in things … but you accept my personality … so I'm happy to hear that you like me … but … can you give me more time?" It's a wish that he's willing to grant her. And soon afterward, she's at his desk, asking him if he'd like to go out with her.

It's not always smooth sailing for the couple. They have fights and break up, and Yumiko is constantly struggling with her own insecurities and worries about whether she's making the right decision. Just as in real life, however, their relationship doesn't exist in a bubble but is influenced by the advice of friends, especially Toshio and Yoko. These two are the kind of friends who

Love Roma's appealingly unfussy artwork, seen on the cover of the first Japanese edition of Minoru Toyoda's relationship comedy.

will carefully plan out a double date and then conveniently get "lost" along the way, allowing Hajime and Yumiko the opportunity to draw closer together.

Their networks of friends and their perseverance through the tough times help the couple to form a closer, stronger bond, progressing far enough to the point where the question of sex becomes viable. Their discussions are just as frank as their confessions of love. Hajime says at several points in the series that like most boys his age he entertains thoughts of sex, while Yumiko feels she's not quite ready to take that step yet and worries that it makes her less of a girlfriend to be thinking that way.

Sweet, affecting and funny, *Love Roma* proves that romance manga doesn't have to feature supernatural beauties, robots or gender reversal. While all of those have their place, it's refreshing to see less melodramatic emotional heights depicted here, with art that's as unpretentious as the storyline.

Lupin III

Monkey Punch; *pub* Futabasha (Jp), Tokyopop (US, UK), Madman (Aus); *ser* Weekly Manga Action (1967–72 14 vols, 1977–81 17 vols); *age* 16+

The manga exploits of master thief Arsène Lupin III resonated with Japanese audiences across three decades and spawned three anime TV series plus numerous films and TV specials, including one film, *Castle of Cagliostro*, directed by famed anime director Hayao Miyazaki. Not bad for a title that was only supposed to be a three-month contract project.

Yet aside from Miyazaki's movie and a short run for the anime adaptation on Cartoon Network, *Lupin III* hasn't struck the same chord in the West. It's not for lack of trying: Tokyopop released *Lupin* in late 2002 in one of the initial waves of the "100% Authentic Manga" initiative. But after publication of the first fourteen volumes, sales of the second half of the series, released as *Lupin III: Most Wanted*, were low enough that Tokyopop cancelled it halfway through its planned seventeen-volume run.

Lupin III was an anomaly in Tokyopop's relaunch, a series geared more to adults in a line that was marketed largely towards teenagers – a factor that may have contributed to the series fizzling out. What's more, the characters involved in the series' core rivalry, Lupin and Inspector Koichi Zenigata, were inspired by fictional characters unfamiliar to today's younger readership: Lupin is the grandson of gentleman thief Arsène Lupin, star of a series of French novels by Maurice Leblanc written between 1907 and 1939, while Zenigata is the descendant of coin-tossing policeman Heiji Zenigata, featured in novels by Kodo Nomura from 1937 to 1959.

Monkey Punch's Lupin, however, is a product of the Swinging Sixties, not only a skilled thief but also someone who fancies himself as a ladies' man and prides himself on being able to get any woman into bed, though he's not quite as successful at the latter as he likes to think. Fujiko Mine, Lupin's love interest, knows that she can double-cross him as many times as she can help him because he'll stick with her either way. In fact, you're just as likely to see him flying at an unsuspecting woman, cartoon hearts fluttering all over the panel, and getting slapped for his efforts, as winning her over and getting right down to it, clothes flying everywhere.

Lupin's eternal foil, Inspector Zenigata, is a man whose success rate in catching criminals is far lower than that of his predecessor. His desire to capture and lock up the master thief is only rivalled by his grudging admiration for the way Lupin keeps wriggling out of his traps. While Zenigata is resolved to follow the rules, Lupin plays fast and loose with them, sometimes enlisting the help of his gang, crack marksman Daisuke Jigen and renegade swordsman Goemon Ishikawa XIII.

The series is loaded with rapid-fire gags and subtle visual sleights of hand that keep readers on their toes. Monkey Punch has cited as influences the comics published in *MAD Magazine* and Mort Drucker's parodies of Hollywood films, and his characters do have an angular, Western quality to them. Aside from obvious gender differences and a few minor facial details, they also look very similar to one another – a similarity used to great effect in stories like "Zenigata Gets Lucky", in which Lupin poses as Zenigata to steal a teleportation device. What fools the players in the story – and readers in turn – is that Lupin wearing a hat looks exactly like Zenigata. Artistic ambiguities like this are sometimes confusing and require several read-throughs to fully comprehend, but make the point of discovery and revelation so satisfying once it's reached.

In the end, it's the rivalry between Lupin and Zenigata that has driven the series all these years. If for some reason Zenigata should capture Lupin, the thief will find a way to escape, and the chase will begin anew. Monkey Punch told an interviewer with the Tokyo Foundation in 2005 that it's for that reason that he believes that the story of *Lupin III* can never end. "If I had to end it, they would be equal," he said. "Both would fall or both would win. Or maybe they'd both just get very old."

Maison Ikkoku

Rumiko Takahashi; *pub* Shogakukan (Jp), Viz (US, UK); *ser* Big Comic Spirits (1980–87); *vols* 15; *age* 16+

Maison Ikkoku is the most straightforward series Rumiko Takahashi has produced to date. No alien girls appear, like in *Urusei Yatsura*; there aren't any *Ranma ½*-style outlandish fighting displays; and it lacks the fantasy elements of *Inuyasha* or *Mermaid Saga*. At 162 chapters and a run of a little under seven years, *Maison Ikkoku* is also one of Takahashi's shorter series. What it does offer is a touching romantic comedy about two flawed young adults brought together by chance, and the meddling neighbours who get in the way of their budding romance.

Bereft of any gimmicks, a series' success or failure rests upon its characters and the situations in which they find themselves, and Takahashi builds a strong cast here. Her protagonist is Yusaku Godai, of whom she once said: "He's like the embodiment of a typical teen trying to make it in the world. Sure it's a comedy and a love story, so some of it is more exaggerated or deformed, but I think he is never a pathetic character, but more of a character you want to encourage or help." As the series opens, he's a prospective college student who has failed to get a high enough entrance exam score multiple times. Just as he decides he's had enough and is about to move out of the ramshackle Maison Ikkoku apartment complex to start over, though, an attractive woman moves in: the apartments' new manager, Kyoko Otonashi. And just like that, Yusaku's heart is set a-flutter and he's convinced that she is the destined love of his life ... forgetting the girl he's recently dated who loves him dearly and considers him her boyfriend, Kozue Nanao. Inexperienced in relationships, this is one of his inevitable mistakes. Since he's afraid of hurting the feelings of people he loves, his struggle with letting Kozue go to pursue Kyoko becomes a subplot that lasts five years in the story's timeline – close to the entire series.

But Kyoko is dealing with her own issues. She's already a widow at 21, having dated a teacher six years her senior while at high school and marrying him after graduation, only to see him die six months after the wedding. Her parents and her in-laws would love for her to move on with her life, but she can't quite bring herself to let go. Also, while she may seem sweet and loving on the outside and is willing to forgive her tenants' numerous faults, she also can get jealous quite easily and tends to hold grudges – traits that often come into play when Yusaku upsets her in some fashion. Yusaku is two years younger than her, his lack of maturity highlighted when a suave tennis instructor with a sparkling smile, Shun Mitaka, makes a play for Kyoko. The difference between Shun's behaviour and the bumbling efforts of Yusaku is stark, and the two men develop an intense rivalry over the course of the series.

Providing much of the comic relief are the apartments' neighbours – nosy housewife Hanae Ichinose, alcoholic bar hostess Akemi Roppongi and mysterious voyeur Mr Yotsuya – who tend to butt in every time there's an inkling of a possible spark between Yusaku and Kyoko

and can transform the most innocuous situations into full-blown arguments. They've adopted Yusaku's apartment as their unofficial party room even when he's trying to study for critical exams. And when they're not partying, Akemi's usually passed out in the hallway drunk, or Yotsuya's crawling into Yusaku's room through a giant hole in the wall to "borrow" stuff or just outright spy on him.

Once Yusaku's and Kyoko's eyes meet in the first volume, you feel sure that those two are right for each other. But getting to that point involves numerous twists and turns along a six-year journey that, in another nod to the realism of the manga, plays out in roughly the same time period as *Maison Ikkoku*'s original serialization.

Monster

Naoki Urasawa; *pub* Shogakukan (Jp), Viz (US); *ser* Big Comic Original (1994–2001); *vols* 18; *age* 16+

Many of the manga covered here are founded on stories that highlight the fantastic or extraordinary through momentous events – fighters with amazing skills beat each other up across continents, groups of people struggle to survive under post-apocalyptic conditions, and romances spring up under comedic circumstances.

Monster has a single character with an unusual skill: Johan, a serial killer able to mentally manipulate weak-willed criminals into carrying out slayings and then killing themselves to make it seem as if the cases are murder-suicides. But where a lesser mangaka might put a character like Johan front and centre in their manga, Naoki Urasawa chooses instead to keep Johan largely shrouded in the background, appearing only occasionally. We see the aftereffects of Johan's manipulations and perhaps flashbacks to the actions that spurred the reactions, but rarely do we see the event as it happens.

That Urasawa would keep his most powerful character as a behind-the-scenes master manipulator is testament to his writing skill and makes a statement in itself: *Monster* is not about momentous events, but builds its suspense through seemingly insignificant events, albeit with something slightly askew. And while Johan is certainly a key presence throughout the series, it's the way the rest of the series' cast reacts to what he does that builds his increasingly terrifying presence.

The opening chapters establish a morally ambiguous world. Dr Kenzo Tenma is a skilled Japanese surgeon working at a German hospital that operates more under a hypocritical oath than the Hippocratic oath – the hospital's director orders his staff to prioritize rich, famous or politically influential patients, even when someone else is in urgent need of care. Tenma follows the corporate line in the first chapter, saving an opera singer while letting a Turkish labourer die, but his guilt on seeing the labourer's family in mourning prompts him to take a stand and operate on a boy shot in the head rather than the town's mayor, as requested. The decision ends up costing him a promotion, his job and his girlfriend, the director's daughter Eva.

Urasawa quickly establishes that every decision his characters make has some consequence down the line, sometimes immediate, other times gradual. The young boy who was saved turns out to be the first time we see Johan; after Tenma, who was in charge of Johan's care, is fired, the director and his lackeys die of mysterious causes. We later find out that Anna, Johan's twin sister, wanted to kill her brother. He's been heralded as the second coming of Hitler, after all, an orphan raised to be a soulless killing machine under the auspices of an East German experimental programme.

A bunch of seemingly disparate stories get swept up in the overarching search for Johan: Anna, now under the alias Nina Fortner, wants to find her brother so she can kill him, end the madness and erase the memories of Johan's massacre years ago. Tenma, who once saved lives in a hospital, is now a fugitive doctor intent on bringing his former patient to justice. Inspector Lunge, a brilliant investigator with a photographic memory, is convinced that Tenma is the killer, using the "Johan" persona as a front, and is determined to bring the doctor to justice. Eva, now on a downward spiral, just wants Tenma back because he was the only person she feels has ever truly loved her.

As the series edges towards an inevitably tragic ending, Urasawa manages to keep all of these characters' stories uniquely their own while weaving them into a complex, challenging plot. A masterpiece among contemporary manga thrillers.

Naruto

Masashi Kishimoto; *pub* Shueisha (Jp), Viz (US, UK), Madman (Aus); *ser* Weekly Shōnen Jump (1999–); *vols* ongoing; *age* 13+

To a generation of Western manga fans who have come of age in the past seven years, *Naruto is* manga. The series' popularity in Japan, where more than 4,250,000 tankōbon were sold in 2008, has carried over elsewhere, with new volumes regularly charting on *USA Today*'s list of the top 150 bestselling books. Viz, in an effort to nudge the series closer to the Japanese release schedule and discourage the download of fan-scanned and translated chapters from the Internet, accelerated its release schedule of *Naruto* books in the US, first in the autumn of 2007, then again in early 2009.

Kishimoto's character designs have changed how contemporary audiences view ninjas. These aren't the ninjas stereotyped so often in the Western world, the ones shrouded in black and wearing masks, carrying around throwing stars, knives and katana blades, skulking around in the darkness and assassinating targets at will. The ninjas of *Naruto* wear normal clothes, headbands rather than hoods, get hired to carry out missions… at least they still carry around throwing stars, knives and katana blades.

Naruto is a mischievous teenager when we first meet him, a Ninja Academy student who aspires to be the strongest ninja, or kage, ever to lead Konohagakure (Hidden Leaf Village). The only problem with that – unbeknownst to him – is that the villagers already know him as the vessel for the Nine-Tailed Fox, the demon spirit who, twelve years prior, nearly destroyed their village and killed a good number of their friends and loved ones. The possibility that the spirit could emerge someday leaves most of the adults fearful and their children – Naruto's peers – openly mocking him.

The teammates he gets in cell 7 are certainly worthy of helping him reach his goal. Sakura Haruno acts as the brains of the operation, while Sasuke Uchiha is the top Ninja Academy graduate from his class. With Naruto's energetic, go-get-'em attitude and under the guidance of their ninjutsu instructor Kakashi, they should be the best roving band of ninjas out there.

Of course, it's more complicated than that: Naruto has a crush on Sakura, but Sakura won't give him the time of day, preferring to swoon over the ice king Sasuke. The fact that Sakura likes Sasuke makes Naruto burn with jealousy, while Sasuke feels utter disdain for both of them, certain that Sakura's crush and

Naruto's sense of reckless abandon are preventing him from achieving his real goal: restoring the legacy of the Uchiha clan and killing his older, more "favoured" brother Itachi. Yet when they do work together, their skills mature and they grow in confidence – as when they are called upon to repel a band of attackers from a village and defend a bridge under construction.

The village/bridge-defending story arc successfully establishes the main themes of friendship, trust and the ninja code of honour, but where the series really hits its stride is in the "Chunin Exam" arc. This arc, in which the junior ninja of cell 7 are enrolled in a series of tests designed to judge their worthiness of promotion to journeymen ninja, fleshes out the universe with the introduction of memorable supporting characters. The variety of different techniques on display, from shadow manipulation and body occupation to doppelgänger creations, ensures that series fans will root for at least one favourite character when the obligatory shōnen manga tournament among characters shows up. (And when it finally does show up, it takes its time, spanning fifty chapters across

The Naruto that nearly was

With dozens of *Naruto* chapters already in print, it might be difficult to imagine everyone's favourite ninja as, well, not a ninja. Yet in what's considered to be the "pilot episode" of *Naruto*, a one-shot piece published in *Weekly Shōnen Jump* offshoot *Akamaru Jump* two years before the series got underway, Masashi Kishimoto portrayed Naruto as a demon fox who lived his daily life in the form of a human boy.

Several elements remained the same between the prototype story and the ongoing series. Naruto was always a ramen-loving mischievous teen who's always getting into trouble, and the Nine-Tailed Fox Spirit still threatened the village, killing off eight of its nine defenders. That's where the similarities ended, though. Instead of being the vessel for the Nine-Tailed Fox Spirit as he is in the ongoing series, Naruto is its son. And while the special ninja techniques that would later make their way into the series are present, here they are used more as appearance-altering tools rather than as battle-enhancing techniques.

The story, in which Naruto helps a down-and-out painter regain the trust he lost when his best friend stabbed him and then killed himself, has its moments but feels rough around the edges, missing the fullness of character that has developed over the series proper. The central themes of friendship and trust in the pilot episode, though, became central to the series as well.

five volumes.) Among the more notable characters are Ino Yamanaka, Sakura's former friend turned friendly rival for Sasuke's affections; Hyuga Hinata, a somewhat quiet girl who harbours a secret crush for Naruto; Gaara, the stealthy, speedy loner assassin; and Rock Lee, whose skill with taijutsu (hand-to-hand combat) is surpassed in his mind only by his overt love for Sakura.

But the most potent of these, and the one who has emerged as the main antagonist of the story, is the rogue power-seeking ninja Orochimaru. His infiltration of the chunin exams and planting of a cursed seal on Sasuke sets in motion what could end up having a tragic conclusion, as Sasuke finds a new source of power within himself and

eventually embraces it, turning his back on his teammates and Konohagakure to pursue his own goals and ally himself with Orochimaru.

Kishimoto has managed to keep his series fresh for a decade now, not only maintaining individual characteristics, looks and fighting techniques for a cast of dozens but also by ageing his characters as his audience ages – the "Shippuden" story arc, which began in volume 28, features characters who have clearly aged more than two years in the story's timeline. Anyone who has followed the series for some time undoubtedly has a favourite ninja with whom they can identify. All of which represents a level of detail unmatched in other shōnen manga series running today.

Nausicaä of the Valley of the Wind

Hayao Miyazaki; *pub* Tokuma Shoten (Jp), Viz (US, UK); *ser* Animage (1982–94); *vols* 7; *age* 13+

Hayao Miyazaki is the world's best-known anime director, co-founder with Japanese publisher Tokuma Shoten of Studio Ghibli, the animation studio that's produced some of the most acclaimed anime of all time, including *My Neighbor Totoro*, *Kiki's Delivery Service*, *Howl's Moving Castle* and the 2002 Academy Award-winning *Spirited Away*.

What's less well-known about Miyazaki is that he originally wanted to be a mangaka. Frustrated by that ambition, he went instead into animation, starting with *Wan Wan Chushingura* (*Watchdog Bow Wow*) in 1963 and serving as key animator for a number of TV series throughout the 1960s and 70s. By 1981, Miyazaki was also coming into his own as an anime director, having directed several *Lupin III* movies. That December, *Animage* magazine revealed that Miyazaki was to serialize a story he wanted to draw – "the story of Nausicaä, a girl who lives in a chaotic age, 1000 years after the collapse of the great industrial civilization."

Twelve years later, the epic was complete. So was Miyazaki's ascension to the anime elite, with the creation of Studio Ghibli and four other movies as well as *Nausicaä* – *Totoro*, *Kiki*, *Laputa: Castle in the Sky* and *Porco Rosso* – added to his résumé. Part of the reason *Nausicaä* took so long to complete was because Miyazaki took time off to work on those films. *Nausicaä* turned out to be the only substantial manga series that Miyazaki would draw. But it is also considered his masterwork, an outlet through which he crafted a longer, more intricate story than could fit into a two-hour movie. Miyazaki earned the 1994 Japan Manga Artists' Association Award for the series, which sold ten million copies in Japan, and went on to be one of the top-selling manga ever released in the US.

In a period when anime and manga were largely dominated by romantic comedies, tales of giant battling space robots or epic martial arts battles, *Nausicaä* was a socially conscious manga filled with complex philosophical, religious and ecological themes. Miyazaki, given the chance to expand beyond an established franchise's canon for the first time with an original property, creates an intricate fantasy world in line with what he would produce in his post-*Nausicaä* anime work. This creativity is evident in such inventions as the Sea of Corruption, an ever-expanding field of poisonous fungi and flora protected by Ohmu, giant mutant insects, and other odd creatures.

The setting is a rather bleak version of the future, one in which humanity has been pushed to the edge of existence on a planet that barely supports them following a cataclysmic war. Yet a new war threatens to envelop the shrinking world that remains, with the Kingdom of Torumekia and its military might challenging the Dorok Empire, an alliance of 51 tribal countries largely ruled by monks. Caught on the periphery of this conflict is the Valley of the Wind, a region on the edge of the Sea of Corruption allied with Torumekia.

The valley benefits from winds coming from the ocean that constantly purify it and protect it from the miasma and poisonous spores. The region's longtime chieftain, rendered an invalid, has been raising his daughter, Nausicaä, for the day that she would take over as leader. The teenage princess certainly has the skills to lead – she's adept with a sword, is clever and resourceful, and handles a *mehve*, a single-person glider, as if it

was an extension of herself. Those skills come in handy when Torumekia calls upon the people of the valley to send a force to help them in the battle against Dorok, and Nausicaä volunteers to lead that force.

Such loyalty, enforced by an ages-old treaty, has its limits. But it turns out that Nausicaä also has the ability to communicate with the Ohmu in the Sea of Corruption, being able to love what many others fear. What the Ohmu reveal to her about the sea and their suffering strengthens her resolve not to join in the cycle of killing. Her true purpose, instead, becomes protecting her people and their way of life and to someday find the utopia known as the Blue Pure Land. This journey challenges her view of the world that she had learned about – a view perpetuated by the other societies out there – and she becomes a changed person for it.

The world that Miyazaki presents here is not black and white; every faction has what it believes are good reasons for acting as they do. "No matter how wise or elaborate the plan, trying to apply it to an era in which you do not live is extremely arrogant. It will not yield satisfactory results. That's something I'm sure of. I didn't want to have Nausicaä just denounce the people who made the world what it was as foolish." Nausicaä's journey demonstrates that destinies often become what we make of them.

Oh My Goddess!

Kōsuke Fujishima; *pub* Kodansha (Jp), Dark Horse (US, Aus), Titan Books (UK); *ser* Afternoon (1988–); *vols* ongoing; *age* 13+

For most people, dialling a wrong number is hardly a life-changing event, but when college student Keiichi Morisato calls the Goddess Technical Help Line by mistake, he ends up with a gorgeous, obedient goddess as his partner. Belldandy shows up in his dorm room to ask him his one allocated wish and he blurts out, "I want a goddess like you … TO BE WITH ME ALWAYS!" And since the hotline's universal computer Yggdrasil carries out every task to the letter, Keiichi now has a perfect girlfriend, who is able to manipulate the computers at Nekomi Tech to make it appear as if she's an exchange student who suddenly transferred into the college.

From these beginnings, Kōsuke Fujishima has crafted a romantic comedy that has run for more than twenty years as one of the archetypes of harem manga. The unconventional start to the relationship between Belldandy and Keiichi makes their romance a somewhat nervous, uncertain one – perhaps maddeningly so even to fans who have followed the series for so many years. Sure, Belldandy loves Keiichi and is eternally devoted to him and he cares deeply for her. It's how to express that love for each other that has provided a constant undercurrent of tension throughout the series to date. As this is shōnen manga, sex isn't a necessary element, but Keiichi has struggled even with deciding the timing of simple displays of affection like kissing or holding Belldandy's hand.

Belldandy's arrival throws Keiichi's life into chaos. While those around him are unaware of Belldandy's status as a goddess, the fact that he's suddenly showing up at college with a beautiful girl attracts attention. Members of the Nekomi Tech motor club kick Keiichi out of their dorm because of their "no girls" policy. The couple eventually find a home at a shrine, though, when a priest sees Belldandy secretly performing a miracle overnight and immediately departs on a spiritual journey, leaving the care of the site to them.

This central plot of a goddess living with a human can only carry the series so far, and creator Fujishima introduces an entire pantheon of goddesses to complicate Keiichi's life, all of whose names come from Norse mythology (as does Belldandy's, an anglicized version of the Japanese translation). The female archetypes, now common to harem manga, begin with Urd, Belldandy's older sister, the brimming sexpot who often tries to push her sister's somewhat shy relationship forward; and younger sister Skuld, the technological genius, who's overprotective of Belldandy and sees anyone having an intimate relationship with her as a threat. Later additions to the cast, including the seductive Peorth in volume 11 and the all-business, no-nonsense Lind in volume 24, have complicated Keiichi's domestic life even further as they've settled into the household. And the group needs all the help they can get, with the demon Marller wreaking havoc and Urd's mother, ultimate demon Hild, also entering the story.

Oh My Goddess! is a landmark title in Western manga history, being one of the few series to be printed in all three formats as the medium evolved – a traditional Western comic-book edition and flopped and unflopped graphic novel formats. Reissuing the series in different formats has helped Dark Horse attract new readers, who are drawn in by the simple setup of Keiichi and Belldandy's relationship in the early chapters. Persist and you get to appreciate not just the growing storyline, but the evolution of Fujishima's art style, too. Gradually, round about the fourth volume, the blockiness of his early drawings gives way to more detailed, refined work. Comparing Belldandy at the start with her depiction in volumes 15 and 30, for instance, you see her progress from being a rather plain-looking girl to a woman who could truly be considered a goddess.

The original Japanese title, *Aa! Megami-sama*, is more accurately translated as "Ah! My Goddess", though "Oh My Goddess!" has been adopted as the favoured title for English-speaking audiences. Fujishima himself has vacillated between the two. No matter what you call it, though, the series is an endearing, enduring manga classic in both Japan and the West.

One Piece

Eiichiro Oda; *pub* Shueisha (Jp), Viz (US, UK, Aus); *ser* Weekly Shōnen Jump (1997–); *vols* ongoing; *age* 13+

t's the second-highest selling *Shōnen Jump* title of all time, behind only *Dragon Ball*, numbering around 2.6 million copies at its peak in the early 1990s and racking up 53 volumes by March 2009. Not bad, really, considering that the adventures of the *One Piece* pirates were supposed to end back in 2002, five years after Eiichiro Oda started the series. But he was having so much fun drawing the story, he simply kept on going.

One Piece has been unadulterated fun for more than ten years running now, with its hero, Monkey D. Luffy, a teenage boy living his dream of sailing the high seas as a pirate. Luffy is the quintessential contemporary shōnen hero, an eternally optimistic guy who hopes to become the best pirate ever, makes friends easily in his quest to reach that goal, and possesses some sort of unusual power to help him get through sticky situations. In Luffy's case, this is the ability to turn his limbs rubbery and use them as powerful weapons, the lingering effects of accidentally eating a Gum-Gum Fruit; its other effect dooms him to sinking should he fall in the water, not exactly the attribute you'd want for a pirate career.

The early part of the series settles into a comfortable rhythm: Luffy will go after some person with extraordinary skill, like the legendary pirate-hunting swordsman Roronoa Zoro, treasure-hunting thief Nami or talking reindeer Tony Tony Chopper, and ask them to join his group, known as the Straw Hat Pirates. That person often laughs off his offer and declines, but that doesn't bother Luffy. He'll just go about his business, taking down some rogue pirate group with a leader who has abilities equally as strange, if not stranger, than Luffy's Gum-Gum powers in the process. And when the once-reluctant invitee has seen what Luffy can do, he or she is more than happy to join the party.

When the Straw Hats finally get their own ship, the *Merry Go*, the story shifts its focus to Luffy's quest to sail the Grand Line ocean and recover One Piece, the fabled lost treasure of Gold Roger. As the series advances, the Straw Hats and their enemies progressively "power up", the creatures and fighting styles grow more exotic, and the settings become grander and more elaborate.

It feels like *Dragon Ball* without the martial arts but with pirates on the high seas, and that's no coincidence: Eiichiro Oda was heavily influenced by Akira Toriyama's *Dragon Ball* when he drafted his story and designed its characters. Yet not only has Oda's creation already lasted longer than Toriyama's – *Dragon Ball* ran for 42 volumes before Toriyama put down his pen – but Oda has yet to show any sign of running out of ideas from a seemingly limitless imagination. New members of the Straw Hats,

including a cola-powered cyborg and a musical living skeleton, have signed on as recently as volume 46. Oda also preserves a sense of fantasy, whimsy and awe in the character of Luffy, a spirit that gradually faded from *Dragon Ball* as the power levels of opponents escalated and the body counts rose. While there are plenty of bloody, prolonged battles in *One Piece*, no one ever dies.

Paradise Kiss

Ai Yazawa; *pub* Shodensha (Jp), Tokyopop (US, UK), Madman (Aus); *ser* Zipper (2000–04); *vols* 5; *age* 16+

High-class fashion in a series like this could never be contained in any run-of-the-mill manga anthology. Leave it to a Japanese fashion magazine, *Zipper*, to serve as the home for a manga about a group of young designers... who know they're being featured in a manga in a Japanese fashion magazine.

Paradise Kiss is nothing if not self-aware. Characters from one of Ai Yazawa's earlier manga series, the untranslated *Gokinjo Monogatari*, make cameo appearances (one even gets a rather descriptive informational box highlighting his appearance, in response to which he promptly complains that the author described him as a "middle-aged

man"), while members of the school/amateur design team Paradise Kiss attend the Yazawa School for the Arts – named after the author. The fashion designs that Yazawa drew are also remarkably authentic – when production began on the *Paradise Kiss* anime, the director hired a fashion consultant to translate the manga's designs to real-world fashion, but the consultant ended up leaving most of Yazawa's original designs intact.

While the world of fashion may take centre stage in *Paradise Kiss*, the series pulses with the energy of josei manga. The setup seems clichéd at first glance – the "ugly duckling transforms into a swan" concept has played out in countless series before and since. But Aizawa steers clear of simple clichés in building her story, capturing the natural anxieties of a teenager who struggles to find an identity that will make her more appealing to her peers and who makes plenty of mistakes along the way. Its appeal lies in something that main character Yukari Hayasaka says late in the series: "My first runway was a lot wider and longer than I thought it would be. I can't believe just putting one foot in front of the other could be so difficult. But, in a way, that's a good analogy for life itself."

Yukari is a high school senior who plays the role of dutiful daughter at the beginning of the series, attending cram school and drooling in secret over her hot classmate, Hiroyuki. All of this changes, however, when she meets some of the members of Paradise Kiss – pierced punk fashionista Arashi, the cross-dressing Isabella (a boy who dresses up in such elegant fashions that people often mistake him for a woman) and cutesy lolita Miwako – who see in her the perfect model for their school festival fashion show.

Yukari doesn't want to do it at first. Why, she reasons, would anyone want her, an ordinary, plain-looking girl, to be their model? Besides, with college entrance exams and studies to tend to, she has no time to deal with such trivial matters. But she finds herself going back there because of the way they

unconditionally accept her and the presence of the group's mysterious leader, George. George, whose appearance is loosely based on the character of Brian Slade in the 1998 film *Velvet Goldmine* (one of Yazawa's favourite films), is, by his own admission, not a nice guy. Often frustratingly inaccessible, his fashions are hard for most to fathom yet beautiful when worn by the right person – and that person is Yukari.

This all makes for a bittersweet coming-of-age story. Yukari's new goal to become a top model puts her directly at odds with her mother's wishes, and she ends up rebelling to the point of moving out of her house. Her grades suffer as a result. There's also the matter of the love between Miwako, her old love Hiroyuki, and her new boyfriend Arashi. While she's already consummated her love with Arashi, she still has feelings for Hiroyuki… who in turn is developing feelings for Yukari… who is falling into a sort of desperate love and desire for affection from George.

Mistakes made in recognizing where true love, affection and acceptance come from help all of the characters grow and mature in the long run. Fashion becomes a metaphor for life. While the characters try to find their way by dressing up as something they're not, the realization that they can be comfortable in their own skin turns out to be the most valuable lesson of all.

Peach Girl

Miwa Ueda; *pub* Kodansha (Jp), Tokyopop (US, as *Peach Girl* and *Peach Girl: Change of Heart*); *ser* Bessatsu Friend (1997–2004); *vols* 18; *age* 13+

By all rights, Momo should be the star of *Peach Girl*. She's the peach in the title, after all, "momo" being the Japanese word for the fruit. But *Peach Girl* is just as much the story of Momo's conniving, manipulative "friend" Sae. The conflict between the two is what drives the series: without Sae, Momo would be more a walking cliché than a sympathetic character; without Momo, Sae's brand of two-faced evil wouldn't be nearly as delicious.

Miwa Ueda fundamentally tells the oft-repeated tale of looking beyond outer appearances to see a person's true beauty. Momo is an outcast because she resembles a ganguro, one of those tanned girls with bleached blond hair who are looked down upon for being shallow and rebellious. But she really has no connection to ganguro culture; she looks the way she does because she's on the swim team, her hair bleached by the chlorine in the pool water and her skin easily tanned from being outdoors so often.

By contrast, Sae is a porcelain-skinned model of Japanese beauty, projecting an image of sweet innocence. And it's this that gives her the benefit of the doubt when she and Momo relate two sides of the same story to their classmates – even when Sae's lying through her teeth. Momo herself is equally convinced by Sae's image, befriending her soon after she enters high school but finding out over time that Sae will do anything to manipulate a situation in her favour – telling Momo a handbag doesn't look fashionable only to turn around and buy it herself, for instance.

Her own image problem has seriously dented Momo's self-confidence. While she's had a crush on baseball player Toji since junior high school, she hasn't acted on it until now because she's been told he doesn't like tanned girls. Once she does approach him, she discovers that he likes her as well. The problem is that Sae's also interested in him… and she'll do whatever it takes to get what she wants. Fortunately for Sae, there's another player who wants into this game of love: Kairi (rendered in the Tokyopop translation as "Kiley"), who has a serious crush on Momo. Kairi is far more outgoing than the staid Toji, and his presence gives Sae the opportunity to meddle, sending Kairi after Momo and leaving Toji susceptible to manipulation.

And thus, a love square forms, with the girls trying to outwit each other in

Courtesy of Kodansha Ltd

Kodansha Comics 別フレ

土田美和

ピーチ 1
ガール

Momo's blonde hair and tan mark her out as a ganguro, but Miwa Ueda's witty script shows there's much more to her than that.

a virtual chess game of relationships while the boys are by and large carried along as their pawns. Ueda's witty script stays tightly focused on these four characters, emphasizing those moments when Momo and Kairi are caught in the wrong place at the wrong time by both Sae and Toji. Sae's more than happy to spread the word about Momo "cheating" on Toji, reinforcing their classmates' notions that Momo is little more than an easy, two-timing ganguro gal. Toji even breaks up with Momo at one point to protect her from further harm to her reputation, even though he can't really believe that she'd cheat on him like that.

Sae doesn't always get the upper hand. When Momo finally gets her revenge on Sae, banding together with Toji and Kairi to reveal her true nature in front of the rest of the school, the result is literally crushing. Ueda draws Sae as a two-dimensional, flattened-piece-of-paper version of her former self as a visual reminder of this. Once Sae gets an idea to put her back on top again (and gets an offer to become a professional model, to boot) – pop! – she's back to her well-rounded self again. Her schemes become more elaborate than ever in the second half of the series, with a drugging and date-rape situation turning the manga away from its otherwise floaty romantic comedy feel. Frequent plot twists make it difficult to guess whether Momo will end up with Toji or Kairi – and whether Sae will ever get her just desserts – which keeps this series compelling right to the end.

Phoenix

Osamu Tezuka; *pub* Osamu Tezuka (Jp, 1967–72), Asahi Sonorama (Jp, 1976–86), Kadokawa (Jp, 1986–88), Viz (US, UK); *ser* COM (1967–72), Manga Shōnen (1976–86), The Wild Age (1986–88); *vols* 12; *age* 16+

There's no disputing that Astro Boy is Osamu Tezuka's most recognized character. Yet it was another of his series, the millennia-spanning *Phoenix*, that the manga master considered his life's work. Serialized from 1967 to 1988, although the foundation for the series was laid as early as 1954 (see box overleaf), it might have run even longer were it not for Tezuka's death in 1989. "The story has been swinging between past and future and eventually it will converge in the present," Tezuka once wrote. "Until it reaches that point, I must continue drawing." Tezuka himself notes in the first story arc, "Dawn", that the story takes place during the time of the Chronicles of Wei from the Three Kingdoms period of China in the third century, considered to contain the first historical account of Japan. The second story arc, "Future", takes the other extreme, depicting humanity on the verge of collapse in the year 3404.

Japanese readers not only had to deal with the series jumping between time periods in its narrative, but also between publications, with *Phoenix* appearing in three different magazines over parts of three decades. It was first serialized in Tezuka's own anthology *COM*, before it shut down in 1972. The artist felt his greatest challenge with *Phoenix* was writing stories that were intellectually challenging, and the series' subsequent move to *Manga Shōnen*, coupled with the emergence of more complex shōjo manga, prompted him to take more chances, some of which he later acknowledged did not pan out. "*Phoenix* in those days became gimmicky to keep up with the trend," he once wrote. "I had been drawing *Phoenix* for over ten years by then, so what I thought was a brilliant new idea seems dated now."

As one of Tezuka's first series aimed at adult audiences, *Phoenix* acts as a link in his evolution from an artist drawing series aimed at children to his later adult-targeted series like *Black Jack*. *Phoenix* was Tezuka's canvas for experimenting with panel layouts. The story arc "Universe" (sometimes known as "Space"), for example, features four astronauts who are forced to abandon their ship in separate escape pods. Once those pods are launched, Tezuka shows each astronaut in separate groups of frames on each page; whenever they join up, their frames join up, whenever they are separate, they are shown separately. The effect even extends to the point where, if an astronaut decides to cut off communication with the others for whatever reason, their frames are shown merely as a string of black boxes.

Each of the twelve *Phoenix* stories Tezuka completed before his death is self-contained; some stories incorporate elements of science fiction, while others are historical fantasies. All are linked by the mythical, immortal phoenix, the bird whose blood supposedly grants eternal life to those who drink it. But immortality and man's quest to seek it interfere with *Phoenix*'s other main theme: the eternal Buddhist reincarnation cycle of death and rebirth. This cycle is embodied in the series' other recurring character, Saruta, a man always destined to suffer yet who manages to persevere in whatever situation he is placed. While he may not be called "Saruta" in every story, his wild hair and large nose signals his presence – acting as a character like those in Tezuka's "star system" (see p.12) and filling different roles in different stories.

The story arc considered the best in the series is also one of Tezuka's most

Phoenix rising: the prototype for a classic

The early influence of Walt Disney's work on Osamu Tezuka could be seen in Tezuka's first, prototypical *Phoenix* series, albeit with a bit more bloodshed and death than the typical Disney cartoon. The stories, published in Kodansha's *Shōjo Club* in Japan between 1956 and 1957 and released in Viz's English translation as the twelfth and final volume, "Early Works", in 2008, featured a less weighty tone than the following series would have.

The time frame is much tighter, from ancient Egypt through to ancient Rome, centring on the reincarnation of love that began when an Egyptian slave girl, Daia, fell in love with a crown prince. The story unfolds with themes that invite comparisons to the Disney-animated movies of the time: the sweet singing voice of Daia that soothes animals, for instance, is reminiscent of Snow White. Talking animals abound, and there's even an evil queen character who is jealous of Daia and wants to bring ruin to what seems to be a predestined love. Of course, the bird itself also makes an appearance, more frequently here than it would in later series, and even bears an egg and raises its offspring before passing into eternity and leaving the task of preserving the legacy to the next generation.

straightforward: the fifth installment, "Karma" (published in 1969–70 in Japan as "Hō-ō", it's volume 4 of Viz's English release). "Karma" profiles the divergent lives of two men in the eighth century. The physically deformed Gao (Saruta's incarnation in this story), tired of being treated like an outcast, goes on a murderous rampage and becomes a merciless bandit. Along the course of his travels, he responds to the kindness of a gifted sculptor, Akanemaru, by cutting off his arm. These characters develop and grow as the story proceeds: Gao

finds redemption through a priest who inspires him to join the priesthood and take up sculpting and carving, while Akanemaru gets caught up in the politics of the time and ends up following a more secular path. By the time the two meet once more, during a competition to build a temple, the gears have been set in motion to deliver a climax that illuminates the Buddhist concepts of karma and the transmigration of the soul. The story is *Phoenix* boiled down to its essence, a contemplation of religious experience in the context of human existence.

Please Save My Earth

Saki Hiwatari; *pub* Hakusensha (Jp), Viz (US); *ser* Hana to Yume (1987–94); *vols* 21; *age* 16+

*P*lease Save My Earth, a romantic drama that spans space and time, has humble origins: Saki Hiwatari's real-life move to a new apartment. As she looked out on her neighbour's yard at dusk one evening, with the sun setting and the stars beginning to twinkle in the sky, she felt at peace, as if she was wrapped in something warm. It was out of an effort to recreate that feeling that her series was born.

Hiwatari effectively blends two stories from different time periods into a single narrative, with the tragedies of one group of characters living in the past

resonating in the lives of a second group in the present. The series' title expresses the desire of seven scientists, the last survivors of an extinct planet who lived on a lunar outpost and observed the Earth, which reminded them of their own planet in its unspoiled form. They agreed never to go to Earth and interact with its inhabitants, regardless of how much they secretly longed to be among them, out of fear that history would repeat itself and their utopia of Earth would be destroyed as well.

The scientists eventually die, doomed by a virus that infiltrates the base. But their spirits survive in six teenagers and a seven-year-old boy living in the twentieth century. Hiwatari quickly establishes the connection between generations, introducing in the second chapter two boys, Jinpachi and Issei, who regularly dream about the scientists. They feel as if they've always known each other from the day they first met in the eighth grade and continued to bond thanks to the shared dreams. Jinpachi feels he's the incarnation of a male archeologist, Gyokuran, in their dreams, while Issei believes he's an introspective female paleontologist, Enju – a situation that Hiwatari acknowledges has the appearance of a boys' love pairing and initially plays for laughs.

While the revelation of a connection happens quickly, Hiwatari is slow to reveal exactly how each of the modern-day characters is linked to the scientists. She frames her narrative from the perspective of Alice, a shy, introspective girl who feels like she shares a special bond with plants and animals but is at a loss to explain these feelings. Alice's journey of discovery is also our journey – unlike Jinpachi, Issei and the others she eventually meets, her dreams are neither as frequent nor as clear. But

Hiwatari hints that Alice is connected to the central figure among the scientists, Mokuren. The first link is obvious: Alice and Mokuren both care deeply about plants. Other connections, however, are established with Alice's interactions with others in their advanced states of awareness. Posing the biggest threat is Rin, the youngest of the twentieth-century group yet the one who is most aware of what happened in the past. Rin knows he was once Shion, Mokuren's fiancé, and presses his advantage to the fullest, psychically manipulating the others into believing lies so he can keep Mokuren/Alice for himself.

Eventually, the group is reunited, but they find themselves engaging in the same cycles of jealousy and revenge they went through in their original bodies. It's a slow grower of a story, but utterly compelling. The concept was so convincing to some readers in Japan that fan letters from people sure that they themselves were reincarnations of the scientists flooded Hiwatari's office at one point. The craze reached such a fever pitch that, starting with the eighth volume, the publisher added a disclaimer stating that nothing in the series was based in reality.

Ranma 1/2

Rumiko Takahashi; *pub* Shogakukan (Jp), Viz (US, UK, Aus); *ser* Weekly Shōnen Sunday (1987–96); *vols* 38; *age* 16+

Kenshiro from *Fist of the North Star* had his share of challenges and challengers in his days wandering the post-apocalyptic landscape. But it's safe to say that he never had to contend with a group of martial arts cheerleaders who fight by throwing pom-poms and batons. He never had to worry about being transformed into a girl, either.

These are just two of the original twists Rumiko Takahashi, a fan of *Fist of the North Star*, put into her take on the martial arts genre, the comedic cross-gender epic *Ranma ½*. The success of *Ranma ½* spawned a host of copycat sex-change, love-triangle shōnen manga. None of those series' heroes, though, could match Takahashi's imaginative creation Ranma Saotome. Ranma is a high school student, a ruggedly tough martial artist and a boy promised in marriage to one of the girls of Soun Tendo's household. The twist is that Ranma is also a girl, doomed to switch genders whenever he's doused with water ever since he fell into a cursed hot spring. At least he remains human, though; his father, Genma, fell into the "Spring of Drowned Panda" and now transforms into a giant panda.

Takahashi's desire to add more variety to her art, rather than a desire to add a plot twist, was her main reason for introducing the transformation mechanism. You can't blame her for wanting more variety in a long-running story: drawing the same characters for sixteen to twenty pages per month, every month, must get tedious after a while.

The story is infused with heavy doses of the double-take, slapstick comedy that Takahashi developed over her career, honed through years of drawing *Urusei Yatsura* and *Maison Ikkoku* (see box overleaf). Sure, there's traditional kick-punch-chop action, but there are also martial arts battles utilizing skills like rhythmic gymnastics, ice skating, cheerleading and Japanese tea ceremonies. Ranma also not only must be wary of people wielding jugs of water, but also of the presence of his other weakness: cats. As a child, Ranma was traumatized when Genma, hoping to train him in the "cat-fist" discipline, tied a fish sausage to him and tossed him into a pack of hungry cats.

The surrounding cast of dozens of characters is just as quirky. Take Ryoga Hibiki, who has held a grudge against Ranma ever since he kept snatching the

Rumiko Takahashi

Manga artist, 1957–

Osamu Tezuka may be Japan's most beloved manga artist, but when it comes to the English-speaking market, that honour may well rest with Rumiko Takahashi. While her first series translated for an American audience, *Urusei Yatsura*, may not have generated the sales numbers Viz had hoped for, subsequent releases, including *Maison Ikkoku*, *Ranma ½* and her most recent series, *Inuyasha*, gained a sizeable readership. *Inuyasha*, one of the series that benefited the most from the boom in translated English manga, turned out to be so popular that Viz slapped yellow "From the creator of *Inuyasha*" stickers on everything the company had in print by her.

Takahashi's popularity isn't limited to the English-speaking market, of course. Virtually everything she's touched has been turned into an anime series, including her shorter *Rumic Theater* and *Mermaid Saga* stories, and she's the highest earning mangaka in Japan. Yet back when she was attending high school in her hometown of Niigata, the only drawing she did was in the margins of her notebook. Manga creation began as nothing more than a hobby, but she grew serious about pursuing drawing as a career while attending Japan Women's University in the mid-1970s. She enrolled for two years at Gekiga Sonjuku, a manga school known for the demanding nature of its founder, Kazuo Koike of *Lone Wolf and Cub* fame. Under Koike, she drew hundreds of pages and learned the importance of showcasing interesting characters and letting them dictate the flow of her stories. Studying at Koike's school would lead her to another mentor: horror manga author Kazuo Umezu, under whom she would work as an assistant for two years.

Takahashi first published several short manga stories as part of the Japan Women's University Manga Club in 1976, then decided against working at a conventional office job in favour of becoming a professional mangaka. It was a decision from which her parents tried to dissuade her. Fortunately, her work caught the eye of the right people at Shogakukan, who invited her to write a story for *Shōnen Sunday*. That story was *Urusei Yatsura*, which debuted in 1978 and began a publishing relationship with the magazine that has lasted now for more than twenty years.

Since 1978, Takahashi has helped shōnen and seinen manga find its sensitive side. Romantic tension, sometimes blossoming into full-blown love, features in many of her major works. This cross-pollination of romance and action, along with a healthy dose of slapstick comedy and tense drama, has broadened her appeal among male and female audiences alike both in Japan and around the globe.

Inuyasha

pub Shogakukan (Jp), Viz (US, UK); *ser* Shōnen Sunday (1996–2008); *vols* 56; *age* 16+

When junior high-school girl Kagome gets dragged into a well on the temple grounds where she lives, she finds herself whisked away to another era, one in which she is believed to be the reincarnation of a great priestess. With the half-demon, half-human Inuyasha (reluctantly) at her side, she must help reassemble the shattered Shikon Jewel, all the while fending off evil demons who desire the jewel's powers. As Takahashi's longest series to date, it meanders somewhat, but this time-travelling tale between feudal and modern-day Japan has its moments too.

Mermaid Saga

pub Shogakukan (Jp), Viz (US, UK); *ser* Shōnen Sunday (1984–94); *vols* 4; *age* 16+

The influence of Kazuo Umezu's horror fantasies is evident in this story about a race of mermaids who can grant eternal life to those who kill them and eat their flesh… but at a horrific cost. Those who become immortal continue to feel physical pain and also must suffer the emotional anguish of seeing their loved ones age and die. Yuta, a 500-year-old immortal, and his travelling companion Mana wander Japan and help those cursed by the mermaids' powers.

One-Pound Gospel

pub Shogakukan (Jp), Viz (US, UK); *ser* Weekly Young Sunday (1987, 2001, 2006–07); *vols* 4; *age* 16+

Kosaku Hatanaka is the first professional boxer to come out of Mukaida's Gym. This normally would be cause for celebration, but Coach Mukaida actually considers the eternally hungry, overweight Kosaku one of his biggest disappointments. It would take divine intervention to save Kosaku from his cycle of gluttony… and appropriately enough, it comes from Sister Angela, a rather cute nun to whom he has been confessing his sins. How she feels about him, however, evolves as the series progresses. Series fans endured a near twenty-year wait for its conclusion. It was worth it though, for the same charming, slice-of-life humour that Takahashi used in *Maison Ikkoku*.

Urusei Yatsura

pub Shogakukan (Jp), Viz (US); *ser* Shōnen Sunday (1978–87); *vols* Jp 34, US 9 (cancelled); *age* 13+.

Takahashi's first major hit series earned her Shogakukan's Best New Manga Artist award and established her as a force on the manga scene. It's an unusual story about a lecherous teen, Ataru, who saves the Earth from invading aliens only to be forced into a marriage with the gorgeous tiger-striped-bikini-clad alien girl Lum. The first few chapters can test your tolerance of slapstick humour and random gags, but the series improves thanks to Takahashi's growing grasp of comic timing.

last piece of bread at their junior high cafeteria. He was supposed to have had a final showdown with Ranma already, but he never made it due to his poor sense of direction, ending up instead at Jusenkyo and falling into the "Spring of Drowned Pig". Another rival, Tatewaki Kuno, loathes Ranma as a boy but loves him as a girl, often accusing him of spiriting away "the pig-tailed girl" without realizing they're the same person.

But perhaps the most difficult challenge for Ranma lies in his fiancée, Akane Tendo, a tomboyish type with a hot temper that emerges whenever Ranma upsets her; her dreadful cooking is almost as dangerous. Yet for all the public squabbling they engage in, there's an undercurrent of romance between the two, shown in the ways they look out for each other every now and then. Adding emotional subtlety beneath all the wham-bam action and comedy is something Takahashi has excelled in throughout her career, and her characters gain more depth and reader sympathy as a result.

Rose of Versailles

Riyoko Ikeda; *pub* Shueisha (Jp), Sanyusha (US); *ser* Margaret (1972–73); *vols* Jp 10, US 2

Rose of Versailles is regarded as the Holy Grail of shōjo manga in the West, a treasure that many readers would love to read in its entirety but can't due to the lack of a complete English translation. While it was the first commercially translated manga to be available in North America – the first two volumes were translated by Frederik L. Schodt in 1981 as a tool for teaching English to Japanese speakers – no other commercial translations are available. It has been rumoured that the rights holders are charging a high price for the licence and no publisher wants to take a chance on releasing a series that is more than 35 years old and might not appeal to the coveted teenage readers of today.

It's a pity, because this tale of pre-revolution France during the reign of Louis XVI and Marie Antoinette deserves to have a wider audience as one of the foundational manga series of the early shōjo period. In Japan, the series was adapted into both live-action and animated TV series and feature films, and an estimated 1.5 million people saw a stage production between 1974 and 1979 (see opposite).

Most of the characters featured in this largely historical romantic drama are based on real people, with one major exception: Oscar François de Jarjayes, the sixth child – and sixth girl – to be born to a family that has traditionally sent its sons to serve in the royal palace guard. The girls' father, convinced he must take matters into his own hands, decides to raise his youngest daughter as a boy so that she (acting as a he) can carry on the legacy.

Many of the early pages are also given over to profiling the alliance between Austria and France that led to the marriage of Marie Antoinette and Louis XVI. Marie loses her Austrian privilege, relegated to simply being the French king's wife out of duty, not love. During her first trip to the palace, Marie sees Oscar and is immediately taken with the tall, powerful "man" and the confident manner in which he carries himself. And for good reason: Oscar's ambiguous sexuality means she appeals to both men and women.

This passing encounter sets in motion a fascinating study in contrasts between the two women. They do eventually meet and become fast friends, and while their lives intersect during key events throughout the series, their paths couldn't be any more different. Marie Antoinette is the free spirit trapped within the rigid structures of the French monarchy. Oscar, while destined to be a member of the palace guard as a man, enjoys the privileges of men that could never be enjoyed by the ladies of the royal court.

TOSHIFUMI KITAMURA/AFP/Getty Images

An image of Marie Antoinette from Ikeda's 1970s manga forms the backdrop for the Takarazuka theatre's production of *Rose of Versailles* in Feburary 2006.

How these two deal with their feelings in the midst of their duties and obligations is a major theme throughout the series. Oscar learns from Marie the value of looking for a reason to love beyond obligation – lessons that Marie ultimately cannot apply to her own life, stuck as she is in a marriage of obligation while pining for the Swedish count, Axel von Fersen. When von Fersen leaves her to assist with the war for independence in the US, Marie ends up living a life of sheer excess to compensate and ultimately brings about the ruin of the monarchy. By contrast, Oscar, with her freedom to explore wherever her heart leads, ends up falling in love with her family servant, Andre, while also harbouring feelings towards a peasant girl, Rosalie. Oscar ultimately gives up everything to fight for what she truly believes in – a luxury that Marie Antoinette, with all her palace trappings, is never able to attain.

Anyone who paid attention in history class knows there's not going to be a happy ending. But with its detailed historical setting providing the framework for a tale of inevitable tragedy and forbidden love, *Rose of Versailles* set the standards for shōjo manga for years to come – one that's tragically still largely unavailable to English-language manga fans.

Sailor Moon

Naoko Takeuchi; *pub* Kodansha (Jp), Tokyopop (US); *ser* Nakayoshi (1992–97); *vols* 18; *age* 13+

Sailor *Moon* was the first magical-girl series to make a significant impact on the English-language manga market. Part of this success was thanks to the anime adaptation (albeit in heavily edited form), which began airing in North America and Australia in 1995 and in the UK in 1999. So when Tokyopop (then Mixx Entertainment) announced that *Sailor Moon* would be a key part of its US *Mixxzine* anthology launching in 1997, fans of the anime had an idea of what they would be getting: the story of a group of teen girls who could transform into world-saving champions of justice and peace. Granted, the art was not very good and the story got progressively weaker the longer it lasted, but it was more *Sailor*

Moon, and that's what girls in the West wanted to read.

The series' "chosen one", who gets to save the world from the forces of evil time and again (and lands the hottest guy in the series to boot), is Serena, known to her friends as "Bunny" and to hardcore *Sailor Moon* fans who keep track of the differences between the Japanese source material and English adaptations as Usagi Tsukino. "I guess I cry easily, but I'm a regular, cute girl!" she chirps.

Serena learns over a nine-chapter span that she is the reincarnation of Princess Serenity, who lived on the moon in a kingdom known as the Silver Millennium. Several millennia ago, the Silver Millennium repelled an attempt by the Dark Kingdom to take the universe's most powerful artefact, the Silver Crystal. The battle ended up obliterating both kingdoms, but the dying wish of the princess's mother, Queen Serenity, ensured that her daughter, her guardians and her daughter's true love, Prince Endymion of Earth, would all be reborn in the future.

And so, according to Queen Serenity's will (not to mention the will of the author who meticulously plotted all of this out beforehand), everyone reappears in reincarnated form in the twentieth century: Serena and her guardians (known as the Sailor Senshi) arrive intact, although Serena and Luna – Princess Serenity's advisor, reincarnated as a talking cat – have to hunt them down

in their new forms as schoolgirls. The Sailor Senshi primarily act as support characters filling specific stereotypes – among them are a shy-but-smart girl, a tough tomboy and a focused Shinto priestess. Of course, the Silver Millennium's enemies have returned as well, so the team led by Serena/Sailor Moon must use their special powers to repel the evil forces and protect the Silver Crystal.

It's a simple story, one that Takeuchi designed to last just fourteen chapters. But the series was doing so well the editor insisted she continue, and her story instead ran for 52 chapters, adding characters like Princess Serenity's daughter Rini (who travels through time and transforms into Sailor Chibi Moon) and the outer Sailor Senshi Uranus, Neptune and Pluto, and increasingly dangerous enemy groups such as the Black Moon Clan and the Death Busters.

But amidst the attacks and multiple deaths and reincarnations that take place throughout the series, one element remains constant: the steady, often tragic love between Serenity and Endymion. The prince is reincarnated in the modern day as Darien, a guy who starts off teasing Serena and ends up dating her, while his transformed form is Tuxedo Mask, the suave, sensitive, debonair defender of Sailor Moon and the Sailor Senshi. What makes their love tragic is that it hardly ever seems to last. In the past, Endymion died in the battle between kingdoms, prompting Serenity to commit suicide. In the present, Tuxedo Mask is cursed and Sailor Moon grabs an enchanted sword and stabs herself. Yet their love endures, no matter how many times they end up dying and coming back to life.

Serenity and Endymion's story echoes that of Western fairy tales, with a prince who is willing to protect his princess no matter what the cost, often arriving at precisely the right time to sweep her off her feet. This modern spin on the classic fairy-tale formula gave *Sailor Moon* an edge in the emerging manga market. While the series may have been overtaken in popularity by modern-day shōjo hits like *Fruits Basket* (see p.122), the fans who enjoyed *Sailor Moon* in its prime still remember the series fondly and have shared their affection with others, helping to expand the audience for manga.

Slam Dunk

Takehiko Inoue; *pub* Shueisha (Jp), Gutsoon! Entertainment (US, 5 vols, suspended), Viz (US), Madman/Chuang Yi (Aus); *ser* Shōnen Jump (1990–96); *vols* 31; *age* 13+

Manga has a strong influence on other forms of popular culture in Japan. Football, sumo wrestling, boxing and baseball are among the many sports that have been featured in manga over the years, and all have benefited from heightened awareness and a surge in those wanting to learn how to play after seeing their manga heroes pulling off dramatic feats.

Slam Dunk did exactly this for the game of basketball, attracting numerous teenage boys to the sport. The manga itself was so popular that in a poll conducted to celebrate the tenth anniversary of the Japan Media Arts Festival in 2006, it was voted the top manga series of all time. Its English-language translation, on the other hand, is unique in that a territory other than the US – namely, Australia – received a complete translation of all 31 volumes first. The first effort in the US to translate the series, in Gutsoon! Entertainment's *Raijin Comics* anthology in 2002, lasted five volumes and a few extra chapters before the company went out of business in 2004. Viz recently re-licensed the series for *Shonen Jump* and began releasing books in 2008.

Inoue's three-year stint on his high school's basketball club served as the inspiration for *Slam Dunk*. It wasn't just his knowledge of the sport that went into the manga, but also something of his own experience. The artist has admitted he isn't that good at playing, and that one of the reasons he joined was that he thought it would help him meet girls – the same reason his main character, Hanamichi Sakuragi, joined the school basketball club. And in this sports manga, the losing streak that builds up to a thrilling win against the odds is more to do with girls than basketball. Hanamichi has quite an impressive record, with fifty girls turning him down since junior high, partly thanks to his reputation as a delinquent punk.

He's hopeful that Haruko Akagi, his first female friend at Shohoku High School, might be different. Haruko's a huge basketball fan, so Hanamichi immediately takes up the game he'd previously hated, thanks to an earlier crush rejecting him for a basketball player. There's one other obstacle for Hanamichi to overcome before he can ask her out, one that runs through the series: the reason she likes basketball so much is because she has a crush on another player, Kaede Rukawa.

So once Hanamichi manages to get onto the basketball team – first by getting several lucky breaks to beat the team captain (Haruko's brother, Takenori) in a one-on-one pickup challenge, then

cleaning up the gym and locker room – a heated rivalry develops between the two. His early days on the court are also exercises in frustration and futility, as he lacks the basic skills necessary to even handle the ball and dribble it. Suffice it to say that it takes a while – and several instances of quitting in disgust – before he finally gets the hang of it. When he does, he becomes quite the natural.

What emerges from all of this is a ragtag bunch that has little chance of winning the national high school championship, with talented players like Kaede neutralized by players who either are inexperienced or who have off-court issues that keep them from doing their best on the court. Seeing them run around in the opening volumes as they struggle to put their individual problems aside to function as a team unit, you're left wondering how such a group valuing individual success over team priorities could possibly succeed. But this is sports manga. So of course this bunch of misfits will eventually bond, start winning games, gain more respect in the process, and eventually become a legitimate threat in the national championships. Watching them do so – and in the process embodying the shōnen principles of friendship, perseverance and victory – is a thrill and a delight, both for basketball fans and for fans of sports in general.

Takehiko Inoue

Manga artist, 1967–

Takehiko Inoue's manga career to date has by and large been defined by two distinct subjects: basketball and swordsmen. Considering one of Inoue's hobbies is playing basketball and his successful *Slam Dunk* (see p.182), *Buzzer Beater* and *Real* all come out of that, the sports-themed manga make sense. The swordsmen theme only emerged when he decided to take a break from basketball and his editor handed him a novel about famed swordsman Musashi Miyamoto as a means to relax. He had planned to stop drawing manga altogether, but a more serious series focusing on the human condition, the stellar swordsman study *Vagabond* (see p.188), resulted instead.

Inoue had a desire to draw since early childhood but felt coming out of high school that he wasn't skilled enough to go into the fine arts, so instead took up writing; but he carried on drawing and sent samples to the *Shōnen Jump* rookie artist contest. Around the same time he served as an assistant to Tsukasa Hojo, who was drawing the classic series *City Hunter*, and learned the basics of drawing manga.

This experience paid off when, in 1988, Inoue earned the Osamu Tezuka Prize for best new manga artist with his debut work, *Kaede Purple*. A short story about basketball, it was the foundation for what would become *Slam Dunk* and the award just the first of a number Inoue has earned over the years for his various titles. Inoue's next professional series work was on Kazuhiko Watanabe's *Chameleon Jail*, followed by his own wildly popular *Slam Dunk*, which ran until 1996.

The distinguishing qualities of Inoue's manga are his constantly evolving art style and an impeccable sense of timing. His artistic talent grows considerably during *Slam Dunk*, while in *Vagabond* the artist switched to a brush style midway through a story arc about Musashi's main rival, Kojiro, because he felt he couldn't express emotions properly with a simple pen-and-ink style. As for the timing, every one of his chapters ends on a cliffhanger and slowly builds to a climax.

The translated version of *Vagabond* has been a consistent hit among older readers; its characters even adorn the walls of the US flagship store of Japanese bookseller Kinokuniya in New York City in a mural the artist drew for the store in 2007.

Buzzer Beater

Self-published and translated into English at www.itplanning.co.jp/bbimages/body.img/BE0/FBEAT0.HTML; 80 installments

Inoue's follow-up to *Slam Dunk* was a short story also about basketball, but this time crossing into the science fiction genre. A millionaire recruits Earth's top players for an all-star team with the hope that they will win the Intergalactic League Championship and bring it back to the planet that created the game. The rest of the universe has bypassed Earth from a talent standpoint, though, and the humans will have to bring their "A" game – and so much more – if they hope to stand a chance. At one point ESPN, the US cable sports network, serialized the manga on its home page.

Real

pub Shueisha (Jp), Viz (US, UK); *ser* Young Jump (2001–); *vols* ongoing

Real is Inoue's third basketball-themed series, but very different, as its name suggests, taking on more serious themes in a tale inspired by the Paralympic Games. A team of wheelchair-bound athletes are brought together by fate and the love of the game; its members are a former sprinter who lost his leg to cancer, a former basketball team captain injured in a traffic accident, and a high school dropout with a sense of guilt over how his motorcycle accident left a female friend paralysed. The three find in their common interest of basketball a way to deal with a society that has marginalized them. *Real* won a Japan Media Arts Festival Excellence Prize in 2001.

To Terra

Keiko Takemiya; *pub* Asahi Sonorama (Jp), Vertical (US, UK); *ser* Manga Shōnen (1977–80); *vols* 3; *age* 13+

Keiko Takemiya released *To Terra* during a time when many anime, manga and movie creators were exploring elements of space travel and science fiction. But while most of her fellow creators were starting their stories on Earth and expanding outward into the unknown, unexplored reaches of space, Takemiya wanted a story that operated from a different perspective, placing Earth at the centre of her story and casting her characters as outsiders who longed to return to their former home. Her story further flowed from a dream she had about the concept of a "Maturity Check" and her desire to depict the terrors of covert attempts at "educating" an entire society through indoctrination and propaganda.

The Maturity Check is part of a coming-of-age ritual known as "The Awakening", which all fourteen-year-olds must go through in the grim Superior Domination (SD) era of the future, when the once-fertile Earth is running out of resources. In an attempt to preserve and manage what's left, mankind has chosen to leave the planet, creating a generation of caretakers who will later return to "Terra" – the former

Earth – and lead humanity into a new utopian age. That's the story that the computer system known as Universal Control has perpetuated, anyway.

Few within this system recognize these processes as being part of a totalitarian regime, of course. There is, however, one faction that has evolved and mutated beyond Universal Control: the Mu, a group that has developed extraordinary psychic and telepathic powers. They know how the computers are manipulating humanity and long for a day when they can break free of Universal Control's oppression and return to Terra on their own.

Takemiya's central character is Jomy Marcus Shim, a fourteen-year-old Mu boy with whom she identified in his struggle to carry out a revolution on his own. Jomy's telepathic powers, activated during his Maturity Check, are powers he doesn't understand himself. Guided by the Mu and their leader, Soldier Blue, Jomy learned the truth: on Ataraxia, the only world he has ever known, children are no longer born, but rather engineered by computers. They are kept strictly segregated from most adults, assigned to foster parents and monitored closely by Universal Control. On their designated

Awakening days, adolescents connect directly to Universal Control for a Maturity Check, during which they learn about the system governing them and receive job assignments in adult society. Those judged to be the purest achieve elite status and become candidates for a mission to return to Terra to re-establish the human presence there. But there are two side effects to the Awakening: the memories of their first fourteen years of life are purged completely, and while they are still able to love others, they are ordered to suppress this urge.

Takemiya could have taken this conflict between the Mu and Universal Control and turned it into a straightforward story of good versus evil, but she instead adds a layer of moral ambiguity. Though the Mu are supposed to be the freer of the two forces at conflict, they have a tendency to consider themselves the superior race, initially dismissing Jomy as being unworthy of leading them because he's "just another human". It's this prejudice that becomes a major theme within the series, infecting even those characters who emerge as "perfect" representatives of their respective races – for the Universal Control humans, Keith Anyan; for the Mu, Tony and other children born of Mu parents. Both of these factions' representatives take their battles to extremes that bring tragedy to all involved.

Throughout the manga, the panel layouts reiterate the plot – neatly ordered in times when a straightforward

© Keiko Takemiya and Vertical, Inc.

Jomy at first refuses to accept he's a Mu in Keiko Takemiya's dystopian tale of totalitarianism versus freedom in the bid to recolonize Earth.

narrative is called for, jagged and chaotic to depict confusing moments like when telepathic messages being broadcast conflict with Jomy's own thoughts. The storyline can be confusing, especially when it jumps around in time with little warning, but it moves inexorably toward its conclusion. The question Takemiya leaves you to consider is one of whether anyone is fit to inherit Terra, given the sins of the past that have carried over to the present.

Vagabond

Takehiko Inoue; *pub* Kodansha (Jp), Viz (US, UK), Madman (Aus); *ser* Morning (1998–); *vols* ongoing; *age* 16+

Revered feudal-era swordsman Musashi Miyamoto has been the subject of countless samurai movies and is known in Japan as the author of the classic martial arts strategy text, *The Book of Five Rings*. Yet for all that has been portrayed of Musashi's mature fighting skills as an enlightened, confident swordsman, not much is known about how he became the man he is remembered as today. In *Vagabond*, Takehiko Inoue takes on the challenge of portraying Musashi's evolution, going back to a time when Musashi was merely an impetuous young man named Takezo Shinmen.

The artist based *Vagabond* on Eiji Yoshikawa's *Musashi*, visualizing the characters as he read the novel and identifying the concepts he would use to flesh out his story. After working on *Slam Dunk* (see p.182) for six years, Inoue wanted to draw something with a more serious tone, a running commentary on the human condition and the continuing cycle of life and death. And so when we first meet Takezo, he's a seventeen-year-old boy left lying amongst the dead on the battlefield after the Battle of Sekigahara. The battle, which took place in 1600, saw the Tokugawa clan score a decisive victory over the Toyotomi clan, effectively becoming Japan's rulers for the next 250 years. Unfortunately for Takezo, he – along with another young man from his home village of Miyamoto, Matahachi Hon'iden – was recruited to fight for the Toyotomi side. Thus liberated from their former obligations, the two are now free to resume pursuit of the goal they had once set themselves: to leave their home and make a name for themselves.

How they go about achieving this task is where their paths diverge both physically and philosophically. Takezo believes pursuing the way of the sword, inflicting death and destruction upon those who stand in his way, is his sole calling in life. Matahachi aspires to be like Takezo but ultimately falls prey to the ways of the flesh, running away at the first sign of danger and preferring drinking and sex to honing his swordfighting discipline. The contrast between the two helps emphasize why it's Musashi and not Hon'iden remembered as the heroic figure today.

By telling the story of Musashi's youth, Inoue is freed to tell the story he wants to tell, rather than sticking with the idealized tradition. Musashi isn't automatically handed victories against his opponents because of who he is and what he means to Japanese history; instead, he must struggle to develop his skills, earning each and every victory in its own right. For instance, early in what is known as the "Kyoto" story arc, in chapters 22–32, Musashi encounters the Yoshioka school of swordfighting and, seeking a challenge, takes on the best fighters the school has to offer. He ends up battling brothers Denshichiro and Seijuro to a draw, mostly because a drunken Matahachi wanders back into the picture (unbeknownst to Musashi) and accidentally sets the dojo on fire. The conflict is not resolved until the "Yoshioka" story arc, more than 140 chapters later, during which time Musashi learns new techniques at other martial arts schools.

The other characters develop as well during this time: Otsu, once betrothed to Matahachi but abandoned for another woman, searches for Musashi so she can seek comfort from her childhood friend. Matahachi deals with the shame of not only running away with a prostitute, but also burning down the Yoshioka dojo. And Granny Hon'iden continues her quest for vengeance against Musashi, believing he let her grandson die on the battlefield, unaware that Matahachi actually survived and ran away. One story arc even removes the spotlight from Musashi completely, focusing instead on developing the back story behind his arch-rival, Kojiro Sasaki.

As a manga series focusing on a swordsman's journey, comparisons are inevitable between this and two other series in our canon, *Blade of the Immortal* (see p.94) and *Lone Wolf and Cub* (see p.147). *Vagabond* falls somewhere between the two, offering the epic scope and cinematic deliberateness seen in *Lone Wolf and Cub* combined with the focus on multiple characters and shifting points of view of *Blade of the Immortal*. There is some irony in what Inoue does with his series – by dealing with the pre-enlightened Musashi, he captures the essence of the enlightened form.

5

Beyond Manga

anime, live action, videogames

With manga, as with any popular intellectual property, an increase in demand results in pressure for more products. Unfortunately the guiding hand of the creator sometimes gets lost in the shuffle. But whether the end result is a brilliant extension of the original conceit or leaves fans disappointingly unfulfilled, manga remains a deep well of content that anime and live-action film producers return to time and time again. It's a chicken-and-egg scenario in many cases, with manga inspiring anime inspiring more manga, and since the 1980s videogames have joined in the mix too.

Much of the manga covered in this guide has made it to the screen in animated form – for more in-depth coverage, check out the companion *Rough Guide to Anime*. This chapter takes a look at manga's influence on the visual and digital arts and highlights some transformative examples along the way.

Manga to anime: page to screen

Ever since *Astro Boy* first flew across the TV screens of Japanese households in 1963, fulfilling Osamu Tezuka's dream of producing Japanese animation (which would come to be known the world over as anime), there has existed a certain synergy between anime and manga. Whenever a manga series breaks out and begins to captivate a larger audience, the chances of it becoming adapted into an anime series grow. In fact, about sixty percent of anime adaptations can trace their origins directly to a successful manga series. Often the anime series becomes so popular that the manga is overshadowed, as is the case with the now classic anime *Neon Genesis Evangelion* (see p.197).

In Western markets, the trend is reversed to an extent, with most readers first exposed to the corresponding anime series on TV. The manga series *Dragon Ball*, *Sailor Moon*, *Naruto*, *Bleach*, *Death Note*, *Fullmetal Alchemist* and *Inuyasha* all entered widespread public consciousness in this way, and it's no secret that manga series are marketed alongside the anime whenever possible. *Love Hina* (see p.150) has been one of the more pervasive manga series in recent years to have expanded onto multiple fronts, including the requisite TV series (not to mention the additional merchandise

– soundtracks, action figures, art books, key rings, posters and assorted knick-knacks).

Feature-length anime are naturally riskier projects for the companies involved. Creator-led movies like Katsuhiro Ôtomo's *Akira* or Hayao Miyazaki's *Nausicaä of the Valley of the Wind* (see pp.78 and 162), however, garnered critical acclaim around the world and drew many Western fans to manga for the first time.

Manga on TV

The most common manga-to-anime transformation is the **TV series**. Most manga adapted into anime series follow the formula of 13-, 26- or 52-episode seasons (based on the allotted schedule on a given network). Some of the more popular anime series air for several seasons and the rare mega-success can stretch into hundreds of episodes (see *Crayon Shin-chan* on p.195). Individual episodes clock in at about 25 minutes, though shorter episodes have gained popularity in the past few years. **OVAs** (or OAVs) – Original Video Animations – are direct-to-video episodes that are produced as an addendum to anime series, or as special one-offs.

Considering manga are often produced by individual artists, whereas anime series are the work of multiple production teams – who may outsource some of the animation, too – it's not surprising that the manga and related anime series often run to different production schedules.

Mangaka and anime adaptations

Most manga creators are thrilled when their series are adapted into anime. Wataru Yoshizumi and Miho Obana, the authors of *Marmalade Boy* and *Kodomo No Omocha* (otherwise known as *Kodocha*) respectively, both gushed in their manga commentaries about meeting the actors cast to voice their characters, and even about creating new characters specifically for the anime. However, there have been incidents where a mangaka was not particularly happy with the creative licence taken by the anime production team. Masami Tsuda's dispute with director Hideaki Anno over the direction of *Kare Kano* was one such example (see p.196). Rintaro, the director of the animated adaptation of Osamu Tezuka's *Metropolis*, had to wait until the author died before he could push ahead with his production. Tezuka had no intention of animating the story, believing that his work before *Astro Boy* generally lacked the quality needed to turn it into animation. Rintaro, who had worked on Tezuka's *Kimba the White Lion* and *Astro Boy*, was determined to produce the film – which was ultimately met with global critical acclaim.

When the anime series begins to outpace the source material, there are two ways of dealing with the problem, both of which send shivers of horror up fans' spines: the "recap" episode and the "filler" episode. **Recap** episodes are just as the name implies: characters pause to reflect on their recent adventures, complete with copious amounts of recycled footage from previous episodes. **Filler** episodes, on the other hand, are single episodes – or in some cases, weeks-long story arcs – with stories that never appeared in the manga, created by the anime production team. These episodes can flesh out existing characters or introduce new characters, leaving the door open in case another filler arc needs to be produced in future.

The most notorious series for using extended filler arcs are probably the most popular of the *Shōnen Jump* serializations – *Naruto*, *Bleach*, *One Piece* and *Dragon Ball* – although other multiple-season series, including *Fullmetal Alchemist*, *Crayon Shin-chan* and *Ranma ½*, are guilty of filler arcs from time to time. In the case of *Dragon Ball*, however, the filler arcs became a running joke among series fans – with the fights featured in the manga already over the top, the anime simply extended them to ridiculous lengths. Multiple episodes would cover a single battle, or even one particular fighting technique. *Naruto*'s filler arcs lasted so long that fans started drifting away from the series en masse. It took a major reboot in the manga

© Simon Richmond

KYOTO
手塚治虫ワールド

©Tezuka Productions

A sign for Osamu Tezuka World in Kyoto, Japan, sporting the artist's most famous anime and manga characters.

(known as the Shippuden story arc), where the characters aged and matured several years, for the anime to reset itself to the new manga storylines – and get back on track.

In other instances, manga series continue well beyond their anime counterparts. Whether it is a case of money running out, a dip in the popularity of a show, the creator putting a cap on anything other than the manga, or whether the differences in the manga and anime were just too great for the liking of the fans – unfinished sagas continue, diverge or get revamped in some form or another. In the case of the vampire saga *Hellsing*, the animated TV series was not up to snuff for some fans and was revamped in the *Hellsing Ultimate* OVAs, which hewed closely to the storyline laid out in the manga. Some ongoing manga series, like the dark fantasy *Berserk* (see below), are known in fan circles for their lost potential: the anime series ended at a key moment, but rumours of more episodes could revive the cycle of creation/reinvention once again.

Manga on TV: some highlights

Berserk

Kentaro Miura; *pub* Hakusensha (Jp), Dark Horse (US); *ser* Young Animal; *vols* ongoing; *age* 18+

When the main character (named "Guts", no less) is introduced as a baby born from a corpse hanging from a tree, you know this series won't be heavy on the hearts and flowers. And indeed, the battle-scarred warrior with a massive sword, together with a story of ambition, loyalty and betrayal, makes for a brutally violent – and incredibly enjoyable – dark fantasy epic.

Ripe for adaptation, the anime series glossed over much of the over-the-top violence and downplayed the manga's supernatural elements. *Berserk* would go on to gain an international cult following, spawn a videogame, action figures and other merchandise – and yet the series came to a sudden halt. Whether it was lack of funding, lack of viewers, or whether the manga simply wasn't being produced fast enough, the end result is one of the most painful cliffhangers in recent anime history. The series stops at a climactic moment when the hero has suffered a great loss as his brothers-in-arms have been decimated, the woman he loves is about to be raped by his leader and best friend, who has been driven mad by demonic influences and his own lust for power. To continue the saga, fans need to turn back to the manga, which is still being produced today.

Crayon Shin-chan

Yoshito Usui; *pub* Futabasha (Jp), CMX (US); *ser* Weekly Manga Action; *vols* ongoing; *age* 18+

Shinnosuke Nohara, also known as "Shin", is a rather precocious five-year-old boy who hits on women, pulls his pants down to do "butt cheek" and "Mr Elephant" dances, and otherwise makes the lives of his teachers, parents, friends and even his dog a living hell – in short, a Japanese Bart Simpson. Shin-chan manages to inject himself into any situation and wreaks havoc in a way that only an innocent-looking kinder-gartener can.

Shin-chan has been a part of Japanese manga readers' lives for close to two decades now, but the history of the English-language adaptations has been far less consistent. Much of the difficulty in translating such a series rests in how much the series' humour relies on Japanese cultural references and puns, as well as more easily translated toilet humour. ComicsONE solved the problem by localizing cultural references wherever possible. When the licence transferred to DrMaster, nothing was done with the series and the rights lapsed.

The anime, which began in Japan in 1992 and continues to air new episodes to this day, has an even more muddled translation history. The first version was broadcast in the original Japanese with English subtitles on KIKU, a UHF station serving Hawaii, from 1993 to 2001. An English-dubbed version, with some edits for content, aired in the UK and Ireland in the early 2000s. Then, there's the English-dubbed version produced by FUNimation, shown as part of the Adult Swim line-up on the US Cartoon Network in 2007. The original Japanese script was largely tossed out, the resulting series rife with raunchy cultural references – a sort of *Family Guy* for the anime set. Ironically, it was on the coat-tails of this version that the CMX manga was released. Aside from nods to FUNimation's renaming of the cast, CMX's translation is arguably even more conservative and closer to the source material than ComicsONE's (although no real context for the Japanese cultural references is provided). The result is that the anime and manga, at least in the English-speaking market, are quite separate experiences, and serve to demonstrate how various markets treat the same material in diverse ways.

Excel Saga

Koshi Rikdo; *pub* Shōnen Gahosha (Jp), Viz (US); *ser* Young King OURs; *vols* ongoing; *age* 13+

A battle is brewing over control of the city of Fukuoka. On one side is the underground organization ACROSS, led by Lord Ilpalazzo, who sends two agents, Excel and Hyatt, to take over. Unfortunately Excel is a hyperactive young woman who tries too hard to impress Ilpalazzo, while her anaemic partner Hyatt has a disturbing tendency to die repeatedly. Defending Fukuoka is the Department of City Security, led by the fabulously mustachioed Kabapu and backed up by a quartet of civil service workers – Watanabe, Sumiyoshi, Iwata and the token female, Matsuya – and a pair of androids named Ropponmatsu.

Whereas the manga is a straightforward parody of life and culture in Japan, the anime pushed the levels of wackiness almost to the point of incomprehensibility, though this merely extended its appeal to hardcore fans. Otaku in-jokes referenced geek culture – from the movie *Aliens*, to anime like *Gundam* and *Sailor Moon*.

The anime also added several characters not in the manga, including The Great Will of the Macrocosm, a small, swirling galaxy-like circle with arms that resurrects key characters who get killed; and Nabeshin, a cool hero type in a giant Afro and flashy suit whose resemblance to real-life series director Shinichi Watanabe is purely intentional. Rikdo loved the series concept so much that he approved a running gag where he would add a stamp of approval to whatever the characters would be doing in each particular episode. (As thanks, he gets killed in the show several times.)

Widening the gap between the relatively tame manga and the anime is the notorious episode 26, aptly titled "Going Too Far". With nudity, lesbianism, bondage, paedophilia and a spot of ultraviolence, the show never made it to air in Japan, but was included on local and international DVD releases.

Kare Kano (His and Her Circumstances)

Masami Tsuda; *pub* Hakusensha (Jp), Tokyopop (UK, US); *ser* LaLa Magazine; *vols* 21; *age* 13+

Yukino Miyazawa is used to being the object of everyone's affection: taking care to present herself as utterly perfect, she has reigned as the top student in her class for years. She's also expert at playing the ingénue in front of her friends, while being spoiled and bratty otherwise. When Sōichiro Arima transfers into her class and usurps her crown, she's initially quite upset. Sōichiro discovers her imperfections, and despite her initial resistance, the two soon find themselves falling for each other.

This slice-of-life, teen love story would seem to be the perfect candidate for a straightforward shōjo-flavour-of-the-month adaptation, but the truth turned out to be much more complex. The manga-to-anime adaptation was the first such project to be taken on by anime studio Gainax and director Hideaki Anno after their controversial hit series *Neon Genesis Evangelion* and its two film sequels. Anno played up the romantic comedy aspect of Tsuda's story and threw in quick cuts animated in different styles to accentuate the different moods – a direction that Tsuda reportedly disapproved of, because she wanted to see the emphasis more on the straight teen romance.

The dispute grew significant enough that Anno ended up leaving the production partway through the series, with Kazuya Tsurumaki taking over directing duties for the remaining ten episodes. The anime series (in typical Gainax style) grew increasingly surreal and "artsy" towards the final episodes. Though the inventive and stylistic use of onscreen text and overall lofty treatment of typical teen fare was to be commended, the end of the series left much unresolved and many scratching their heads at what the symbolism and overwrought emotion (or lack thereof) was really meant to signify.

Neon Genesis Evangelion

Yoshiyuki Sadamoto; *pub* Kadokawa Shoten (Jp), Viz (US, UK), Madman (Aus); *ser* Shōnen Ace; *vols* ongoing; *age* 13+

Neon Genesis Evangelion: Angelic Days

Gainax (story), Fumino Hayashi (art); *pub* Kadokawa Shoten (Jp), ADV Manga (US); *ser* Asuka; *vols* 6; *age* 13+

Arguably the greatest anime series ever created, *Neon Genesis Evangelion* features a trio of seemingly normal teenagers with some deep-rooted psychological issues lurking beneath – Shinji, Rei and Asuka. These kids, recruited by NERV (staffed by adults who are easily as screwed up as they are), are placed in biomechanical suits known as EVAs and sent to battle "Angels" – odd alien creatures that seem bent on triggering an apocalyptic event known as the Third Impact (the first two, of course, destroyed Tokyo).

Fans also know that the ending of the series – equal parts surreal, unnerving and indecipherable – took someone with doctorates in psychology, mythology, theology and astrophysics to even attempt to analyse. A pair of follow-up movies released theatrically did little to clear up the confusion but added a whole new level of violence and sex to the official canon. As a review in the first issue of *Newtype USA* magazine succinctly put it, "Asuka goes crazy, Rei gets big, everyone dies." It would appear a new "Rebirth of Evangelion" series of four movies, beginning with *Evangelion 1.0: You Are (Not) Alone*, will be tweaking the franchise canon once again.

Few fans, however, realize that the manga version of the *Evangelion* story predates the anime: it was first serialized in *Shōnen Ace* in December 1994, supposedly to serve as a promotional tool for the anime series

beginning in October 1995. Why hardly anyone realizes this is because the manga's release cycle has been akin to slow torture. At the time of writing, a total of eleven volumes' worth of material had been released over the past fourteen years.

Fortunately for the publisher, *Evangelion* has turned into a self-sufficient, multi-billion yen franchise with a patient readership. Besides, any item with the image of female characters Asuka and Rei is guaranteed to sell. Sadamoto, the mangaka and anime's character designer, has tweaked his designs further for the print version, also taking the opportunity to alter their personalities and motivations. Rei, for instance, is a quiet, enigmatic character in the anime, while she's more talkative and "human" in the manga, and Asuka's verbal abuse and overall sass toward Shinji is toned down.

Another iteration in manga form exists, with a trail back to the source material that is nearly as complex as *Evangelion*'s "Instrumentality Project" itself. Not only was *Neon Genesis Evangelion: Angelic Days* produced post-original manga and anime, it was also partially based on an *Evangelion* videogame, *Girlfriend of Steel 2*. In this story, there's less blood and more romantic comedy, and the absence of Sadamoto/Anno is telling – Fumino Hayashi provided the art while the studio provided the story in an almost NERV-lite capacity.

Anime to manga: screen to page

It's inevitable that anything that stirs fans into a tizzy will get a second go-round in some form or another. Usually it's manga turned into anime, but just occasionally

.hack//Legend of the Twilight follows main characters Shugo and Rena as they explore "The World", the MMORPG at the centre of Project .hack (see p.205).

a successful anime series is adapted into manga form – though rarely for artistic reasons. More likely the franchise is in desperate need of extension and the resulting manga tends to be unspectacular at best. Given a property's popularity, it's a sure bet that any manga will be followed by a slew of merchandise.

In the case of the *Cowboy Bebop* anime, a slow-burner that reached intense heights of popularity in Japan and the US (where it was the first series to debut on Cartoon Network's Adult Swim), the finality of the denouement made any further episodes unlikely. A movie was produced in 2003 – set between episodes 22 and 23 of the 26-episode series – and two short manga series retelling the stories in the series were produced after the show was done (see opposite).

The "retelling and side stories" model of anime-to-manga also applies to popular series like the fantasy epic *Escaflowne* (see p.200), and the prolific sci-fi romantic comedy *Tenchi Muyo!* (see p.201), which expanded into its own universe of media and merchandise. Slightly different in origin is *The Melancholy of Haruhi Suzumiya* (see p.200), which began as a series of Japanese light (young adult) novels, became an anime smash and an Internet sensation (with over two thousand Haruhi-themed YouTube clips), making way for videogames and dramatizations on CD. Different manga iterations are currently being produced.

Another route still is that of *Di Gi Charat* (see opposite), basically a cute concept promotional image that erupted into a flurry of anime, manga, videogames and merchandise (all at the same time), becoming the mascot of the otaku-haven Gamers stores in Japan.

Anime to manga: some highlights

Cowboy Bebop: Shooting Star

Hajime Yatate (story), Cain Kuga (art); *pub* Kadokawa Shoten (Jp), Tokyopop (US); *ser* Asuka Fantasy DX; *vols* 2; *age* 13+

Cowboy Bebop: A New Story

Hajime Yatate (story), Yutaka Nanten (art); *pub* Kadokawa Shoten (Jp), Tokyopop (US); *ser* Asuka Fantasy DX; *vols* 3; *age* 13+

Spike, Jet, Faye, Ed and Ein – the crew of the *Bebop*, a bunch of bounty hunters looking for a big payday and their next meal, each with a tragic backstory that belies their happy-go-lucky travels. Stacked with kung fu, space cowboy action, and sex appeal, *Cowboy Bebop* was a stylish breakthrough anime directed by Shinichiro Watanabe, with Studio Sunrise's vibrant animation and art design.

Another crucial element in the series' coolness was Yoko Kanno's music – so much so, in fact, that the retelling in these manga short stories struggles for life. Fans have been clamouring for a prequel for years, and whether this happens in manga or anime form is yet to be seen. The one spark on the horizon is the 2009 announcement of a US produced live-action film (with Keanu Reeves set to star as Spike).

Di Gi Charat

Koge-Donbo; *pub* Broccoli Books (Jp, US) also Viz and Studio Ironcat (US); *ser* Degenki Daioh; *vols* ongoing

Di Gi Charat Theater: Dejiko's Summer Vacation

various; *pub* Broccoli Books (Jp, US); *ser* From Gamers; *vols* 1

Di Gi Charat: Piyoko is Number One!

various; *pub* Broccoli Books (Jp, US); *ser* From Gamers; *vols* 1

Cute, cute and more cute. Di Gi Charat (aka Dejiko) is an adorable catgirl who engages in surreal adventures with her sidekick, floating blob Gema, her best friend Puchiko, and her rival bunnygirl Rabi-en-Rose. As a meta-marketing tool, the *Di Gi Charat* series is unparalleled: not only are the characters official Gamers store mascots, their early adventures are actually set within stores.

There have been subsequent movies, OVAs, anime, trading card games, videogames, and cosplayers donning bells and ears en masse. Six different incarnations of the manga series exist in English; two were never completed due to Broccoli Books going out of business, while a third released by Studio Ironcat features a forgettable English translation. The manga, like all iterations of the property, does not rely heavily on an intricate storyline, but luxuriates in the juxtaposition of adorable and weird to spin its sugary magic.

The Vision of Escaflowne

Katsu Aki; *pub* Kadokawa Shoten (Jp), Tokyopop (US, UK), Madman (Aus); *ser* Shōnen Ace; *vols* 8; *age* 13+

Messiah Knight (aka Hitomi) – The Vision of Escaflowne

Yuzuru Yashiro; *pub* Kadokawa Shoten (Jp); *ser* Monthly Asuka Fantasy DX; *vols* 2

Escaflowne – Energist's Memories

various; *pub* Kadokawa Shoten (Jp); *ser* Monthly Asuka Fantasy DX; *vols* 1

What teenage girl doesn't dream of being whisked away from high school and into a magical land? Hitomi finds herself on the planet Gaea where the Zaibach empire is threatening to take over. With the tortured Van and the pretty-boy Allen at her side, Hitomi discovers that her own newly discovered psychic powers are the secret to awakening the giant mech, Escaflowne.

The anime series suffered a delay in production, reduced episode counts, and a split personality, mixing the traditionally shōnen action genre with the traditionally shōjo romantic genre. This mix also carried over to two very different manga adaptations. The more shōnen *The Vision of Escaflowne* was developed before the shōjo elements were added to the anime and resulted in a markedly different feel and a much more curvaceous heroine than was ultimately put on screen. Later, two shōjo series, *Messiah Knight (aka Hitomi) – The Vision of Escaflowne* and a collection of mini-stories titled *Escaflowne – Energist's Memories*, were followed by a movie, a series of light novels, and drama CDs. The one uniting factor – each adaptation varied wildly from the original anime series.

Haruhi Suzumiya

Mizuno Makoto; *pub* Kadokawa Shoten (Jp); *ser* Shōnen Ace; *vols* 1

The Melancholy of Haruhi Suzumiya

Gaku Tsugano; *pub* Kadokawa Shoten (Jp), Yen Press (US); *ser* Shōnen Ace; *vols* ongoing; *age* 13+

The Melancholy of Haruhi Suzumiya-chan

Puyo; *pub* Kadokawa Shoten (Jp), Yen Press (US); *ser* Shōnen Ace, The Sneaker; *vols* ongoing; *age* 13+

Haruhi Suzumiya is oddly obsessed with the supernatural and forms the "SOS Brigade" to investigate mysterious happenings in and around her high school. She drafts in classmate Kyon, who sticks around to protect the helpless victims of Haruhi's accusations, and recruits three more members who are, unbeknownst to her, the embodiment of the weird and supernatual. Artificial human Yuki, time-travelling Mikuru and Itsuki, who has ESP, are in fact secret agents sent to keep watch over Haruhi, who just happens to be able to shape the universe to her liking. The members of the club do their best to keep her occupied and preserve life as we know it.

Needless to say, the cute girls and the intriguing storyline caused the anime series to become a global smash. Based on a series of bestselling light novels, the anime took the conceits to some ridiculous highs and was extremely well received, spawning all the usual merchandise. The manga adaptations, on the other hand, did not fare as well. The first attempt, diverging significantly from the original source, was cancelled after only one volume; the second series continues today and seems aimed at a younger age group, but doesn't manage to capture the wacky spirit of the anime. A third series, *The Melancholy of Haruhi Suzumiya-chan*, takes a different approach with a series of four-panel comic strips that parody the series.

No Need for Tenchi!

Hitoshi Okuda; *pub* Kadokawa Shoten (Jp), Viz (US), Madman (Aus); *ser* Comic Dragon Jr; *vols* 12; *age* 13+

The All-New Tenchi Muyo!

Hitoshi Okuda; *pub* Kadokawa Shoten (Jp), Viz (US); *ser* Comic Dragon AGE; *vols* 10; *age* 13+

The one that started the "harem" genre of anime, the *Tenchi Muyo* series, movies, OVAs and various spin-offs have been around since 1992 and continue to be produced today. Tracking the different versions – not to mention the debate on what's canon and what isn't – would require an extensive flow chart. All you really need to know is that Tenchi Masaki, a seemingly normal Japanese teenager, finds himself surrounded by a load of women from space who eventually all manage to fall in love with him. Throw in aliens, demons, *Star Wars*-esque weapons, transforming cat-rabbits, magical girls, the space-time continuum, a mysterious royal bloodline – and you've got a modern classic.

The debate over whether Tenchi is truly meant to be with space pirate Ryoko, or any one of the other women vying for his affections, has gone on for over fifteen years. What hasn't been hotly contested is the fact that the manga is absolutely non-canon. Though based on the first two OVA series, the new storylines and other elements (including a Ryoko clone), do not carry over into the anime series.

Manga into live action

Manga normally reach the screen via animated adaptations, but there are some select works where flesh and blood actors have brought the monochrome tales to life. A wide variety of manga has made it into live-action movies and TV series – shōnen as well as shōjo titles – with varying levels of success. There are far more titles made in Japan and other Asian companies than ever reach English-speaking audiences, however.

That might change, though, with a batch of high-profile titles under development in Hollywood. Whether or not these films ever make it has yet to be seen – it's not the first flurry of interest from US studios, after all. But with 2009's *Dragonball Evolution* film, the recent *Transformers* franchise and the revival of *Street Fighter* on celluloid, anime and manga properties do seem to be following the trend of American comic-book heroes' path to the cinema screen.

In particular, Leonardo DiCaprio is set to produce live-action *Akira* and *Ninja Scroll* films, Steven Spielberg is attached to a live-action *Ghost in the Shell*, and *Cowboy Bebop* looks set to blast off with Keanu Reeves as the lead. Infamously, *Neon Genesis Evangelion* was announced in 2003 with a global production team and concept art by Weta Workshop (famous for *The Lord of the Rings* and

King Kong). At the time of writing, development of this proposed trilogy was still moving forward, keeping fans on tenterhooks.

Hollywood dreams are all well and good, but on a smaller scale, several Japanese live-action adaptations have come to pass. Scoring a number-one box-office smash was the *Boys Over Flowers* (see opposite) live-action film. Other titles to have reached the big screen, albeit with limited releases in the West, have been a trilogy of *Death Note* movies, also released on DVD.

Smaller-screen live adaptations can sometimes work better, as was the case with Rumiko Takahashi's *Maison Ikkoku* (see p.156), which spawned nearly one hundred anime episodes beginning in 1986, although a live-action movie the same year was abysmal: badly acted, poorly scripted and edited, and deviating significantly from both the manga and anime. More than twenty years later, TV Asahi produced a couple of feature-length TV dramas, cleverly set in the present with flashbacks to the 1980s, that have been far better received.

Nana (see p.72) is another manga to have a successful anime series, plus (not surprising considering the rock music theme) soundtracks and tribute albums. The 2005 live-action film and accompanying soundtrack led to a pan-Asian *Nana* craze, grossing more than ¥4 billion in Japan; the sequel, however, wasn't up to scratch.

The rest of Asia shouldn't be overlooked either: Hong Kong and South Korea have both worked on adaptations of *City Hunter*. Meanwhile, Japan, Taiwan and South Korea have all produced extremely successful, separate TV dramas of *Boys Over Flowers*.

Live-action manga: some highlights

Battle Angel Alita

Yukito Kishiro; *pub* Shueisha (Jp), Viz (US); *ser* Business Jump; *vols* 9; *age* 13+

Battle Angel Alita: Last Order

Yukito Kishiro; *pub* Shueisha (Jp), Viz (US); *ser* Ultra Jump; *vols* ongoing; *age* 13+

It's amazing what can be found in the trash sometimes. Daisuke Ido, searching for useful scrap that he can use in his job as a cybermedic, discovers the intact head and upper torso of a female cyborg placed in suspended animation. After fixing her up, he gives her the name Alita ("Gally" in the original Japanese), in honour of his recently deceased cat. The problem with Alita is that she seems to have lost her memory, save for her innate knowledge of a Martian martial art, which comes in handy in the rough-and-tumble environment of the Scrapyard.

The final hundred pages of *Battle Angel Alita* were a rushed mess that Kishiro put down to his being burned out and forced to cut the series short in 1995. A five-year hiatus and a move to a different magazine set things right again, essentially wiping those hundred pages from the series canon and recontinuing from there.

In any event, the story was captivating enough to convince James Cameron – of the *Terminator* and *Titanic* movies – to purchase the option to make a live-action film out of the first three volumes, but the project has never made it past the planning stages.

Boys Over Flowers (Hana Yori Dango)

Yoko Kamio; *pub* Shueisha (Jp), Viz (US); *ser* Asuka Fantasy DX; *vols* 36; *age* 13+

Makino Tsukushi is the daughter of a working-class family who's managed somehow to get into Eitoku Academy, a school mostly attended by society's elite. Accordingly, Makino's treated rather rudely by most of her classmates. She takes all of this in her stride and even thrives on it, an attitude that catches the attention of two members of "Flower 4" or "F4", a group of the school's most eligible, wealthiest hotties: the quiet violinist Rui Hamazawa and the temperamental Tsukasa Domyoji.

How these relationships play out amid the backdrop of social differences drives the story forward and has accounted for much of its popularity, not only in manga form but also in subsequent anime and live-action TV dramas. Some fans of its separate series in Taiwan, Japan and Korea aren't even aware of its manga roots, enjoying the attractive casts' work on its own merit.

City Hunter

Tsukasa Hojo; *pub* Shueisha (Jp), Gutsoon! (US); *ser* Weekly Shōnen Jump; *vols* 35; *age* 13+

In this popular shōnen manga Ryō Saeba is one of the most efficient "sweepers" in Tokyo's Shinjuku district, a gun-for-hire working to rid the city of its criminal elements. All anyone needs to do to employ his services is write a message on a chalkboard in Shinjuku Station and he'll take the case – especially ones involving beautiful female clients. It's a pity his pickup skills – which often involve the term "mokkori" (a Japanese "sound" word that indicates an object rising quickly) – aren't as finely honed as his crime-fighting skills, which include a sixth sense for danger and keen marksmanship. That's probably why he needs Kaori Makimura, the adopted sister of his dead partner and friend, to keep him in line.

The manga spawned four anime series, two OVAs, three specials, one animated film, and a live-action film starring the legendary Jackie Chan. Controversy surrounded the 1993 film when Chan publicly denounced it (though it was a success in Hong Kong) and called out director Jing Wong in the press. Wong in turn took a shot at Chan in his subsequent film.

In 1991, the Hong Kong film *Saviour of the Soul* took elements from *City Hunter* by including characters from the manga, but little of the plot points. *Mr Mumble* in 1996 did the opposite – sticking close to *City Hunter*'s original conceit, but changing the characters' names. Recently announced was a co-production between Fox Television and South Korean SSD to produce a new live-action adaptation.

Videogames and manga

The issues of source material, intellectual property and marketing savvy come full circle in the case of videogames. Successful manga/anime series all hope to expand into more profit-generating areas, whether it's videogames, trading cards or other merchandise. With videogames, it's not simply a case of sticking a favourite character on a key ring: there's a lot more at stake in terms of time and cost, and so manga (and anime) creators often play a major role in the games industry. For example, *Dragon Ball* creator Akira Toriyama designed the characters for *Dragon Quest* – one of the most successful RPG videogame

franchises; and Yasuhiro Nightow, creator of *Trigun*, designed characters, while *Oh My Goddess!*'s Kōsuke Fujishima provided mechanical designs, for the videogame *Gungrave* (a mediocre third-person shooter, but a critically acclaimed anime series).

Manga, anime, games – any one can be the starting point. Take *Pokémon*, the game which launched a worldwide craze that expanded into manga, anime and beyond, earning Nintendo a fortune in the process (see p.47). More complex videogames with finely crafted storylines and dynamic character designs are essentially manga/anime made interactive. The journey that players invest in and the cut scenes that flesh out the stories often leave them wanting more – hungry for anything that can expand on this established universe or embellish what is already revealed (exponentially so in the *Higurashi* series – see p.206). Manga and anime can certainly inspire videogames but the reverse holds true as well.

After decades of experience, production companies are much wiser about how they approach the consumer. Whether they launch on multimedia fronts (see *.hack*, below), combine already successful properties in innovative ways (see *Kingdom Hearts*, p.206) or follow up a concept with something a little different (see *Yu-Gi-Oh!*, p.207), there is a definite design to the madness.

Character art for Laharl in PS2 game *Disgaea: The Hour of Darkness* (developed by Nippon Ichi, published by Koei and Atlus USA, 2004)

Videogames and manga: some highlights

.hack//Legend of the Twilight

Tatsuya Hamazaki (story), Rei Izumi (art); *pub* Kadokawa Shoten (Jp), Tokyopop (US, UK); *ser* Comptiq; *vols* 3; *age* 13+

Project .hack (pronounced "dot hack") is a microcosm of multimedia launched by producers CyberConnect2 and Bandai in 2002. *Project .hack* invaded multiple fronts including videogames, card games, anime, novels, manga, and tons of merchandise. This assault across geek culture was a meta-contextual web gone wild, spearheaded by icons like Koichi Mashimo (famed anime director of *The Irresponsible Captain Tylor*, *Sorcerer Hunters*, *Noir* and *Tsubasa Chronicles*) and Yoshiyuki Sadamoto (character designs – best known for his work on *Neon Genesis Evangelion*).

With the PlayStation2 game *.hack//Infection* (the first of four) and the anime series *.hack// Sign*, the world was introduced to "The World" – a fictional massively multiplayer online roleplaying game (MMORPG). Players interact with "The World" using virtual reality headsets and game controllers. Most characters in the *.hack* franchise are known only by their virtual avatars (game characters) that exist within "The World", but the storylines also include their "real world" players as characters. (Confused yet?)

Brain-meltingly complex, the *.hack* world (including the "sequel" to *Project .hack*, called *.hack Conglomerate*) has spun off at least seven manga series and specials, including what is considered the most canonical and tied to the main storyline of *Project .hack* – *.hack//Legend of the Twilight* –

which follows the player characters Shugo and Rena as they delve deeper into the mysteries (and chibi cuteness) of "The World".

Other manga series and titles include *.hack//XXXX* – which adapts the storyline laid out in the four original *.hack* videogames; *.hack//4 Koma* – a four-panel parody comic; and *.hack//Link*, which takes place after the end of *.hack//G.U.* (a further series of three videogames) in a new version of "The World".

Disgaea

Arashi Shindo; *pub* Ichijinsha (Jp), Broccoli Books (US); *ser* Comic Zero-Sum; *vols* 1; *age* 13+

Character art for Flonne in *Disgaea: The Hour of Darkness* (developed by Nippon Ichi, published by Koei and Atlus USA, 2004)

Disgaea 2: Cursed Memories

Hekaton; *pub* ASCII Media Works (Japan), Broccoli Books (US); *ser* Dengeki Maoh; *vols* Jp ongoing, US 2 (cancelled); *age* 13+

Laharl is Prince of the Netherworld. When he awakens from a two-year seed-sleep he finds his father dead, and the throne empty. With the help of his father's servant Etna (a demon-girl) and Flonne, a hare-brained angel (and possibly, trained assassin), Laharl plans to become the new Overlord.

One look at the successful *Disgaea* series of tactical roleplaying games and you can instantly spot its anime- and manga-worthiness. The adorably impish character designs and rollicking storyline made this an easy spin-off. The anime, though well received, deviated dramatically in many instances from the storyline of the game. The manga was guilty of much of the same – random jokes and gags, personality changes, and a softer character design style – but it maintains the sugar-and-spice of the original game concept.

Higurashi: When They Cry

"Ryukishi07" (story), various (art); *pub* Square Enix/Kadokawa Shoten (Jp), Yen Press (US, UK); *ser* Gangan Powered and others; *vols* ongoing; *age* 13+

Produced by a collective known as 07th Expansion, *Higurashi* began as a "sound novel" game – an interactive fiction using static images and text, with the emphasis on music and sound effects. The series focuses on a group of young friends and a murder mystery taking place over the past four years in their otherwise sleepy village.

The series of games were separated into four "question" and four "answer" arcs – *Rashomon*-like, the corresponding arcs would reveal a different perspective on the events of the overarching story. The popularity of the games led to a manga series that adapted and expanded on the four arcs. Eight different manga artists worked separately on the stories by "Ryukishi07", the pen name for a member of 07th Expansion. Additional manga side stories served as supplements to the games and continued the mystery with new characters and storylines. On top of that there have been several anime series, novels, videogames, and a live-action movie adaptation with a sequel forthcoming – all featuring exclusive story arcs that deepen the intrigue of the fiction.

Kingdom Hearts

Shiro Amano; *pub* Famitsū PS2 (Jp), Tokyo-pop (US); *vols* 4

Kingdom Hearts: Chain of Memories

Shiro Amano; *pub* Famitsū PS2 (Jp), Tokyo-pop (US); *vols* 2

Kingdom Hearts II

Shiro Amano; *pub* Famitsū PS2 (Jp), Tokyo-pop (US); *vols* 5

Take one spunky hero, named Sora, who is desperate to save his home and friends from shadow creatures named the Heartless, give him an awesome weapon called the Keyblade, and you've got the makings of the next *Final Fantasy* game (not to mention drop-ins by Cloud, Sephiroth, Squall, Yuffie and other FF characters). But toss in Mickey, Goofy, Donald, Tinkerbell, Simba, and a host more – now you've got a work of mad genius. A joint venture between Square and Walt Disney, the *Kingdom Hearts* RPG must have sounded like a fever dream when it was first announced. But 5.6 million-plus copies (and two sequels) later, it's become one of the most successful RPG franchises in history.

A manga series for the game and each of its sequels (*Kingdom Hearts: Chain of Memories* and *Kingdom Hearts II*) was produced, retelling much of the story of the games, with some embellishments and omissions, though it's all in keeping with the spirit of the franchise.

Yu-Gi-Oh!

Kazuki Takahashi; *pub* Shueisha (Jp), Viz (US, UK); *ser* Weekly Shōnen Jump; *vols* 38

Yu-Gi-Oh! is probably best known as the second most successful Japanese trading card game. What surprises many is that the game was in fact a plot device created within the fictional world of the *Yu-Gi-Oh!* manga. In the manga, the main character Yugi Mutou ("Moto" in the English translation) is given pieces of an ancient Egyptian artefact known as the "Millennium Puzzle". Upon finally reassembling the puzzle, he is possessed by the spirit of an ancient pharaoh and he and his friends try to discover the secret of the pharaoh's lost memories. The game, called "Duel Monsters" (originally known as "Magic & Wizards" in the Japanese), is a fantasy card game used by characters in the manga to battle each other.

Of course, a real-life version of this fictional game was inevitable. But whereas in the manga the battles are used to drive the plot forward and have no concrete rules system, the actual card game and its electronic counterpart have distinct rules of combat.

6

The players

manga publishers

Any discussion of English-translated manga publishers must start with the largest market and what has traditionally been the first stop for licensed Japanese material: the US. There has been an explosion of publishers licensing and producing manga in the US market in recent years, rising from just five in 1998 to close to thirty a decade later.

While each has tried to carve out its own niche, the truth is that all are locked in the game to win ever-diminishing slices of the readership pie. The market is inevitably heading towards saturation point, and it's likely that by the time this book sees print, one or more of the publishers profiled in the following pages will have joined those already in the dustbin of manga history (see boxes on pp.222 and 240). The bulk of this chapter is taken up with profiles of US manga publishers but it includes a number of manga publishers native to or specializing in other regions, including Europe, Australia and New Zealand.

Aurora Publishing

Est. 2007
aurora-publishing.com

As the market for translated manga nears saturation point, new publishers are increasingly avoiding going head-to-head with the more established, "all-audiences" publishers and are instead focusing on niches within the market as a way of carving out a distinct identity. One of the more mainstream efforts of recent years is Aurora Publishing, a subsidiary of Japanese publisher Ohzora. The top publisher of female manga franchises in Japan, it was a natural step for Ohzora to try to capture the hearts of women and girls in English-speaking markets too.

Aurora has launched three imprints, aimed at different segments of the female readership. The main Aurora line is the catch-all imprint, focusing primarily on shōjo titles, while **Deux Press** handles the steamier yaoi series and **Luv Luv Press** focuses on josei. Of the three, Deux appears to have the most aggressive publishing schedule, with between one and four volumes of manga releasing every month in 2008.

The question is whether the company can gain enough of a foothold to survive in an already crowded market. A high number of bookstore returns coupled with the economic downturn in 2009 saw the company selling the extras directly to conumers online at a discount to try to recover its losses. Its titles are largely unfamiliar to the casual manga fan and lack an obvious hook to grab readers. They also have an unmistakeably "Japanese" feel to them: while they don't contain any blatantly incorrect uses of English, the translations still feel a bit stilted. Past attempts at marketing josei to English-language readers, including Tokyopop's Passion Fruit line, have largely been met with indifference, and it remains to be seen whether Aurora's experience will be any different.

Nightmares for Sale

Kaoru Ohashi; *ser* Honto ni Ata Kowai Comics (2002); *vols* 2; *age* 16+

Shadow and his assistant, Maria, run a pawnshop that offers loans in exchange for people's valuables – loans that often end up giving someone exactly what they deserve, even if they don't expect it. The whole pawnshop setup is a rather forgettable part of the manga, however, often being pushed aside in favour of standard horror-manga-with-a-morality-lesson fare.

Walkin' Butterfly

Chihiro Tamaki; *ser* Ease Comics (2004); *vols* Jp 4, US ongoing; *age* 18+

Meet Michiko, a young woman with a large chip on her shoulder. She hates being too tall, she hates it when people call her attention to being tall, and she especially hates it when people tell her she can't do something. So when she accidentally stumbles into a fashion show on a pizza-delivery run gone wrong and gets laughed at, she wants to prove her critics wrong. It's a quest with unmistakeably mature overtones, as she navigates her way past a drug-filled situation and strips naked in front of an agency talent chief to prove how serious she is about modelling.

Bandai Entertainment

Est. 2004
bandai-ent.com

Bandai Entertainment may be a prominent anime publisher, but it's yet to make big waves in the manga scene. Ever since the company announced its manga line, new releases have trickled out like drops of water from a dripping tap. It's easy to forget the division even exists… until another special edition volume of the *Eureka Seven* anime is packaged with a new volume of the manga adaptation.

Eureka Seven – along with the spin-off series *Eureka Seven: Gravity Boys and Lifting Girl* – is, in fact, one of very few manga series to be released since that announcement. *Witchblade Takeru*, a Japanese manga adaptation of a popular US comic book series, came out in 2007. And in 2008 *Code Geass* and *Ghost Slayer Ayashi* were both released in conjunction with anime DVDs. Bandai has also licensed the *Lucky Star* manga on which its popular anime series is based. Add in a couple of "film manga" (books containing screenshots from anime with word balloons added) and that's pretty much the entire Bandai manga catalogue to date.

It's clear Bandai considers its primary aim to be anime production and distribution, with the manga branch being simply a nice cross-promotional perk. That said, the few manga titles it has released at least have the advantage of some degree of name recognition among anime fans.

Code Geass: Lelouch of the Rebellion

Ichirou Ohkouchi and Goro Taniguchi (story) majiku (text and art); *ser* Monthly Asuka (2006); *vols* Jp 5, US ongoing; *age* 13+

An adaptation of the popular anime series with a shōjo spin, this series follows young Lelouch Lamperouge, a prince in the Holy Empire of Britannia, who turns on his lineage after his father fails to prevent the assassination of his mother and the crippling of his sister. The character designs for the original anime were by CLAMP.

Eureka Seven

Jinsei Kataoka and Kazuma Kondou; *ser* Shōnen Ace (2005–06); *vols* 6; *age* 13+

Manga based on the anime, featuring a fourteen-year-old-boy who lives a dreary life in a dreary town and dreams of one day leaving it all behind to do some lifting (like surfing, but in the air) with a renegade group known as Gekkostate. His dream comes true when a giant mechanical suit piloted by a beautiful girl named Eureka crashes into his grandfather's garage. Together they take off on an adventure that raises issues of racial and religious tolerance, although these are not explored in the same depth as in the original anime.

Lucky Star

Kagami Yoshimizu; *ser* Comptiq (2004–); *vols* ongoing; *age* 13+

These four-panel comics are the source material for the popular *Lucky Star* anime. They lack the numerous inside jokes that Kyoto Animation loaded into the anime (as well as the banter of the "Lucky Channel" segments that gave the anime extra comedy flair). However, the basic stories remain the same: four high-school girls – die-hard anime/manga/videogame fan Konata, the friendly-yet-clumsy Tsukasa, her spunky twin Kagami, and the proper, rich, intelligent Miyuki – share everyday experiences.

Witchblade Takeru

Yasuko Kobayashi (text), Kazasa Sumita (art); *ser* Champion Red (2006–); *vols* ongoing; *age* 18+

As established in the original comic book, the Witchblade is an ancient weapon that has bonded with women throughout history and granted them the power to become unstoppable killing machines when confronted with evil. (It also has the power of va-va-voom sexiness, as the women lose much of their clothing in the transformation process.) The bearer of the Witchblade this time around is Takeru, a high-school student raised in a Buddhist convent, who fights off *oni* (traditional Japanese demons) with its help.

Chuang Yi

Est. 1990
chuangyi.com.sg

Chuang Yi started out as a relatively modest operation licensing and translating manga from Japanese into simplified Chinese for its home base of Singapore. But the worldwide phenomenon that was *Pokémon* prompted the

company to expand into other Southeast Asian and Pacific markets in the late 1990s, and to begin translating manga into English. In 2003 it began distributing manga in Australia and New Zealand. A distribution deal with Madman Entertainment has brought a nice cross-section of popular shōnen and shōjo titles to the region, including *Astro Boy*, *Fruits Basket* and *Fullmetal Alchemist* (see pp.82, 122 and 123) and the adapted-from-anime *.hack//Legend of the Twilight*, *Rahxephon*, *Tenchi Muyo!* and *Samurai Champloo*.

The arrangement has meant that while the US is only now beginning to get translated *Slam Dunk* (see p.182) volumes for a second time from Viz (the first time was through the failed Gutsoon! venture), Australian readers have had the complete series available for several years now. Also completed in Australia before its US run was the twelve-volume Yuki Nakaji series *Love for Venus* (released by CMX under the title *Venus in Love* from 2007).

CMX

Est. 2004
dccomics.com/cmx

For good or ill, two words have come to symbolize this imprint of US comics publisher DC Comics: *Tenjho Tenge*.

TenTen, as it's commonly known, is a moderately popular school-based shōnen series notable for two things: a character who appears at first to be a small girl but can transform into a hot, busty babe, and frantic fight scenes in which said babe gets her clothes ripped off in very revealing ways. There are other women, and other fights, and other strategically placed rips and tears, and… well, you get the idea.

For some reason, though, the CMX powers that be decided *TenTen* should have a "T" rating, meaning it was suitable for age thirteen and upwards. They asked series creator Oh! Great for input into how the art could be changed to achieve that broader rating. The resulting product was digitally blurred in some areas, while elsewhere images were more closely cropped to cut out offending portions.

Oh! Great might have approved of the changes, but US fans who knew what had happened certainly didn't. The controversy came to a head at the 2005 Comic-Con International in San Diego, where fans confronted CMX representatives over the issue during the company's panel session. Later in the series' run, the rating was changed to an older teens (16+) rating, but the PR damage had already been done.

Since the *TenTen* controversy, things have been relatively quiet at CMX. Aside from a few notable successes such as the comedy kogal romp *GALS!*, a portion of the "boy-meets-girl-on-train" franchise *Densha Otoko*, and the silent adventures of tiny dinosaur Gon, the company's catalogue is filled with relatively obscure titles that English-speaking fans probably never realized they wanted translated in the first place.

If only they knew what they were missing. CMX has emerged as a treasure trove for classic shōjo manga from the 1970s and 80s, material that transcends the usual dreamy high-school romance fare. And its list as a whole is admirably eclectic, ranging from well-known series such as *Crayon Shin-chan* (see p.195), mysteries such as *Chikyu Misaki* and adaptations of *tokusatsu* (live-action superhero) series like *Kikaider Code 02*, to the Victorian-era setting of *Emma*. Fred Gallagher's popular online global manga *Megatokyo* has also found a home at CMX after periods at Studio Ironcat and Dark Horse.

Emma

Kaoru Mori; *ser* Comic Beam (2002–06); *vols* 7; *age* 16+

Kaoru Mori is a self-confessed Anglophile, and her meticulous attention to historic detail shows in this series set in London just before the turn of the twentieth century. Emma, a girl from a poor Yorkshire seaside village, is training to be a proper English maid when she falls in love with William Jones, the eldest son of a wealthy and socially ambitious merchant family. While her feelings are reciprocated, the social divide constantly threatens to snuff out the fledgling spark of love.

GALS!

Mihona Fujii; *ser* Ribon (1999–2002); *vols* 10; *age* 13+

Ahh, Japanese kogal culture, that subset of high-school girls known for their conspicuous consumption and uniform of knee-high baggy socks, platform shoes, designer accessories and heavy make-up. Ran Kotobuki, the lone rebellious daughter in a family of police officers, is a kogal, as are her friends Miyu and Aya, two girls with shady pasts. This series sets out not to condemn kogals but to praise them, showing readers the true meaning of loyalty and friendship… with a helping of comedy on the side.

Gon

Masashi Tanaka; *ser* Weekly Morning (1992–2002); *vols* 7

None of the animals in *Gon* ever utters a single sound effect or word of dialogue. Quite frankly, no one has to. The old cliché that actions speak louder than words is the basic premise behind this series, which features the adventures of a small, short-tempered yet kind-hearted dinosaur who goes around the world interacting with native fauna and helping his newfound friends out of predicaments. Winner of a 1998 Excellence Prize at the Japan Media Arts Festival.

Musashi No. 9

Miyuki Takahashi *ser* Kirara Seize/Mystery Bonita (1996–); *vols* ongoing; *age* 13+

Ultimate Blue, a covert group so powerful that it's known as "the other United Nations", defends the Earth against militants and criminals who would dare to disturb the peace. Among its field operatives is Agent Number Nine. She kicks butt and takes names with the best of them, despite being just sixteen years old. At the heart of the series is her struggle to deal with criminals while protecting those people who appear normal but have within them some element that could change the world.

Samurai Commando: Mission 1549

Harutoshi Fukui and Ryo Hanmura (text), Ark Performance (art); *ser* n/a (2005); *vols* 2; *age* 16+

After a training accident, a unit of the modern Japanese army find they've somehow been transported back to feudal-era Japan. Seizing the opportunity to change history for the better, a military commander promptly kills Nobunaga Oda, a pivotal figure in Japanese history. But – as is always the way in such stories – the future doesn't change in quite the way he hoped. Now it's up to another army task force to leap back in time and stop the commander before history is irreversibly rewritten.

Dark Horse

Est. 1988
darkhorse.com/zones/manga

Like CMX, Dark Horse's manga division is part of a larger comic book publisher, though it has been around far longer than DC's venture. In fact, Dark Horse was one of the very first US publishers to enter the manga market, beginning in 1988 with Kazuhisa Iwata's *Godzilla*.

Since then, Dark Horse Manga has gained a reputation as the go-to publisher for quality action, science-fiction and horror manga. That said, its longest continuously running series (in fact the longest-running series in the entire English-language manga industry), *Oh My Goddess!* (see p.164), has been successful because it appeals to both male and female audiences. The series *What's Michael?*, about the everyday adventures of an adorable cat, also stands out for being accessible to a wide age range.

In a long-running partnership beginning in 1988, Dark Horse co-produced manga with publishing and production house **Studio Proteus**. Close to 60,000 pages were produced through the alliance, with the companies splitting the profits and the US copyrights down the middle. The partnership ended in 2004, when Dark Horse bought Proteus from Toren Smith, who had become disenchanted with the way the manga market was heading.

The bankruptcy of the distributor LPC Group in 2002 hurt Dark Horse, limiting exposure of its titles right around the time competitors Tokyopop and Viz kick-started the modern manga boom times. The company that had been such a dominant force in the 1990s manga market became less so during this time. Periodic distribution hiccups continue to this day: promised shipping dates for new *Oh My Goddess!* volumes have slipped without notice from time to time. Dark Horse is also decisive in pulling the plug on series that underperform, with *3X3 Eyes*, *Museum of Terror* and *Cannon God Exaxxion* being three of the more prominent titles to get the chop in recent years. Still, the company presses on, continuing to introduce new series and products to the marketplace. A recently announced deal with CLAMP promises more intriguing projects to come.

3X3 Eyes

Yuzo Takada; *pub* Kodansha (Jp), Dark Horse (US); *ser* Young Magazine (1987–2002); *vols* Jp 40, US 9 (cancelled)

Yakumo Fujii's father disappeared four years ago while on an expedition to Tibet. Since then, Yakumo has tried to move on with his life as an average high school student, but soon finds himself entangled with a three-eyed girl named Pai, who claims she's a member of a race blessed with eternal life and that Yakumo's father gave her a letter explaining all of this before he died. And then a monster attacks the city, Yakumo saves Pai but dies in the process, and Pai resurrects him by bonding her life with his. Now, the two are on a quest to become human. The series earned the Kodansha Manga Award for shōnen in 1993.

Gunsmith Cats

Kenichi Sonoda; *ser* Afternoon (1991–97); *vols* 8; *age* 18+

Kenichi Sonoda is a fan of American culture – particularly the cars and guns – and this manga combines the two in one big action-packed blowout. Welcome to Chicago, where two women, Rally and Minnie-May, run a gunsmith shop. Rally's a bounty hunter, while Minnie-May's a prostitute-turned-explosives expert. Together, they hunt down assorted riffraff across the city in a never-ending battle against the criminal underworld. The series continues under the title *Gunsmith Cats Burst*, also published by Dark Horse.

Hellsing

Kohta Hirano; *ser* Young King Ours (1998–); *vols* 10; *age* 16+

A series in which British Protestants battle it out against Catholic killer nuns, inquisitors and Nazi vampires, amongst others. Working for Hellsing, an organization that protects the UK from vampire attacks, are agents Arucard, a vampire working for the good guys, and Seras Victoria, a former police officer. Expect a healthy dose of gothic violence, lovingly crafted down to the last bloody detail.

Del Rey

Est. 2004
randomhouse.com/delrey/manga

Having struck a deal with Japanese publisher Kodansha to bring some of its top titles to the US, in 2004 publishing giant Random House launched a manga division, Del Rey.

Random House isn't the only big-time trade publisher to see growth in the manga market and decide to get a piece of the action. AD Vision and DC Comics tried it with their ADV Manga and CMX imprints and, at first, Del Rey looked in danger of making the same mistake of underestimating manga fans. Among its first releases was Ken Akamatsu's *Negima!* As readers of Akamatsu's previous series, *Love Hina*, will attest, fan service – mostly of the accidental-burial-in-pillowy-breasts and panty-flash varieties – are Akamatsu's romantic-comedy bread and butter. *Negima!*, about a young magician who becomes a teacher at an all-girls school, stuck closely to that formula.

Word got out that Del Rey was going to be altering ten panels in the first volume to cover up implied nudity. While Akamatsu expressed his surprise and amusement in his blog, manga fans were incensed over what they saw as censorship, no matter how few panels were involved. But rather than stick to its guns, Del Rey recanted and left the manga untouched, albeit with shrink-wrap and an age-restriction sticker as a concession to the more conservative US market. It's a strategy that might have served ADV Manga and CMX better. It certainly worked for Del Rey, swiftly propelling it into the public consciousness for all the right reasons.

The company started off with only four titles, but all four had considerable pedigrees. Along with *Negima!*, there were the latest ongoing crossover series by CLAMP, *Tsubasa Reservoir Chronicle* and *xxxHolic* (see pp.100–101), as well as a new chapter in the sprawling giant robot saga that is the Gundam universe, *Mobile Suit Gundam SEED*. The Kodansha partnership has yielded a number of hidden gems and fan favourites since then, including *Love Roma* (see p.152), *School Rumble*, *Genshiken* (see p.134), *Nodame Cantabile*, *Mushishi* and *Basilisk*. Sure, there are a few clunkers – just try wading through the fan service overload of *Pastel* and *Gacha Gacha*, or the sugary sweetness of *Mamotte! Lollipop*. But Del Rey treats all its titles equally, with translation notes regularly included in the back of the books.

Random House published a selection of Del Rey titles under the **Tanoshimi** imprint in the UK in 2006: *Basilisk*, *Ghost Hunt*, *Guru Guru Pon-chan*, *Negima!*, *Tsubasa Reservoir Chronicle* and *xxxHolic*. However, the number of Tanoshimi titles available lagged behind the full Del Rey catalogue available in the US and the imprint was retired for economic reasons in January 2009.

In 2007 Del Rey made a foray into the OEL manga market with the release of Avril Lavigne's *Make 5 Wishes* (see p.54), featuring the pop star as the imaginary friend of a troubled young girl. The publisher has since added *Odd Thomas*, a collaboration between author Dean Koontz and artist Queenie Chan, as well as manga versions of *X-Men* and *Wolverine*, released in conjunction with Marvel Comics.

Basilisk

Futaro Yamada (story), Masaki Segawa (text and art); *ser* Young Magazine Uppers (2003–04); *vols* 5; *age* 18+

Inter-clan rivalry in seventeenth-century Japan has never been as action-packed as in this story, which features ten members from each of the rival Kouga and Iga ninja clans facing off to determine which grandson of Tokugawa Ieyasu will ascend to the shogunate. But there's a *Romeo and Juliet*-style twist: Gennosuke of the Kouga clan was betrothed to Oboro of the Iga clan and whether their love can survive the war remains the thread of tension throughout this series.

Mushishi

Yuki Urushibara; *ser* Afternoon Season/ Afternoon (1999–); *vols* ongoing; *age* 16+

Primordial life forms known as *mushi*, neither plant, animal nor fungus, drift through the world undetected by most people – but occasionally show up to wreak havoc on the few who do have the ability to see them. One of those people is Ginko, the main character in this series. There's no overarching plot, only a chronicle of Ginko's wanderings as he traverses rural Japan, helping those in need, then going on his way, taking care not to linger because he would otherwise attract too many *mushi* to himself.

Nodame Cantabile

Tomoko Ninomiya; *ser* Kiss (2001–); *vols* ongoing; *age* 16+

Shinichi Chiaki is a perfectionist when it comes to music, hoping someday to study abroad to become a conductor. One night, when he's passed out in front of his apartment after drinking his sorrows away, Megumi "Nodame" Noda finds him and brings him into her messy apartment. She is everything Shinichi hates… and yet she has the ability to play the piano by ear. When Shinichi is assigned to conduct her and a bunch of other loser students in an orchestra, hilarity ensues.

School Rumble

Jin Kobayashi; *ser* Weekly Shōnen Magazine (2002–); *vols* ongoing; *age* 16+

This school-based manga proves that hardened delinquents can feel love, too, as Kenji Harima pines for energetic school cutie Tenma Tsukamoto. But Tenma has her own unrequited crush on Oji Karasuma, a boy who is so focused on whatever task is at hand that he never notices Tenma flinging herself at him. A strong supporting cast flesh out what is turning into a rather complex romantic shōnen comedy.

Digital Manga Publishing

Est. 1996
dmpbooks.com (main site)
junemanga.com (Juné imprint)

Educational manga

Nestled among the countless yaoi titles and more traditional manga in **DMP**'s catalogue are several rather unconventional series, designed to educate as well as entertain. In the *Edu-Manga* series, readers join Astro Boy and his friends as they travel through time meeting historical figures including Helen Keller, Anne Frank, Beethoven, Einstein and Mother Teresa. The *Project X* series, based on a popular documentary series in Japan, is more straightforward in its presentation, profiling three business successes: the Datsun Fairlady Z, the 7-Eleven convenience store chain, and Momofuku Andou's development of Cup Noodle. Finally, *Pop Japan Travel: Essential Otaku Guide* takes readers on a typical Pop Japan Travel tour, offers a few dos and don'ts… and then adds a little dramatic embellishment. These series certainly help to fulfil DMP's goal of sharing Japanese pop culture in non-traditional ways. But at a more basic level, they're simply a means of challenging the stereotype that comics make kids stupid. Following are two other publishing ventures which likewise aim to turn manga into a teaching tool.

Manga University *(est. 1998, mangauniversity.com)*
An imprint of Japanese publisher Japanime, Manga University is home to an ever-expanding catalogue of instructional books. The company's flagship series is *How to Draw Manga*, licensed from Japanese publisher Graphic-Sha, while *Kana de Manga* and *Kanji de Manga* teach fans how to read the three Japanese alphabets of hiragana, katakana and kanji. There's also *The Manga Cookbook*, a guide to making 27 Japanese dishes. In 2007, Japanime ventured into more traditional story manga with two OEL titles: *Moe USA*, about two American girls who find a pair of enchanted maid costumes when they begin working at a maid café in Japan, and *Harvey and Etsuko's Guide to Japan*, a travelogue series of sorts where a mouse from outside Tokyo visits a friend in the city.

No Starch Press *(est. 1994, nostarch.com)*
This San Francisco-based publisher expanded its offerings in what it calls "geek entertainment" – mostly books about computing and programming – by licensing several edu-manga from Japanese publisher Ohmsha's *Manga de Wakaru* ("Understanding Through Manga") series. No Starch's releases began with *The Manga Guide to Statistics* in October 2008, in which heroine Rui learns about data categorization, standard deviation and other statistics fundamentals as a way of impressing her dream love, Igarashi. The series has since expanded to include books on databases and calculus (and yes, the stories are equally whimsical).

Digital Manga Inc., the parent company of Digital Manga Publishing, has for the past decade been on something of a mission to introduce English-speaking audiences to Japanese pop culture. An anime and manga news site, **Akadot.com**, came online in 2000, and a retail component was added soon afterwards. **Pop Japan Travel**, a travel service that took anime and manga fans on tours of Japan, launched in 2003. But at the heart of the enterprise is, of course, DMP's manga list.

Released in 2003, DMP's first four titles – *The Ring*, *Hellsing* (see p.215), *Trigun* and *Berserk* – were co-branded releases with Dark Horse and sold well. Less successful were the first two series released under its own banner: the seinen series *Ikebukuro West Gate Park* (an adaptation of a Japanese TV series) and *Worst*. There was a hiatus of close to two years between the releases of the third and fourth volumes of *IWGP*, while *Worst* was cancelled after its licensed run of three volumes (out of a total of seventeen). DMP has also published a number of educational manga (see box opposite).

But the company struck gold with its investment in what was at the time an under-represented genre: yaoi. DMP president and publisher Hikaru Sasahara would later admit to *Publishers Weekly* that he didn't even know about the genre until the president of Tokuma Shoten pointed out that it had existed for thirty years. Figuring the fan bases in Japan and the US were similar, he decided to give it a shot, and the first three titles – *Only the Ring Finger Knows*, *Desire* and *Passion* – rolled out in late 2004.

The strategy paid off. According to Sasahara, "*Only the Ring Finger Knows* sold instantly, almost twelve thousand units with almost no promotion … I grabbed another five titles in the boys' love genre without even checking their marketability. All [sold] tremendously well."

Just how "tremendously well" became apparent in 2006, when the publisher not only created a new imprint, **Juné**, to handle the increased volume of yaoi titles, but also spawned a sister company, **801 Manga**, to handle more explicit yaoi series. Now it's found its niche, DMP goes from strength to strength.

Only the Ring Finger Knows

Satoru Kannagi (text), Hotaru Odagiri (art); *ser* Chara (2002); *vols* 1; *age* 16+

A tradition at the high school that Wataru attends dictates that a couple will wear similar rings to demonstrate their love for each other. While Wataru has a ring, he's also blissfully single… that is, until he finds out that another boy, Yuichi, has the same style of ring. This series is a fine way to learn about the conventions of yaoi storytelling, as the two boys alternate between feelings of repulsion and attraction to one other.

Princess Princess

Mikiyo Tsuda; *ser* Wings (2002–06); *vols* 5; *age* 16+

In an all-boys school, the students vote to choose guys who will dress up as girls – or "princesses" – and offer support and eye candy to everyone else throughout the school year. It's Toru Kouno's first day at the school. He's a reasonably attractive guy. Inevitably, hijinks ensue as he's dragged kicking and screaming into the princess programme.

Speed Racer: Mach Go Go Go

Tatsuo Yoshida (text), Jiro Kuwata (art), 1968; *vols* 2

Speed Racer was the first publication in DMP's Platinum line, which releases manga in premium packaging. Here, the racing adventures of Speed, the Mach 5, his friends Trixie, Spritle and Chim-Chim, and rival/brother Racer X are presented in translated manga form for the first time, as two hardbound books in a slipcase.

DrMaster

Est. 2005
drmasterbooks.com

DrMaster is nothing if not enthusiastic about its publishing programme. A mission statement posted on its website gushes about how, "with ambition in their eyes and a love for art melded with fantastic storytelling", its experienced staff have built up the company with the aim of bringing the best manga and manhua from Japan and China to US readers. They're proud of "brazenly going against the grain and laughing in the face of conformity".

Umm… right. Joking aside, the tiny publisher – there are only six full-time employees – has gained a reputation for quirky thinking. But the proof is in the pudding, and – setting aside a few

minor hiccups during the transition of licences from **ComicsONE** (see box on p.222) – the quality of its products has been consistently good. Since it's a niche publisher, however, it can be difficult to find its books on store shelves.

After finishing up what ComicsONE started with the 26-volume *Iron Wok Jan* (see p.142), DrMaster has focused its efforts on shorter series that run for about ten to twelve volumes. In its early days, the publisher did go in for the odd bout of cheesy fluff – such as *Hinadori Girl*, about a cute servant android who gets into a platonic love triangle with her boy owner and his little sister, and *Tori Koro*, a series of four-panel comics whose humour apparently got lost somewhere along the way. But there have been signs of improvement since – more recent releases have included the outrageous comedy *High School Girls*, the creepy supernatural tale *Lunar Legend Tsukihime* and the gritty earthquake survivalist drama *Metro Survive*.

High School Girls

Towa Oshima; *ser* Manga Action/Comic High! (2001–); *vols* Jp 8, US 9, on hiatus

High School Girls is loosely based on the author's own experiences at an all-girls school. Friends Eriko, Yuma and Ayano are attending a girls school for the first time, but their dreams of a kinder, gentler school experience are shattered when they find out just how slovenly some girls can get. Fortunately, they find a fast friend in the ostentatious Kouda, and hilarity ensues. Discussions of menstrual cycles, bikini lines and other feminine hygiene issues will either titillate readers or turn them off.

Lunar Legend Tsukihime

Tsukihime Project (story), TYPE-MOON (text), Sasaki Shōnen (art); *ser* Dengeki Daioh (2003–), *vols* ongoing; *age* 16+

Shiki Tohno has the ability to see "death cracks", which run through all living creatures on the planet. He also has the power to cut through those cracks, instantly destroying the item or person through which they run. He ends up joining forces with a female vampire, Arcueid, when she tells him about the world's true nature, filled with vampires, magicians and other creepy-crawly creatures, and together they battle vampires in an effort to protect their world.

Fanfare/ Ponent Mon

Est. 2003
ponentmon.com

Fanfare/Ponent Mon specializes in nouvelle manga, a hybrid Japanese/Franco-Belgian movement that emphasizes slice-of-life stories. Forged in an alliance between UK publisher Fanfare and Spanish firm Ponent Mon in 2003, it produces translated editions of manga for both the Spanish and English-language markets.

Its books are pricier than many US-produced titles, but for that you get sophisticated content and top-end presentation, with larger trim sizes and higher-quality paper than the standard manga fare. Most releases are single, self-contained volumes, the exception to date being *The Times of Botchan*, a historical fiction series based on the life of early twentieth-century novelist Natsume Soseki.

If only it were easier to find those books; despite an arrangement with Biblio Book Distributors in 2006, the sight of a Fanfare/Ponent Mon book on a store shelf in the US remains a rarity. The situation is far better in the UK.

Blue

Kiriko Nananan; *ser* Come Are! (1996–98); *vols* 1; *age* 13+

Blue follows the course of a friendship between two girls. Their feelings blossom into love but soon secrets and mistrust threaten to tear the girls apart. The art is minimalist – the teens are the only elements of the story drawn in detail, with other characters merely hinted at through disjointed dialogue bubbles and sentence fragments. This gives the story room to breathe, while heightening the emotional intensity.

Disappearance Diary

Hideo Azuma; *ser* n/a (2005); *vols* 1; *age* 16+

In this autobiographical account, mangaka Azuma reveals how he deals with the continual abrasive nagging of his editors: cut off all contact with them and drop out of society for long stretches at a time. He's been homeless. He's worked as a gas pipe layer. He's gone into rehab for alcoholism. But as long as the work comes in on time, the editors are okay with it. The book won the Grand Prize for Manga at the 2005 Japan Media Arts Festival and the Grand Prize at the 2006 Osamu Tezuka Cultural Awards.

An elegy for defunct publishers

Not all the companies that have entered the US manga market have enjoyed the success of Tokyopop and Viz. Here are some of the more notable flame-outs of recent years.

Broccoli Books *(publishing run 2001–08)*
Broccoli first rose to prominence in Japan, thanks mostly to the mascot character of its Gamers stores, alien princess catgirl Dejiko. Expansion to the US meant a whole new region for Dejiko and her anime/manga franchise, *Di Gi Charat*, to conquer, and when Broccoli's translated manga division opened for business in 2003, *Di Gi Charat* was a major part of the launch. But publishers cannot survive on cute catgirls alone. So Broccoli began picking up other licences, and in 2007, it branched out to yaoi with its Boysenberry imprint, rolling out three single-volume titles: *Delivery Cupid*, *Pet on Duty* and *Sex Friend*.

Broccoli's books were high quality, printed on a bright paper stock. The company was also considered one of the more fan-friendly publishers, offering free dust jackets, bookmarks and other goodies as mail-in offers with their books. But the truth was not enough people were buying the books. Other US divisions of the company were doing similarly badly, and so, with falling revenue and no prospects for turning the situation around, in 2008 Broccoli International shut down its US operations.

ComicsONE *(publishing run 1999–2005)*
Inspired by the dot.com boom, in 1999 wireless gaming businessman Robin Kuo launched ComicsONE with a clear goal in mind: to be the first to successfully sell manga as downloads from the Internet. After about a year, Kuo was obliged to admit defeat, and switched over to the more conventional print channels. The company eventually found its niche licensing full-colour manhua from Hong Kong, including adaptations of the *Crouching Tiger, Hidden Dragon* and *Shaolin Soccer* films.

On the manga side, there were a few niche successes, such as *Crayon Shin-chan* (see p.195), *Iron Wok Jan* (see p.142) and *High School Girls*. But ComicsONE's offerings were largely unexceptional. Translations and print quality were maddeningly inconsistent, and series that weren't doing well were dropped without warning. Others were delayed for months at a time and were difficult to find on store shelves. Financial troubles were apparently to blame. In late 2004, ComicsONE announced a deal transferring many of its titles to a new publisher, DrMaster. The story of DrMaster since then can be read on p.220. The final word on ComicsONE's fate came from an ICv2.com report in March 2005: "ComicsOne has stopped paying its bills and has disappeared".

Gutsoon! Entertainment (Raijin Comics) *(publishing run 2002–04)*
It certainly wasn't for lack of ambition that *Raijin Comics* failed. The debut cover of America's first weekly manga anthology declared: "The Dream Team Has Come!" And the launch line-up included several series that had found major success in Japan, including *Fist of the Blue Sky* and *First President of Japan*. However, the price of this authentic manga experience was $4.95 per issue, or a hefty $189.60 for an annual subscription. Readers gravitated instead towards Viz's monthly *Shonen Jump*, which debuted around the same time and offered the more buzz-worthy *Dragon Ball Z* and *Yu-Gi-Oh!* for the same cover price.

Signs of trouble began to emerge in early 2003, when a sister publication, *Raijin Game & Anime*, ended its print run and was folded into the main publication. That summer, the publisher announced *Raijin Comics* would switch to a monthly cycle, in response to a reader poll. But the magazine remained the same size, meaning the manga on offer each month was reduced by 75 percent. Meanwhile, the cover price rose to $5.95. Less than a year later, it was announced that the comic would go "on hiatus" while the team sought "ways to broaden the appeal of our publications". The publishers never did return from that brainstorming session. And the dream was officially dead.

Studio Ironcat *(publishing run 1997–2005)*
Internal fraud, walkouts by disgruntled employees, a lone hit series lost when distribution squabbles arose… it's a wonder Studio Ironcat managed to publish anything at all. Manga artists Kuni Kimura and Steve Bennett IV founded the company in 1997 with financial backing from fellow artist Masaomi Kanzaki. The publisher took its name from Kanzaki's manga – perhaps an odd choice in retrospect, since many (most notably critic Jason Thompson) consider *Ironcat* one of the worst manga ever made. Over the next few years, the company turned out mostly shōnen titles under the Ironcat imprint and hentai manga through its SexyFruit imprint. But the problems began to mount up. Kimura was the first to go in 1999, accused of embezzlement, though no charges were ever filed. Soon afterwards Kanzaki left, taking his manga and its name with him, forcing the company to rebrand itself as I.C. Entertainment. The company was eventually able to get the Ironcat name back, and scored the print rights to Fred Gallagher's *Megatokyo* in late 2002. But distribution was poor, and Gallagher took *Megatokyo* to Dark Horse in 2003. Ten key employees left in July 2003, alleging unfair working practices and unfairly withheld pay. The publisher clung on until 2005, but was finally forced to call it a day.

Prison life in all its mundane detail is the subject of Kazuichi Hanawa's autobiographical *Doing Time*.

Doing Time

Kazuichi Hanawa; *ser* Ax (1998–2000); *vols* 1

Hanawa, a model gun aficionado, was arrested in 1994 on firearms violations after trying out some of his guns in the hills. While serving his sentence, he chronicled prison life through sketches and drawings; the result became *Doing Time*. There's no real narrative line, but instead a series of detailed stand-alone pieces in which he analyses a particular event, the behaviour of his cellmates, or his confined surroundings.

The Walking Man

Jirō Taniguchi; *ser* Morning Special (1990–92); *vols* 1

A man walks through the streets of Japan. That's pretty much the entire plot of this manga. His journey is uneventful, punctuated by everyday occurrences such as stepping in puddles, retrieving a boy's toy aeroplane from a tree, and watching birds fly past. But Taniguchi manages to imbue these simple situations with depth and resonance. A simple, mostly dialogue-free presentation adds to the charm.

Yukiko's Spinach

Frédéric Boilet; *ser* Furansugo Kaiwa (2000–01); *vols* 1; *age* 18+

Boilet is one of the leading artists of the nouvelle manga movement. This story, about a French artist living in Japan and the young Japanese woman who acts as his muse and lover, is about as intimate as manga can get, depicting a series of special moments between the two. Yet there's a pervasive air of sadness, as the artist slowly realizes that the woman will never love him as much as he loves her. The photorealistic style is more detailed than traditional manga art.

Go! Comi

Est. 2005
gocomi.com

The Go! Comi story begins with *The Almost Legendary Shannon*, the dream project of writers David Wise and Audry Taylor. The tale concerns a high-school girl who accidentally pulls the legendary sword Excalibur from a stone at a Renaissance fair. Wise and Taylor knew the style in which they wanted the project to be illustrated: both were anime fans, and Wise, a former writer for US cartoons including the first *Teenage Mutant Ninja Turtles* series, was heavily influenced by anime and manga after meeting Osamu Tezuka in 1980. And so, in 2004, the couple secured up-and-coming artist You Higuri to do the artwork.

As for finding *The Almost Legendary Shannon* on bookstore shelves: don't bother looking. It has yet to be released, on hold because of Higuri's surging popularity in Japan. However, Wise and Taylor have meanwhile launched Go! Comi, drawing on connections with editors, artists and publishers made during their time in Japan. They had always planned to publish *Shannon* themselves, and decided to license other works as a way of keeping the self-publishing dream alive. Wise became CEO of the new company, and Taylor its creative director. The couple scored

a coup when ex-Tokyopop editor Jake Forbes agreed to join the venture.

Go! Comi's launch line-up included four shōjo manga: *Cantarella*, *Her Majesty's Dog*, *Crossroad* and *Tenshi Ja Nai!* (*I'm No Angel!*). Since then, the company has carefully expanded its catalogue, opting to license hidden gems and building on word of mouth rather than picking up whatever happens to be popular at the time. Go! Comi also emphasizes quality, working closely with the original creators whenever possible and offering extensive translation notes, polished production values and full-colour pages where available. But perhaps the greatest strength of the company is its translation and script-writing team. "Practically every one of us was a professional writer long before coming to manga", Wise told *Comic Book News* in 2006. "We know how to write dialogue that reads well, that flows, we know how to give characters distinct individual voices while remaining faithful to the original Japanese."

Go! Comi is beginning to supplement its main manga list with global manga. Aimee Major Steinberger's *Japan Ai: A Tall Girl's Adventures in Japan* is more of a sketchbook diary than a manga, but is an intriguing addition to the list. Wendy Pini's *Masque of the Red Death* is the publisher's first venture into offering original manga content via the Internet. And who knows – perhaps some day soon, readers will be able to pick up *The Almost Legendary Shannon*, too.

After School Nightmare

Setona Mizushiro; *ser* Princess (2004–08); *vols* ongoing; *age* 16+

Ichijo is suffering an identity crisis: while the upper half of his body is male, the bottom half of his body is distinctly female. Attending a school programme in which students live out their worst nightmares doesn't help matters. There are two questions driving this compelling drama. First, will Ichijo embrace his male or his female side? Fledgling romances with members of both sexes rely heavily on the answer. And, second, why do students who "graduate" from the programme have all trace of their existence erased from the memories of those left behind?

Cantarella

You Higuri; *ser* Princess Gold (2000–); *vols* 10 (Jp on hiatus); *age* 16+

Cardinal Rodrigo Borgia's desire to become Pope once led him to sell the soul of his infant son to the devil. That son, Cesare Borgia, has grown older and now finds himself shunned by his father, hated by his brother and loved by a sister who is kept away from him. With a demonic side rising within him and a thirst for vengeance and destruction slowly taking him over, it may be up to a would-be assassin to slay Cesare's demon-possessed body while sparing and freeing his soul.

Crossroad

Shioko Mizuki; *ser* Princess (2003–05); *vols* 7; *age* 16+

Kajitsu's home life has never been a bed of roses. Her grandmother has just died, her dad is a deadbeat, while her mum gallivants around town switching boyfriends as often as she changes her clothes. But when her two stepbrothers show up – with a brand-new baby sister in tow – Kajitsu is forced into family life. If home truly is where

the heart is, they'll have to find it pretty quickly if they're to survive.

Infinity Studios

Est. 2004
infinitystudios.com

Another publisher born out of the ComicsONE collapse (see box on p.222), having helped co-produce an adaptation of the *Peigenz* manga before the company went under, Infinity Studios has had the same sort of love-hate relationship with fans as its former partner.

And this despite a mission statement on Infinity's website that declares its founding intention "to always put the consumers first and to change the negative image the industry was beginning to acquire by both the fans and the Asian publishing industry". While *Peigenz* was plagued with the same typographical errors and inconsistent print quality that dogged ComicsONE titles in that publisher's final days, Infinity has steadily improved its products to the point where it's one of the better publishers in the industry today.

Yet it still seems unable to deliver sufficient quantities of its manga in a timely, consistent manner. For example, *Iono-sama Fanatics* volume 1 was released in May 2007; at the time of writing there is no sign of a second volume. The third volume of *Ninin Ga Shinobuden* was released in January 2008 and went out

Literary manga

Drawn & Quarterly *(est. 1989, drawnandquarterly.com)*
A number of small-press, alternative North American comics publishers have been dabbling in manga licensing of late, amongst them Drawn & Quarterly. Based in Montréal, Canada, the company is devoted to publishing literary comics. So far, its manga catalogue is decidedly small, comprising three volumes of short stories by Yoshihiro Tatsumi and Seiichi Hayashi's *Red-Colored Elegy*. All were published in Japan between 1969 and 1973 and were considered to be gekiga at that, pretty much ensuring that only the hardest of the hardcore manga fans (and perhaps scholars and manga critics) would pick these series up from store shelves.

This might seem like commercial folly, but the books have sold in respectable numbers. Credit artist Adrian Tomine, who recognized Tatsumi – one of the *gekiga* movement's most important artists – as a major influence on his work and on the American literary comics movement of the 1980s in general, and pushed for the publication of his work in the West.

Last Gasp *(est. 1969, lastgasp.com)*
Based in San Francisco and born out of the American countercultural movement of the late 1960s, Last Gasp is another publisher that primarily releases alternative, "underground" comics. In 2004, however, it entered the manga market, picking up the rights for *Barefoot Gen* (see p.88), previously held by Penguin Books, re-translating and re-publishing the first four volumes and then getting down to the task of producing the remaining six volumes in English for the first time. *Barefoot Gen* was Last Gasp's only manga offering until 2007, when it released *Town of Evening Calm, City of Cherry Blossoms*, Fumiyo Kouno's award-winning manga about the aftermath of the atomic bomb dropping on Hiroshima. More recently, the company has branched out from accounts of the World War II bombing, licensing two manga by Junko Mizuno, *Pure Trance* and *Fancy Gigolo Pelu*, and *Tokyo Zombie* by Yusaku Hanakuma, a horror-comedy about two factory workers and jiu-jitsu enthusiasts dealing with a zombie infestation.

of stock shortly afterwards. Significantly, a blog that once kept readers posted on publication delays and an online reader forum that were both active as of September 2007 have since disappeared.

In an effort to battle sagging customer confidence, Infinity launched a new e-book programme in February 2008, through which customers could get their hands on electronic versions of titles thought to have been abandoned by the publisher. Unfortunately, the series on offer are unexceptional at best. Worse, in an inexplicable inconvenience, customers aren't able to download the files once they buy them; instead, the publisher burns a copy to DVD and pops it in the post. While this method may free Infinity from the uncertainties of print publishing, the lack of the instant gratification one expects from the Internet means it has little to offer customers. The e-book listings, tellingly, have not been updated since December 2008.

Blood Alone

Masayuki Takano; *ser* Dengeki Daioh (2004–); *vols* ongoing; *age* 13+

By day, young Misaki lives with the older Kuroe at his apartment, where they laze about and enjoy each other's company. There's even a hint of blossoming romance between the two. The night brings a different story, though: Misaki has a vampiric streak within her – and Kuroe is a private investigator and vampire hunter. The story, while slow and methodical in its development, is a gripping combination of romance and suspense.

Iono-sama Fanatics

Miyabi Fujieda; *ser* Dengeki Teioh (2004–06); *vols* Jp 2, US 1 (on hiatus); *age* 13+

In a small kingdom far, far away, Queen Iono dreams that some day she will have a harem full of beautiful girls with long, black hair who love her just as much as she loves them. As it happens, Japan is full of girls who fit that description. So off she goes with her harem in tow, recruiting the willing and not-so-willing into a group in which yuri hijinks aren't just recommended for survival, they're virtually required.

Ninin Ga Shinobuden

Ryoichi Koga; *ser* Dengeki Daioh (2000–06); *vols* 4; age 16+

Shinobu is training to become a ninja. She's a kind-hearted yet somewhat clumsy girl who always has the best of intentions. Unfortunately for her, she's training under the auspices of Onsokumaru, a yellow, blobby, shape-shifting creature who, despite being a perverted, lazy, greedy slob, is somehow the master of his own ninja dojo. Alongside her new friend Kaede, Shinobu fights for truth, justice… and obligatory fan service for the ninjas and the audience.

Madman Entertainment

Est. 1997
madman.com.au

For residents of Australia and New Zealand, Madman *is* anime, controlling 98 percent of the DVD market in that region. It makes sense, then, that the company is the region's dominant force in manga too, with more than three hundred items in its growing catalogue. Madman's dominance in the market is such that US companies Viz and Tokyopop license their products to Madman for distribution in the region. Madman also distributes the products of Singapore-based publisher Chuang Yi.

If a series is popular or being pushed heavily in the US, it's likely to be carried by Madman as well. Current American favourites such as *Fruits Basket*, *Naruto* and *Fullmetal Alchemist* (see pp.122, 159 and 123) are among the titles represented, as well as the classic *Astro Boy* (p.82). However, since Madman is pulling from different sources for its manga, release schedules vary wildly. Release dates for *Naruto* volumes lag far behind those in the US, for example. Yet being in Madman's region also has its perks: the first volume of *Fruits Basket* author Natsuki Takaya's earlier work, *Those With Wings*, was available in English here nine months before Tokyopop's release in April 2009. Living in Australia or New Zealand doesn't always have to mean relying on delayed imports or international orders via the Internet.

Media Blasters

Est. 2004
media-blasters.com

Before entering the manga market, Media Blasters had established itself as a player in the anime scene, licensing and distributing a wide range of anime, from mainstream hits such as *Rurouni Kenshin* (vagabond swordsman with a violent past vows to protect the weak without killing to atone for the lives he's taken) and *Magic Knight Rayearth* (adapted from the CLAMP manga) to hardcore hentai.

Media Blasters' anime strategy had been to start with hentai anime and edgy live-action films before moving on to more mainstream stuff, and its manga wing followed suit. Its first manga, announced in January 2004, was *Flesh for the Beast*, an anthology based on an original live-action horror film that featured seven stories by American comics creators and one by manga duo Studio Zombie. A few months later, the company announced it had licensed *Skyscrapers of Oz*, its first yaoi title, and in short order started picking up sexually explicit yaoi titles, as well as edgy shōnen and seinen titles that eternally teetered on the brink of bad taste.

However, while sales of the yaoi titles were good, the more mainstream shōnen/seinen stuff wasn't doing so well. And so, three years after the manga line debuted, the shōnen line was cut back and the yaoi line further expanded to make up the lion's share of what's being produced by the company today.

Media Blasters hasn't completely given up on the mainstream manga market. A trio of non-yaoi licences were announced in 2007, including *Fujoshi Rumi: Mousou Shoujo Otaku Kei* (see below). Still, Media Blasters' focus looks set to remain with its yaoi line for the foreseeable future.

yaoi, yuri and hentai specialists

ALC Publishing *(est. 2003, yuricon.org/alc.html)*
ALC Publishing is the home of translated Japanese manga, original anthologies and light novels – all, as its website boasts, 100% **yuri manga**. Publisher Erica Friedman, herself a proudly out lesbian, is yuri manga's most vocal advocate: she founded the convention Yuricon in 2000, and her blog at okazu.blogspot.com is the premier source of all things yuri-related on the Internet.

ALC launched in 2003 with Rica Takashima's *Rica'tte Kanji!?* Next came the first volume of *Yuri Monogatari* (*Lily Tales*), an annual anthology of yuri stories that are largely by dōjinshi creators in Japan, North America and Europe. While the stories may contain adult situations and themes, they are never outright pornographic.

Eros MangErotica *(est. 1994, eroscomix.com/manga)*
It all started with a bit of temptation. Literally. *Temptation*, Hiroyuki Utatane's tale of sexual dominance, violence and emotional trauma was the first **hentai** manga published in the Eros MangErotica line. Part of alternative comics publisher Fantagraphics' adult imprint Eros Comix, Eros MangErotica has gone on to become one of the dominant players in the US hentai manga market today.

It's even been suggested that the profits from this line have helped keep the more prominent Fantagraphics side of the business afloat. However, as one of the very first companies to introduce manga to the English-speaking world, Eros MangErotica must also take some of the blame for fostering the "manga equals porn" belief that lingers, to a certain extent, to this day.

Icarus Publishing *(est. 2002, icaruscomics.com)*
Another English-language publisher currently licensing and releasing **ero-manga** (publisher Simon Jones would prefer that you not call his products "hentai manga", thank you very much), Icarus Comics launched its bimonthly ero-manga anthology *Comic AG* in 2002. While the anthology remains the publisher's core product, a number

of series that previously appeared in those pages have been reprinted and collected in trade paperbacks as well.

As is to be expected with products of such an extreme sexual nature, finding Icarus's publications on store shelves can be tricky. Icarus recently opened a digital distribution system in an attempt to get its manga into the hands of more people, posting complete copies of the first few issues of *Comic AG* on BitTorrent sites and allowing users to download them for free. Like ALC Publishing's Erica Friedman, Jones is a vocal advocate for what his company publishes, and his blog has become a popular source of information on ero-manga in general.

Yaoi Press *(est. 2004, yaoipress.com)*
A **yaoi** specialist, as the name suggests, Yaoi Press is also the only publisher to entirely forego licensing Japanese properties in favour of an all-global-manga approach, picking up titles from American and European creators. Publisher Yamila Abraham founded the company in 2004 after a lifetime spent drawing and writing her own yaoi even before she knew what "yaoi" was.

Titles are geared towards girls and women aged thirteen to fifty and range from sweet romances to hardcore sex-filled flings. The most popular titles to date are Abraham and Studio Kosaru's *Winter Demon*, about a snow demon who makes a pact with a monk to defend his village; KŌSEN's *Stallion*, a single-volume story about a cowboy and a Native American who team up to take on a cowboy who wronged them both; and the *Yaoi Hentai* anthology. Designed for audiences aged eighteen and older, *Yaoi Hentai* gained notoriety in the US when "family-friendly" store chain Wal-Mart inadvertently offered copies for sale on its website.

In 2007, Yaoi Press joined forces with Korean manhwa publisher **NetComics** in an online publishing deal in which its less sexually explicit titles can be read for a small fee on NetComics' website (netcomics.com).

Fujoshi Rumi Vol.1 page 58 © NATSUMI KONJOH 2004

Fujoshi Rumi sees the eponymous female otaku try to turn her yaoi fantasies into reality.

Apocalypse Zero

Takayuki Yamaguchi; *ser* Weekly Shonen Champion (1994–96); *vols* Jp 11, US 6; *age* 18+

Another post-apocalyptic, Tokyo-got-levelled-again epic. As usual, a remnant of humanity is struggling to survive, and up pops a badass hero destined to save the world. In this case, it's the teenage Kakugo, a skilled martial artist who has iron balls embedded in his body and armour inhabited by the souls of World War II test subjects. The hook here is the revolting rogues' gallery that confronts him – from a seven-ton fat naked woman to a monster who attacks with huge genitalia – and the equally disgusting ways in which he dispatches them. It's either pulp fiction genius or eye-gougingly awful, depending on your tolerance for such things.

Fujoshi Rumi: Mousou Shoujo Otaku Kei

Natsumi Konjoh; *ser* Comic High (2006–); *vols* ongoing; *age* 16+

Takahiro has a crush on Rumi. The good news is she's interested in him. The bad news is that her interest in him is not as a boyfriend, but as the perfect partner to class playboy Shunsuke in her yaoi fantasies. Rumi is a *fujoshi*, one of those anime and manga fans known in Japan as "rotten girls" for the way they place heterosexual characters into homosexual situations. With popular girl Yoko also coming out as a closet *fujoshi* and teaming up with Rumi, Takahiro may never get what he wants. The two girls, though? Different story. Maybe.

SelfMadeHero

Est. 2007
selfmadehero.com

The formula that UK-based SelfMade-Hero has used to carve its niche in the manga market is simple: take abridged forms of the plays of William Shakespeare as adapted by Richard Appignanesi and have some of the UK's best manga-inspired artists – including some from Sweatdrop Studios – render them in a graphic novel format that appeals to teens. The Manga Shakespeare concept debuted in January 2007 with *Romeo and Juliet* and *Hamlet*; as of August 2009, fourteen of Shakespeare's plays had been adapted to the format.

The settings of the Manga Shakespeare books certainly aren't what you remember from English literature class. *Romeo and Juliet*, for instance, becomes a struggle between warring yakuza families in Tokyo's hip district of Shibuya; *Macbeth* features samurai warriors in a future post-nuclear world of mutants; and *King Lear* becomes a story of Iroquois tribal displacement on the American frontier circa 1759. While these changes in setting make it seem that much creative licence has been taken, this isn't the case: the Manga Shakespeare books retain the original dialogue and as much of the spirit of the story as possible. It's been a successful approach too, with the books regularly among the bestselling Shakespeare titles on amazon.co.uk.

Seven Seas Entertainment

Est. 2004
gomanga.com

Seven Seas' launch line-up was certainly unusual: *Amazing Agent Luna* by Nunzio DeFilippis, Christina Weir and Shiei; *Blade for Barter* by Jason DeAngelis; *Hai!, Last Hope* by Michael Dignan and Kriss Sison; and *No Man's Land* by DeAngelis and Jennyson Rosero. They were all global manga and they were all published online before making their way to traditional book format in early 2005. It wasn't until later that year that Seven Seas announced its first Japanese licence acquisition, the *Boogiepop* series of light novels and manga.

The approach had its share of detractors: how dare they call themselves a manga publisher without any Japanese manga content? But for company founder Jason DeAngelis, a professed fan of Japanese culture who started off translating manga before moving on to make his own, it was a labour of love. Fortunately for him, while companies such as Tokyopop took flak for daring to apply the name manga to titles created outside Japan, Seven Seas largely flew under the radar.

One controversy, however, was unavoidable. In 2006, the company announced it had licensed the series *Kodomo no Jikan*, about a teacher who finds one of his nine-year-old students has developed a crush on him. Shortly before the first volume of the series, renamed *Nymphet* for the US market, was supposed to be released, word got out that the romance between the two characters could be considered paedophilic. Uproar ensued, and while DeAngelis initially tried to defend the title, saying it was not considered pornographic or paedophilic by any means in its home country, sinking support and order cancellations from major distributors finally led to the publication being cancelled.

Controversies aside, what Seven Seas has brought to the table has been rather impressive. It has some of the best-quality printing standards in the industry. It was the first publisher to launch with an extensive webcomic presence before establishing an identity in print media. It was the first to provide samples of its manga for download to the PlayStation Portable, boasting twelve thousand downloads in the first five days the service was offered. It is also among the few English-language publishers to have an imprint dedicated to yuri, having rolled out the **Strawberry** line in 2007. And it does its bit for creators, too, offering global manga creators full ownership of their properties, in keeping with the Japanese way of doing business.

Aoi House/ Aoi House in Love!

Adam Arnold (text), Shiei (art); *ser* n/a; *vols* 4; *age* 16+

Meet Alexis and Sandy – two college guys who love anime, especially hentai. This gets them in trouble with their dorm mates, who eventually toss them out for repeated infractions of the hall rules. Fortunately for them, another dorm on campus, Aoi House, is advertising for new roommates and offering anime viewings and manga readings. Unfortunately, it's home to a group of young women: the "Y" has fallen off the house sign. What can a couple of homeless fanboys do other than move in and endure whatever happens to them?

Boogiepop Doesn't Laugh

Kouhei Kadono (text), Kouji Ogata (art); *ser* Dengeki Animation Magazine (2000); *vols* 2; *age* 16+

Strange things are happening at Shinyo Academy: female students are running away and disappearing, only to turn up dead. Many of the surviving students believe this phenomenon is caused by the death spirit (or shinigami) known as Boogiepop. Yet all is not as it seems. Viewing the story from different students' perspectives, it's possible to see what is really going on… including the role played by the mysterious creature known as the Manticore.

Tetragrammaton Labyrinth

Ei Itou; *ser* Comic Gum (2005–07); *vols* Jp 5, US ongoing; *age* 16+

Meg is a nun. She and her eternally youthful companion Angela share a strange, strong bond – one which they use to their advantage when they battle the demons that continually plague mankind. Meg, of course, uses the power of God, while Angela relies on the powers of… well… whatever strange force is behind her eternal youthfulness. While the series is advertised as part of the Strawberry line, the yuri element largely stays out of the way in favour of a good story.

Sweatdrop Studios

Est. 2001
sweatdrop.com

Sweatdrop Studios is the UK's most prominent outlet for homegrown manga. Its collective of artists has been generating original content since 2001, when four artists who had been self-publishing individually, Hayden Scott-Baron (alias Dock), Laura Watton, Sam Brown (alias Subi) and Foxy, joined forces to start up the studio. Members also regularly run art workshops at area conventions and present tutorials in *Neo* magazine. The majority of the works published are amateur ventures, and the artists aren't full-time. Several Sweatdrop members have earned honours in Tokyopop's Rising Stars of Manga: UK and Ireland competition, including Emma Vieceli, Sonia Leong and Selina Dean.

Sweatdrop's catalogue of more than a hundred titles includes several themed anthologies, including *Blue Is For Boys* and *Pink Is For Girls* (collections of shōnen and shōjo stories, respectively),

Cold Sweat and Tears (nine short stories themed around emotions), *Stardust* (seven stories in a variety of genres, from slapstick comedy to gothic horror) and *Sugardrops* (thirteen stories with an overriding emphasis on the cute and cuddly). Sweatdrop's series tend to fall well within the boundaries of mainstream shōjo and shōnen fare and are generally suited to teenage and older audiences.

Tokyopop

Est.1996
tokyopop.com

Tokyopop doesn't just want people to read manga. The publisher, which calls itself the "leader of the manga revolution", wants people to *live* manga – not only through printed books, but also through Internet videos, mobile phone content and, perhaps some day, even movies and TV.

This multimedia approach has been in place from the very beginning, when the company's founders, Victor Chin, Ron Scovil Jr and Stuart Levy, met at an AOL entrepreneur trade show in 1996. Chin and Scovil were looking to create an anime and manga website with AOL, and Levy was interested in coming on board. The three men shared a love of manga, a desire to bring it to a wider readership in the US, and a belief that it could prove popular if marketed correctly. While the idea for an AOL site languished, a new publication was born: *Mixxzine*, a manga anthology that set Viz and its *Manga Vizion* anthology squarely in its cross hairs. The four series that launched *Mixxzine* in 1997 – the distinctly shōjo *Sailor Moon* and *Magic Knight Rayearth* rubbing elbows with the rather graphic seinen *Ice Blade* and *Parasyte* – were an odd mix, but the plan all along was to split the magazine into two as soon as that became economically viable.

Tokyopop has always acted boldly, starting with its pick-up of the most recognizable licence at the time, *Sailor Moon* (see p.180). But its lasting contribution to the industry came with a raft of initiatives launched in 2002. The "100% Authentic Manga" strategy, which kept pages in the original Japanese right-to-left format and sound effects untranslated, meant the spirit of the original art work remained intact, gaining Tokyopop an early advantage in attracting Japanese authors and publishers. A push to expand the manga market beyond its traditional corner of the comic-book store put more manga on the shelves of traditional bookstores, where they gobbled up an ever-increasing amount of shelf space. And Tokyopop also expanded its catalogue beyond Japanese manga. With the release of *I.N.V.U.*, it became the first to license manhwa. And it has scooped up a bumper crop of global manga creators through its "Rising Stars of Manga" contest and aggressive recruiting.

However, controversy over changes to series has dogged the publisher throughout its history – despite that "100% Authentic Manga" commitment. The shift of *Sailor Moon* from *Mixxzine* to *Smile*, which left fans scrambling to switch their subscriptions, was one early PR gaffe. Accusations that the publisher prioritized profits over reader concerns came easily when character names in the *Initial D* series were changed, especially when Tokyopop explained its motive: it wanted to position the anime version of the series for possible TV broadcast and felt the changed names would be more palatable to US viewers. The translation of *Miracle Girls* also saw name changes, and, in the case of josei title *Tramps Like Us*, the title of the entire series was changed (the literal translation would have been "You're My Pet").

These days, in a more competitive market, Tokyopop appears to have taken a "scorched earth" approach to publishing manga, throwing a bunch of series at the market in the hope that at least one or two will gain enough traction to be profitable. Japanese series in both regular and yaoi flavours? They have those. Manhwa? They have lots of that, too. Global manga? "Rising Stars of Manga" now exists in US and UK flavours and has introduced different categories – comedy, drama, action, sci-fi, mystery, fantasy, romance and horror – to boot. Four global manga – *Bizenghast*, *I Luv Halloween*, *Riding Shotgun* and *A Midnight Opera* – have been turned into online animation shorts. Four others – *Van Von Hunter*, *Peach Fuzz*, *Mail Order Ninja* and *Undertown* – have appeared in US Sunday newspaper comics sections. The Tokyopop website aims to be the portal for manga fans, while a cellphone site offers the usual assortment of wallpapers and ring tones.

Not all of the expansion strategies have worked out. The **Pop Fiction** line of translated novels struggled to gain an audience and was ultimately cancelled. Meanwhile, global manga series have wrapped up sooner than expected when sales didn't meet expectations.

One result of the company's aggressive publishing schedule is that the market has been flooded with Tokyopop titles. While this worked in the beginning, when there weren't nearly as many titles for fans to choose among, readers now have to search for the gems among the dross. For every hit series like *Fruits Basket* or *Princess Ai*, there are at least half a dozen others that appear on the shelves, flounder around for a bit and then disappear.

In June 2008 the company announced it would be splitting into two divisions. **Tokyopop Inc.** would continue to publish manga, while **Tokyopop Media** would handle comics-to-film and digital initiatives. Thirty-nine people were laid off, including veteran manga editors. Several global manga titles were shifted from print to digital-only distribution, and nine series were cancelled outright. Whether these changes herald

a new streamlined operation or one that collapses under its own weight, only time will tell.

Angelic Layer

CLAMP; *ser* Monthly Shōnen Ace (1999–2001); *vols* 5

A new toy craze has the children of Tokyo all a-twitter: "Angelic Layer", a sort of virtual-reality arena-battling game in which children can buy and customize dolls known as "angels" and send them into one-on-one fights. Entering the fray for the first time is Misaki Suzuhara, who sees a doll named Athena battling on TV one day and is instantly smitten. Guided by the rather eccentric scientist Icchan, Misaki becomes a skilled trainer in her own right, and sets off on an inevitable collision path with the mysterious owner of Athena.

Bizenghast

M. Alice LeGrow; *ser* n/a; *vols* ongoing; *age* 13+

A car accident leaves Dinah without her parents and on the edge of insanity… but with the ability to see ghosts. The skill certainly comes in handy when she and her friend Vincent stumble upon an abandoned mausoleum and are subsequently tasked with helping otherworldly creatures recapture lost souls. The penalty for failure: Dinah will forfeit her own soul. It's a game of high stakes in a dreamlike world.

Manga Sutra / Futari H

Aki Katsu; *ser* Young Animal (1997–); *vols* ongoing; *age* 18+

Three words are sufficient summary for this series: manga sex manual. Makoto and Yura are two newlywed virgins with no reason to stay virginal much longer. Through the suggestions of friends, colleagues and whatever media they can find on the topic, the couple learn how to have a fulfilling sex life. Tokyopop's translation also comes with sex advice from a licensed therapist and aphrodisiac recipes.

Sgt Frog

Mine Yoshizaki; *ser* Monthly Shonen Ace (1999–); *vols* ongoing; *age* 13+

Keroro, the leader of a platoon of frog-like invaders from the planet Keron, has set his sights on the planet of Pokopen as his next conquest. The problem is that "Pokopen" is Earth. Fortunately, Keroro is easily distracted with building model kits of the Gundam robotic suits and other cool toys, and the Hinata family easily subdue him, along with a subsequent wave of attackers, which consists of four of his colleagues. If the Keroro Platoon are to have any hope of conquering Pokopen, they'll have to overcome the Hinatas first… which they'll do right after they've finished the chores assigned to them by the family.

Udon Entertainment

Est. 2000
udonentertainment.com

The past few years have been busy ones for this Canada-based publisher. Udon started out creating comics based on the *Street Fighter* videogame franchise. Then it began licensing manga based on *Street Fighter* and other Capcom properties. Now it's expanded into other areas of the

manga market, as well as branching out into manhwa.

When ICE Kunion, a consortium of three Korean manhwa publishers, dissolved in December 2006, Udon picked up some of the licences left behind. It also picked up *Robot*, a manga/artbook anthology that Digital Manga Publishing dropped due to low sales but which still had a modest following, and added a similar manhwa venture, *Apple*, to complement that series.

In late 2008 Udon announced it would be releasing Kai's *1520*, about two teens from different kingdoms bound by a curse that de-ages them, as part of a digital manga and comic digest posted on the online video streaming site Crunchyroll. Another bold move came with its "Manga for Kids" initiative, which aimed to expand the market for children's manga beyond brand-name fare like *Pokémon*, *Digimon* and *Yu-Gi-Oh!* Udon teamed up with Japanese publisher Poplar to release four series starting in April 2009: *The Big Adventures of Majoko*, in which a young female wizard befriends a human girl; *Ninja Baseball Kyuma*, in which a ninja learns how to play baseball; *Fairy Idol Kanon*, in which fairies compete in singing contests; and *Swans in Space*, the story of a pair of classmates embarking on interstellar adventures as members of the Space

Patrol. It remains to be seen whether these original properties can succeed in a market dominated by heavily promoted franchises.

Vertical

Est. 2003
vertical-inc.com

While most US manga publishers have focused their efforts on picking up the hottest new titles coming out of Japan, Vertical's first offering in 2003 was Osamu Tezuka's religious series *Buddha*, originally serialized in 1972–83. It's not exactly *Naruto*-type sales potential we're looking at here.

But, then, Vertical wasn't founded as a manga publisher per se; rather, its aim is to release to English-speaking markets translations of the best contemporary Japanese books of all kinds. Its position as a publisher of Japanese fiction and non-fiction has helped the company bypass the usual licence-acquisition process. Rather than dealing with Japanese publishing companies, Vertical goes straight to the source – the authors or their estates. The result has been one of the largest collections of translated Tezuka manga, including *Apollo's Song*, *Black Jack* (see p.92), *Dororo*, *MW* and *Ode to Kirihito*. The company has also

picked up two Keiko Takemiya series, *Andromeda Stories* and *To Terra* (see p.186), as well as the *Guin Saga* manga, which ties in nicely with the novels also being released.

After seeing its manga line succeed beyond expectations, Vertical is pushing ahead with expansion, increasing its coverage of more contemporary manga, particularly in the popular shōjo genre.

Andromeda Stories

Keiko Takemiya; *ser* Manga Shōnen (1980–81); *vols* Jp 2, US 3

The marriage of Prince Ithaca of Cosmoralia to Princess Lilia of Ayodoya was supposed to be a blessed event for the inhabitants of the planet Astria. All the celestial signs pointed towards Ithaca being a holy king in what was termed a "papacy". What nobody guessed was that all this would come about only after an invasion by a force of hostile machines, that Ithaca would become a cruel ruler, and that Lilia's unborn child would end up being the one to save them all.

The Guin Saga Manga: The Seven Magi

Kaoru Kurimoto (text), Kazuaki Yanagisawa (art); *ser* n/a; *vols* 3

Guin, a warrior often seen wearing a leopard's mask, has become the king of Cheironia, yet an evil dragon and its seven magi are already conspiring to get him out of there. With the help of a priestess and an elder mage, Guin is ready to take on his opponents' challenge – and if he dies in the process, so be it.

Knocking at death's door

Say what you will about the publishers that have gone out of business over the years – they either informed the public they were shutting down, or flamed out so spectacularly it was clear they weren't coming back. For a handful of others, though, the question of whether they've left the manga stage for good isn't quite so easy to determine.

ADV Manga *(est. 2003)*
When AD Vision announced in 2003 that it would start publishing translated manga, the move seemed to make perfect sense; after all, ADV Films was one of the US's top anime publishers. ADV CEO John Ledford said that the company had licensed a thousand volumes of manga and manhwa. But not many of those would reach consumers. Between 2003 and 2006, 42 series went on months-long, unexplained hiatuses, and another 11 were announced but never released. All the company's manhwa licences disappeared, and even some of its bestselling titles, such as *Chrono Crusade*, *Full Metal Panic* and *Cromartie High School* (see p.31), experienced hiccups. And so ADV Manga has earned the dubious honour of being the publisher with the most highly scrutinized list of delayed or cancelled series in the industry. Ledford has since said it was a matter of bad timing: AD Vision jumped into the US manga market just as established companies were ramping up production. The competition for shelf space was simply too hot. But try explaining that to fans who are still waiting for a handful of volumes to complete their collection of *Steel Angel Kurumi*.

After financial difficulties at AD Vision in 2008 saw the elimination of magazine *Newtype USA* and several anime series, fans feared ADV Manga could be next for the chop. Rumours have circulated that the division has already been secretly shut down, but company spokesman Chris Oarr has insisted this is not the case. Still, as he told *Publishers Weekly* that June, even he didn't know when the next volume of the Eisner-nominated *Yotsuba&!* would come out: "I know we've been criticized for our PR strategy… But right now … it just doesn't serve anybody's purpose [to answer that question]… We don't know, and we're not going to lie about it." (For the record, *Yotsuba&!* did resurface in late 2009 – at Yen Press.) It's a shame, really, because when ADV Manga excels at a series, it really excels – particularly with short series that it can release quickly and on a consistent schedule.

CPM Manga *(est. 1994)*
One of the first English-language manga translators, CPM Manga was an offshoot of Central Park Media, a noted anime video distributor. It launched in 1994 with a global

manga adaptation of the *Project A-Ko* anime, by *Ninja High School* author Ben Dunn. But notable releases were few and far between in the 1990s as CPM focused on its anime.

CPM Manga hit its stride in the early 2000s, releasing several series based on popular anime franchises. Highlights included the swords-and-sorcery shōnen *Record of Lodoss Wars*; another shōnen series, *Slayers*, featuring teenage sorceress Lina Inverse; and spacefaring adventure *Nadesico*. Another branch, CPM Manhwa, handled licences of Korean titles, while the Manga 18 branch translated hentai. In late 2004, however, financial problems began to affect the publisher's release schedules. Central Park Media suspended the CPM Manga and Manhwa lines in 2005 to restructure distribution deals, laying off a number of staff. The collapse of two major retailers didn't help matters, forcing another round of layoffs in 2006. The publisher pressed on, with a few titles trickling out under a new yaoi imprint, Be Beautiful, though the financial problems continued. While Be Beautiful was a strong CPM imprint, in 2007 it was hit by a very public dispute with Libre, the titles' Japanese licensor, who claimed CPM was publishing its titles illegally. CPM Manga has remained silent ever since; with the publisher perilously close to bankruptcy at the time of writing, it would not be surprising to see it vanish completely by the time this book sees print.

DramaQueen *(est. 2005)*

DramaQueen is well on the road to being the yaoi equivalent of ADV: it surfaces once in a while to insist it's still alive and kicking, but fails to follow through with any new releases. The publisher got off to a strong start, releasing both licensed and global yaoi manga, including the anthology *Rush*; *Challengers*, a shōnen-ai comedy about a pretty-boy college student and the office worker who falls for him; and *Audition*, a manhwa about an aspiring rock band. There was also a shōjo manhwa wing, but when a company markets itself as "Purveyor of Fine Man Sex" – as it reportedly did at Yaoi-Con 2006 – it's clear most of its eggs are going in the yaoi basket for the time being.

After the initial flurry of titles, however, the flow of books slowed and finally stopped in late 2007 with little explanation. The silence lasted until April 2008, when company president Tran Nguyen told *Publishers Weekly* that the company had reorganized, a new financial partner had been found, and more yaoi would be making its way to stores shortly. In June 2008, posts by employee Taisa Tolunchanian on the company's online message boards cast doubt on the existence of those new investors. DramaQueen's fate remains unclear.

Viz Media

Est. 1987
vizmedia.com

Arguably the market leader in the US manga market, Viz has in its stable many of the industry's heaviest hitters past and present, including *Bleach*, *Fullmetal Alchemist* (see p.123), *Naruto* (see p.159), *Ranma ½* (see p.175), *Dragon Ball* (see p.116), CLAMP's *X/1999*, *Ouran High School Host Club*, *Nana*, *Honey and Clover* and *Rurouni Kenshin*, to name just a few. Being jointly owned by Shogakukan, Shueisha and Shogakukan's licensing division ShoPro Japan – and thus having access to a steady, largely exclusive pipeline of titles – certainly helps in landing hits of that calibre.

Viz has had quite a while to establish its present dominant position in the market, being one of the first companies to offer translated manga in the US. Its founder was businessman Seiji Horibuchi, who originally worked to export American culture to Japan but soon had the idea of publishing manga in the US. In 1986, he formed an alliance with Shogakukan and Eclipse Comics, which at the time was looking to license several manga but found no Japanese publisher willing to hand over the rights to their series. (The concern at the time was that US publishers would re-edit or re-draw series as they saw fit.) Together, they released three series in 1987: Sanpei Shirato's *Legend of Kamui*, a drama set in feudal-era Japan; Kaoru Shinitani's *Area 88*, an air-combat drama filled with political intrigue; and *Mai the Psychic Girl*, about a teenage girl with telekinetic powers (see p.29). All were released in the traditional American comic-book format.

Sales of those three titles were decent, if unspectacular. There was only so much that Viz could do to penetrate a market still heavily focused on traditional comics. But the company pressed on, publishing manga under its own banner from 1988, first as comics and then in collected graphic-novel editions. In the 1990s it expanded and diversified its catalogue, adding a few shōjo titles to what had originally been a shōnen-dominated line-up. It also launched several magazines, which were instrumental in disseminating manga culture, including *Animerica*, a monthly magazine that profiled anime and manga series and creators; *Manga Vizion* (1995–98), a monthly manga anthology for general audiences, and its replacement *Animerica Extra* (1998–2004); and *Pulp* (1997–2002), a manga anthology for adult audiences. But two properties in particular – *Pokémon* in the 1990s, and the *Shonen Jump* anthology, launched with fan favourites *Dragon Ball Z*, *One Piece*, *Yu Yu Hakusho* and *Yu-Gi-Oh!* in 2002 – have propelled Viz to the forefront of manga fans' minds.

Still, leadership has its disadvantages. While Viz generally avoids editing artwork, readers have been unhappy with the few edits that have been made, notably in *I*"s, where stars cover a character's nudity, and in *Fullmetal Alchemist*, where a character shown on a cross in the Japanese version is shown on a more generic slab of stone. The publisher responded by saying the changes were made to fit criteria for release to a wider US audience and that they had the full cooperation of the original creators. Viz's desire to attract a wider audience has also brought complaints that its translations are not wholly accurate, with long-running series sometimes having wildly varying translations as translation teams are cycled on and off.

Unlike most of the other English-language manga publishers, Viz has for the most part stayed out of the global manga market. An exception was *One World Manga*, a joint venture with the World Bank that addressed such global issues as HIV/AIDS, poverty and the environment.

Bobobo-bo Bo-bobo

Yoshio Sawai; *ser* Weekly Shōnen Jump (2001–07); *vols* ongoing; *age* 13+

It is the year 300X, and the Maruhage Empire is cracking down on anyone who dares to have hair, shaving offenders bald. A new defender of the people emerges in the form of the Afro-ed Bobobo-bo Bo-bobo. With the help of his companions – including Beauty, a girl once saved by Bobobo-bo Bo-bobo; Poppa Rocks, the round creature whose powers lie in his own insanity; and General Jelly Jiggler, with the power of, umm, jiggling jelly – he will take the fight to the Maruhage Empire! That is, if the

group can stop the infighting and be serious about what they're doing – a formidable task in itself.

Dance Till Tomorrow

Naoki Yamamoto; *ser* Big Comic Spirits (1989–90); *vols* 7; *age* 18+

Suekichi Yamamoto is a college student who'd rather work backstage with a theatre troupe than complete his studies. However, if he graduates from college and starts a career, he stands to inherit ¥450 million from his late great-grand-father. Sounds a breeze, but of course there's a complication: Aya, a woman who mysteriously appears at his great-grandfather's funeral and proceeds to drive her way into Suekichi's life… not to mention his pants. As one-night stands turn into longer-term sexual encounters, Suekichi has to figure out a way to get his life back on track.

Even a Monkey Can Draw Manga

Koji Aihara and Kentaro Takekuma; *ser* Big Comic Spirits (1989); *vols* Jp 2, US 1 (cancelled); *age* 18+

This would-be tutorial manga for up-and-coming artists doesn't so much skewer sacred cows as slaughter them, rack them up on a spit, grill them and slather barbecue sauce over them. Few manga clichés are spared as Aihara and Takekuma take on such "important" lessons as how to draw a manga about mah-jongg if you've never played it; and how all shōjo manga are built on the premise of a heroine running out of her house, late for something, with a piece of toast dangling from her mouth. If that's not enough, the authors draw themselves naked. Often.

Sexy Voice and Robo

Iou Kuroda; *ser* Ikki (2000); *vols* 1; *age* 16+

Nico Hayashi is Sexy Voice, a fourteen-year-old girl who works for a phone club, chatting with men who want to talk to what they believe are attractive young women in a non-sexual manner. Iichiro Sudo, also known as Robo, is one of Sexy Voice's clients, a rather average-looking otaku. When Sexy Voice is recruited to help an older man with a shady background, she ends up pulling Robo into her world, commandeering him to help her get around town and act as her muscle on occasion. The real story here is about relationships and communication, all presented in a lavishly detailed Tokyo. Perhaps its only drawback is that Kuroda never finished the series.

Striker (Spriggan)

Hiroshi Takashige (text), Ryoji Minagawa (art); *ser* Weekly Shōnen Sunday (1988); *vols* Jp 11, US 3 (cancelled); *age* 13+

Ancient, powerful artefacts from a civilization technologically superior to our own are being unearthed around the world, and it's up to the ARCAM Corporation's military arm and its Spriggan units to prevent those artefacts from falling into the wrong hands. Yu Ominae is ARCAM's top Spriggan operator stationed in Japan, but he has a tortured past as one of the victims of a CIA/US Army programme that kidnapped children, brainwashed them and stuck them into a covert black ops programme known as COSMOS. This series is one of the most striking examples of Viz's early censorship, as much of the blatant anti-Western sentiment and many violent scenes were cut out.

Yen Press

Est. 2006
yenpress.us

Yen Press may be one of the newer publishers in the industry, but its relative youth is offset by several formidable forces: the imprint is backed by Hachette, the world's third-largest publisher, and led by former DC Comics vice president Rich Johnson and ex-Borders Group graphic novel buyer Kurt Hassler. Having Hassler on board was a major coup for Yen, as he had recently been named the "most powerful person in manga" by online industry analyst ICv2.com.

So far, so good. While the average retail price of Yen's books has been $1 higher than similar offerings from Viz and Tokyopop, its manga has tried to mirror the Japanese releases as much as possible. "My goal is for Yen Press to be as transparent as possible", Hassler told *Publishers Weekly* in February 2007, "and provide fans with as authentic an experience as we can short of learning Japanese." The company has not limited itself to any particular genre, so titles like Keiko Tobe's *With the Light: Raising an Autistic Child* share catalogue space with the latest series from Peach-Pit, *Zombie Loan*, the entire ICE Kunion catalogue of manhwa, and a few global manga creators, including Svetlana Chmakova, fresh from her success with Tokyopop's *Dramacon*.

Signs point to steady growth across these varied markets. In summer 2008 Yen launched a monthly manga anthology, *Yen Plus*, whose initial line-up reflected its diverse blend of titles. Expansion into the yaoi market came with the acquisition of several series by Lily Hoshino, with the first title, *Love Quest*, released in October 2008. Yen is also dabbling in the light novel market, with translations of the *Haruhi Suzumiya* novels courtesy of a partnership with Little, Brown.

Yen's titles are distributed in the UK by Orbit – Little, Brown's science fiction/fantasy imprint. The company has promised that release dates in the UK will closely parallel those in the US.

Alice on Deadlines

Shiro Ihara; *ser* Gangan Wing (2004–06); *vols* ongoing; *age* 16+

A lecherous shinigami is thrown into the buxom body of a young schoolgirl, while the girl's soul is knocked into a nearby skeleton. Hilarity ensues as the shinigami enjoys his new body a little too much for the normally prim and proper girl's comfort.

With the Light: Raising an Autistic Child

Keiko Tobe; *ser* For Mrs. (2000–); *vols* ongoing; *age* 13+

Caring for an autistic child in a world that doesn't quite understand the disorder can create a whole slew of challenges for the parents. Tobe's series doesn't offer any easy answers, but it does provide an enlightening exploration, presenting a variety of perspectives on how parents can deal with the various issues they're likely to encounter.

Zombie Loan

Peach-Pit; *ser* G Fantasy (2003–); *vols* ongoing; *age* 16+

A girl with the gift of "shinigami eyes" – the ability to see lines around the necks of people that signify they're destined to die soon – teams up with two boys who should have died already but are now under the employ of the Zombie Loan agency. This tale of zombie hunters is a darker turn for Peach-Pit, but the stories are action-packed and the mysteries are introduced and resolved in short order.

7

The Information

where to go next

As the market for manga has grown in the West, so too has the number of resources available that explore manga and the surrounding culture. (The book you're reading now is proof of that.) Whether you want to learn more about manga, draw your own or meet other people with similar interests, there's certain to be some book, website or anime convention listed here that meets your needs.

Books

Getting a full perspective on the story of manga would take far more space than is available in this book. If you'd like to learn more about manga – the history, the series, the people in the industry – you can't go wrong with these books.

The Astro Boy Essays: Osamu Tezuka, Mighty Atom, and the Anime/Manga Revolution

Frederik L. Schodt (Stone Bridge Press, 2007)

The newest of Schodt's books devoted to the manga/anime phenomenon takes a tighter focus than his previous two titles (also covered in this section), exploring the life and times of Osamu Tezuka and framing it within the context of his global hit series, *Astro Boy*.

Schodt's first manga title is still the gold standard by which others are measured.

Dreamland Japan: Writings on Modern Manga

Frederik L. Schodt (Stone Bridge Press, 1996)

The spiritual successor to Schodt's seminal work *Manga! Manga!* is a compilation of observations made of the Japanese manga industry over a sixteen-year time period, looking at various manga magazines, artists and their work, and how manga complements other forms of pop culture in Japan. It also looks at how manga has expanded into international markets, including an early look at what was then an emergent market in the US.

500 Manga Heroes and Villains

Helen McCarthy (Collins & Brown/Barrons, 2006)

McCarthy, one of the leading manga experts outside of Japan, frames the global manga phenomenon in the context of five hundred signature characters and groups from manga history. The categories she explores include male and female heroes, male and female villains, teams, otherworldly characters and characters with a real historical basis.

Japanomerica

Roland Kelts (Palgrave Macmillan, 2007)

Lecturer and writer Roland Kelts explores why Western audiences are so infatuated with Japanese pop culture, including anime and manga, framing his journey in the context of interviews with creators, critics and fans in both nations.

Manga Design

Masanao Amano (Taschen, 2004)

A virtual encyclopedia of manga artists, this book showcases the art of 140 artists from Koji Aihara (known most in the Western world for *Even a Monkey Can Draw Manga*) through to Sensha Yoshida (who has yet to have any of his manga published in English). The range of artists profiled is vast and all have made a contribution to Japanese culture, even if their works haven't been translated outside of Japan.

Manga! Manga! The World of Japanese Comics

Frederik L. Schodt (Kodansha International, 1983)

The gold standard by which all books about manga are measured. Schodt's book, despite its age, holds up remarkably well today as a snapshot of the industry at the time, from its origins to the present day, with in-depth explorations of the various genres. Translated selections from four manga series are also included within its pages; it would take years before two of these series, Osamu Tezuka's *Phoenix* and Keiji Nakazawa's *Barefoot Gen,* would receive more robust English translations. Meanwhile, Riyoko Ikeda's *Rose of Versailles* and Leiji Matsumoto's *Ghost Warrior* have yet to be fully translated.

Manga: Masters of the Art

Timothy R. Lehmann (HarperCollins, 2005)

Lehmann explores the manga phenomenon through interviews with twelve creators, each with a distinctive style: Kia Asamiya, CLAMP, Tatsuya Egawa, Usamaru Furuya, Takehiko Inoue, Suehiro Maruo, Reiko Okano, Erica Sakurazawa, Miou Takaya, Jiro Taniguchi, Yuko Tsuno and Mafuyu Hiroki.

Manga: Sixty Years of Japanese Comics

Paul Gravett (Collins Design/HarperCollins, 2004)

A freelance journalist, curator, lecturer and broadcaster who has worked in comics publishing, Gravett offers a thematic look at manga and how it has evolved for different audiences – boys, girls, men, women – as well as underground movements and manga's growth into a major export and global influence. It's a large-format full-colour book that makes use of excerpts from a wide range of manga to illustrate its points.

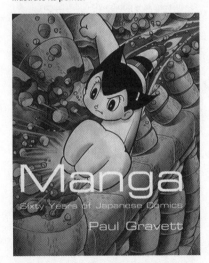

Packed with full-colour illustrations, Gravett covers manga's development in every area, from girls' stuff to hentai.

Manga: The Complete Guide

Jason Thompson (Ballantine Books/Del Rey, 2007)

Thompson, with the help of 24 other writers, meticulously catalogues more than 900 English-translated manga series in all genres – from mainstream shōnen and shōjo to hardcore hentai books – in one volume, rating them from zero to four stars and offering short synopses for each. Essential for the genre completist.

Mechademia

Various; Frenchy Lunning, ed. (University of Minnesota Press, www.mechademia.org)

The first regularly published English-language academic journal comes courtesy of Frenchy Lunning, a liberal arts professor at the Minneapolis College of Art and Design, and offers academic and critical commentary on anime, manga, Japanese pop culture and the fans of all three. Each volume is based on a common theme, like "Limits of the Human" and "Networks of Desire".

The Rough Guide to Anime

Simon Richmond (Rough Guides, 2009)

What this book does for manga, Simon Richmond does for anime. It's a look at the origins of anime and its spread in popularity in the West, along with accounts of the fifty essential anime and biographies of key industry personalities.

Schoolgirl Milky Crisis: Adventures in the Anime and Manga Trade

Jonathan Clements (Titan Books, 2009)

Clements, the co-author of the *Anime Encyclopedia* and *Dorama Encyclopedia*, has spent close to two decades writing about anime and manga as editor of *Manga Max* magazine, contributing editor at *Newtype USA* and currently as a columnist for *Neo Magazine*. A collection of his essays and interviews for those magazines is included here. The title refers to a fictitious anime show that Clements made up to protect his industry insider sources, both innocent and guilty.

Tezuka: The Marvel of Manga

Philip Brophy, ed. (National Gallery of Victoria, 2006)

This hard-bound catalogue was produced in conjunction with the exhibition of the same name, which originated in Australia before heading to San Francisco. Included are 66 samples of the 234 Tezuka art pieces featured in the exhibit, as well as 7 essays focused on Tezuka's work.

THE ROUGH GUIDE to
Anime
the artwork • the stories • the studios
Simon Richmond

Understanding Comics / Reinventing Comics / Making Comics

Scott McCloud (Harper Paperbacks, 1994/2000/2006)

Comics artist Scott McCloud's first book, *Understanding Comics*, was among the first comics-related books to delve into what makes manga unique from artistic and storytelling standpoints. McCloud has since expanded on those thoughts in two follow-up books. All three are excellent resources for learning about comics as a whole and not just about manga.

Watching Anime, Reading Manga

Fred Patten (Stone Bridge Press, 2004)

Patten was one of the pioneering forces in raising awareness of anime and manga in the US in the 1970s and can bear witness to both industries' evolution over the years. This book collects 25 years' worth of essays previously published in fan publications, with some additional commentary from Patten about changes that took place after his original essays were published.

McCloud's iconic self-portrait graces the front cover of this seminal book on the graphic arts.

Books on drawing manga

Toss a rock at any respectable section on art, drawing and cartooning in a bookstore, and it's likely that you'll hit several dozen "how to draw manga" books on the shelves. While the aims of these books are admirable, the truth is that many of them are little more than overglorified basic art books with big eyes, speed lines and exotically coloured hair attached. Which is fine in itself, but for guides on how genuine Japanese artists work, take a look at the following translated titles.

Shoujo Manga Techniques: Drawing Basics / Writing Stories

Hirono Tsubasa and Nene Kotobuki (Drawing Basics), Mako Itsuki (Writing Stories) (DMP, 2005)

A two-volume series that breaks down the entire thought process behind drawing and writing a story suitable for shōjo manga, even going so far as to discuss how to submit work to a prospective publisher.

Draw Your Own Manga: All the Basics / Beyond the Basics / Honing Your Style

Haruno Nagatomo (Kodansha International, 2003)

This series of books is used as the textbooks of choice at Tokyo Animation College, the top school for manga artists in Japan. Translated interviews with artists Takao Yaguchi, Toru Fujisawa, Shinji Mizushima and Monkey Punch are also included.

Shōjo Beat's Manga Artist Academy

Hiroyuki Iizuka (concept), Amu Sumoto et al. (art) (Viz, 2006)

Shōjo artists Shoko Akira, Yukiko Iisaka, Miyuki Kitagawa, Mayu Shinjo, Chie Shinohara, Emiko Sugi, Rie Takada, Masami Takeuchi and Yuu Watase act as guides for the entire process of drawing manga, from conception to publication.

Drawing manga for girls by girls: there's no mistaking the shōjo sensibility of this guide to becoming a mangaka.

Magazines

The early 2000s were peak years for Western readers who got their fill of anime and manga news and reviews from magazines. In 2002, just as the Tokyopop "100% Authentic Manga" initiative was gaining critical mass, four magazines were published regularly: *Animerica*, *Anime Insider* (then known as *Anime Invasion*), *Newtype USA* and *Protoculture Addicts*. In 2009, only the last of these was still running. While *Neo Magazine* in the UK (established in 2004) and *Otaku USA* (2007) have since filled the void, the influence of print publications appears to be waning. Manga anthologies have fared better: Viz's *Shonen Jump* (starting in 2002) and *Shojo Beat* (2005) have remained strong and were joined by Yen Press's *Yen Plus* in 2008.

Neo

neomag.co.uk

Coverage of anime and manga series makes up a good portion of this UK-based magazine, but the editorial content goes beyond just those two areas, covering much of Asian pop culture, such as Japanese, Korean and Chinese entertainment, such as music and live-action movies and TV series, in the process.

Otaku USA

otakuusamagazine.com

Otaku USA boasts a veteran corps of writers and editors that includes Patrick Macias as editor in chief, Jason Thompson as manga editor, and contributing writers such as Casey Brienza, Ed Chavez, Erin Finnegan and Gilles Poitras. This editorial team has helped the publication, one of the newer ones on the market (debuting in 2007), quickly establish itself as a premier source of information for more mature manga fans.

Protoculture Addicts

protoculture.ca

Originally started as a *Robotech* fan magazine, it has since expanded to cover all anime and manga, supplementing its coverage through an alliance with the Anime News Network website. The layouts may not be pretty, but the information provided more than makes up for the generally bland appearance.

Otaku USA's typically vibrant cover catering for the manga/anime/videogame-obsessed US fan.

Shonen Jump / Shojo Beat

shonenjump.com
shojobeat.com

These two monthly Viz publications are the only manga anthologies that have survived – and to all intents and purposes, flourished – ever since they first hit newsstands. *Naruto*, *Bleach* and *One Piece* have been the flagship series for *Shonen Jump* and its collection of manga for ages thirteen and up, while *Shojo Beat* targets an audience of older teen females with titles like *Honey and Clover*, *Nana* and *Vampire Knight*.

Yen Plus

yenpress.us/?cat=4

Yen Press's answer to *Shonen Jump* and *Shojo Beat* is aimed at older teens of both genders, offering a mix of manga, manhwa and OEL manga. Popular titles highlighted in its pages so far have included *Maximum Ride* by James Patterson and NaRae Lee, *Nightschool* by Svetlana Chmakova, *Soul Eater* by Atsushi Okubo and *Higurashi: When They Cry* by "Ryukishi07".

Teen characters aimed at teen readers: Yen Press's *Yen Plus* caters to both genders.

Websites

The Internet has been one of the major influences fuelling the boom in manga, helping spread news faster than ever before and giving fans in remote corners of the world a common venue where they can discuss their favourite series. While there are many sites worth a visit, what follows is a cross-section of the best resources for online news and commentary. In addition to the sites listed here, all manga publishers maintain an online presence – see Chapter 6. Also, check social networking sites like twitter.com, facebook.com and myspace.com – you're bound to find fans with similar interests, or perhaps even industry professionals who maintain a presence there too.

Anime News Network

animenewsnetwork.com
animenewsnetwork.com.au

Since 1998, this site founded by Justin Sevakis has grown and expanded into the premier English-language site for anime and manga news both in Japan and around the world. A comprehensive encyclopedia of anime and manga titles, review columns like Bamboo Dong's "Shelf Life" (for anime) and Carlos Santos' "Right Turn Only" (for manga), Brian Hanson's weekly "Hey Answerman!" column, plus other regular news and commentary features as well as an active online community make it worth a visit every day.

A vast archive of anime and manga info, the ANN front page has daily news updates.

About.com: Manga

manga.about.com

Published cartoonist Deb Aoki hosts this regularly updated, wide-ranging look at all things manga, from an introduction to the form to looks at emerging trends in the market.

Anime Vice

animevice.com

Gia Manry, a freelance journalist and blogger based in Portland, Oregon, first rose to prominence online as a staff writer for the now-defunct animeOnline in 2007. After two years of running her own blog, she was hired as managing editor of Anime Vice, a portal featuring news, reviews, an encyclopedia of anime and manga series and forums. Her writing style comes from the perspective of the average fan, sharing the glee of finding good stuff and cringing in horror at the bad.

ComiPedia

comipedia.com

Having trouble distinguishing between *Shōnen Sunday*, *Shōnen Jump* and *Shōnen Sirius*? This site provides information on all the Japanese manga anthologies, publishers and imprints.

ComiPress

comipress.com

Formerly an offshoot blog of Manga Jouhou, ComiPress has forged its own path since August 2006, reporting on manga news and trends from around the world with an emphasis on the US and Japan.

Icarus Publishing blog

icaruscomics.com/wp_web/

Publisher Simon Jones may be most vocal about ero-manga, but his blog runs the gamut of commentary on current manga issues in every genre, and in both Japanese and Western markets.

Inoue Takehiko on the Web

itplanning.co.jp/newse.html

The creator of *Slam Dunk* and *Vagabond* (see pp.182 and 188), is one of the only mangaka who regularly maintains an English-language website in addition to his native Japanese. Features include Inoue's blog, sketches from current and past series, and the eighty-chapter, online-exclusive story *Buzzer Beater*.

MangaBlog

mangablog.net

Freelance writer Brigid Alverson set up her blog back in March 2005 with the aim of making sense of all the goings-on in the manga world. It currently monitors around fifty different manga blogs, as well as a range of news sites, offers interviews, reviews and also compiles companies' press releases.

MangaCast

mangacast.net

Ed Chavez and team contribute their thoughts on everything related to manga culture, including the latest releases in Japan and the US, previews of upcoming releases, analysis of sales information, and even experiences they're having in Japan.

Manga Jouhou

manganews.net

Publisher press releases and manga reviews complement the site's most valuable resource: a comprehensive database of around seven thousand manga series including info on whether anyone has taken up the task of scanlating unlicensed titles into English.

Mania.com Anime/Manga

mania.com/anime_manga_oav_ova_dvd_category_143.html

Mania's anime and manga coverage has as its foundation the news and reviews once hosted by Chris Beveridge's Anime on DVD website, bought out by Mania in 2008. The simple layout may be missing, but all the old content has migrated over and is now supplemented by fresh news and reviews. Of particular note is the "manga comparisons" database, where you can see all the titles ever published or announced by a given publisher... and whether they're still published or have been cancelled.

Matt Thorn

matt-thorn.com

Thorn, a cultural anthropologist now working in Japan as an associate professor in the School of Manga Production at Seika University, is one of the pre-eminent scholars of shōjo manga. His site offers columns and papers he's on the subject, an interview with Moto Hagio published in *The Comics Journal* in 2005, and other work relating to manga.

The Overlooked Manga Festival

shaenon.livejournal.com/60625.html

Viz editor, freelance writer and online comic artist Shaenon K. Garrity offers a roundup of more than fifty series, complete with selected scans of pages, that she feels were ignored by American readers for whatever reason. Other editors and site visitors chip in with additions to the list.

Okazu

okazu.blogspot.com

The oldest and most comprehensive blog devoted to yuri anime and manga is the online home of Erica Friedman, president of Yuricon and ALC Publishing and proud advocate for all things yuri.

Rumic World

furinkan.com

Everything you ever wanted to know about Rumiko Takahashi, including her major and minor works, her characters and numerous interviews over the years, is included at this site. It's a veritable treasure trove of information on a beloved creator.

Tezuka in English

tezukainenglish.com

When the official Osamu Tezuka website (tezuka.co.jp) converted to an all-Japanese format in 2008, the makeover eliminated what was once a large repository of information in English about the artist and his work, "Tezuka Osamu @ World". Fortunately for Western fans, this volunteer-run site was established in 2005, filling the details void with biographical details, Tezuka-related news, character and series profiles, analytical essays and an active online forum.

Conventions

Most of these events are officially anime conventions but the name is one of convenience more than anything. Calling them "anime, manga and Japanese pop culture love fests" would take far too long. Indeed, many of the events feature some kind of manga component, whether it's tied in with the featured anime, part of the manga lending libraries that sometimes open in conjunction with the event, or in the "artist alley", where the Western version of the Japanese dōjinshi culture comes to life. This is only a small sampling of the events out there; check out AnimeCons.com for a comprehensive listing, including exact dates for upcoming conventions and up-to-date listings of the guests scheduled to attend.

AmeCon

amecon.org

An event started by the Leicester Anime and Manga Club in 2004 has since grown into one of the largest events in the UK, with all 1300 attendee slots for the 2008 convention filled within three weeks of the preregistration period. Its home for the past few years has been on the campus of the University of Leicester.

Anime Expo

anime-expo.org

The largest US anime convention, held in Southern California, has weathered its share of criticism in recent years, with moves to locations in Long Beach and downtown Los Angeles spurring griping among fans about the lack of space. For all intents and purposes, though, the event remains an industry magnet that draws thousands each July.

Anime North

animenorth.com

Running since 1997, the Toronto-based Anime North is Canada's oldest and most prominent anime convention, having in the past hosted artists including Svetlana Chmakova, Ben Dunn and Stan Sakai.

Armageddon Expo

armageddonexpo.com
pulpexpo.com

This is more of a sci-fi convention that happens to have an anime and manga component, but it runs several times each year at various sites in Australia and New Zealand.

Comic-Con International: San Diego

comic-con.org

The granddaddy of them all when it comes to gatherings that celebrate manga, this renowned annual comics convention has welcomed artists from Japan as far back as 1981, when Osamu Tezuka led a delegation of thirty artists to meet and greet fans. While other comics and pop culture icons get the lion's share of the space, July at Comic-Con is often the time when manga publishers unveil their plans for the coming year.

Kawaii Kon

kawaii-kon.org

There's no denying that this small convention has attracted its share of big guests to Hawaii each April. Artists Robert and Emily DeJesus are regular guests; other guests through the years have included Jin Kobayashi, the author of *School Rumble*, and Rikki and Tavisha Wolfgarth-Simons of Studio Tavicat.

MangaNEXT

manganext.com

This convention based in New Jersey may not be as large as some of the other conventions held on the East Coast, but it is the only convention in the US that focuses more on manga than anime. Representatives of Del Rey, Media Blasters and ALC Publishing are regular attendees.

Otakon

otakon.com

Fans on the East Coast have made this convention in Baltimore, Maryland, the second-largest convention in the US. It takes place in August each year.

Project A-Kon

a-kon.com

The oldest convention strictly dedicated to anime and manga that remains in existence today operates out of Dallas, Texas. May 2009 marked its twentieth anniversary.

Supanova Pop Culture Expo

supanova.com.au

As with Armageddon Expo, anime and manga are just two elements in this Australian celebration of sci-fi TV shows, movies, comics, videogames and other pop culture icons. The show runs four times a year in Brisbane, Melbourne, Sydney and Perth.

YaoiCon

yaoicon.com

If you love boys' love manga, this is your dream come true. Held annually in San Francisco, this convention celebrates yaoi in all its glory, from professional releases to fan-created dōjinshi.

glossary & index

Glossary

Note: Japanese does not have plurals, so words are either singular or collective. The noun manga can therefore either refer to a manga or to manga in general – and mangaka can refer to either one or several manga artists.

4-koma or **yonkoma** four-panel comic strip that usually culminates with a gag. Strips are commonly printed vertically and have self-contained plots, although some developments may carry over between strips.

akahon literally "red book", cheaply made books with red-ink covers produced after World War II and often sold from street stalls. Pulp comics – most notably the early work of Osamu Tezuka – were published in this format through the 1960s.

anime Japanese term for animation in general, used in Western markets to refer to animated series/movies with Japanese origins.

bishōjo a beautiful girl character, usually between high school and college age. Also describes manga predominantly populated by such characters, eg *Sailor Moon*.

bishōnen a beautiful boy character, usually between high school and college age. Also refers to manga predominantly populated by such characters, eg *Fushigi Yugi*.

boke the funny man in a manzai comedy routine. See also **manzai** and **tsukkomi**.

boys' love Japanese term for manga that feature platonic relationships between two boys or men. See also **shōnen-ai** and **yaoi**

bunkoban a paperback collection of manga chapters from a single story that were previously serialized in a weekly or monthly magazine (see also **tankōbon**). Bunkoban are printed on thinner, higher quality paper and contain several tankōbon volumes.

chibi Meaning "little", refers to characters drawn in a childlike or squashed manner, usually in comedic sequences. Also known as **super deformed** (SD).

cosplay the fan activity of dressing up as favourite manga, anime or videogame characters.

dōjinshi self-published manga drawn by amateur artists and featuring either original stories or stories involving characters from professional works.

emakimono narrative "picture scrolls" with occasional text, popular in twelfth-century Japan.

fan service artistic elements placed in manga scenes purely to please readers. Commonly refers to lingering close-up shots of the female anatomy.

furigana hiragana and katakana characters written above the kanji to help younger readers learn how to pronounce words they may not be able to read yet. See also hiragana, kanji, katakana and rōmaji.

gekiga literally "drama pictures", a term used in the late 1950s and early 60s for manga featuring more adult and action-oriented themes and more realistic artwork. Today used to describe underground, avant-garde works.

giseigo onomatopoeia; sound effects written in Japanese kana that mimic actual sounds.

gitaigo sound effects written in Japanese kana that represent states of mind or moods, eg "jiiiiiiiiiiiiiiiin" for an uncomfortable silence.

global manga comics drawn in or influenced by manga style, by artists outside Japan. Also known as OEL manga and world manga.

harem manga genre where a single character is surrounded by multiple characters of the opposite sex. The main character is often male (eg *Love Hina*, *Oh My Goddess!*) but can be female (eg *Ouran High School Host Club*).

hentai erotic manga covering a wide array of fetishistic, niche interests. Akin to hardcore pornography.

hikikomori an individual who has chosen to withdraw from social life for extended periods of time. In Japan, some otaku have become hikikomori due to their lack of social skills.

hiragana one of the two Japanese alphabets collectively known as kana, hiragana is used for writing native Japanese words. See also katakana.

international manga see global manga.

josei "young woman", used to describe manga aimed at young adult females aged eighteen to thirty.

kana collective name for the two Japanese phonetic alphabets, hiragana and katakana.

kanji written Japanese language based on Chinese ideograms.

kashihonya Post-war paying libraries where books or comics, usually targeting older readers, could be borrowed for a small fee.

katakana one of two Japanese alphabets collectively known as kana, katakana is used for writing words originating in other languages. See also hiragana.

kibyōshi literally "yellow covers", books containing ten pages of drawings produced from woodblock prints and accompanied by captions.

magical girl or **mahō shōjo** genre in which a girl or group of girls magically transform in order to battle enemies, eg *Cardcaptor Sakura* and *Sailor Moon*.

mangaka manga artist or artists.

manzai a style of Japanese comedy in which a funny man says something silly and a straight man tries to correct his error, often in exasperated vain. See also **boke** and **tsukkomi**.

mecha a term that describes machines in general, but is most often used to refer to the robots and spacecraft of science fiction manga.

ninja a warrior who studies and trains in ninjutsu fighting techniques.

OEL acronym for "original English language manga", used to describe comics drawn in or influenced by the manga style, by artists outside Japan. Also known as **global**, **world** or **international** manga.

omake bonus content that is not part of the main story of the manga, including creator commentaries and margin notes and short, often humorous side stories.

otaku Japanese term used to refer to anyone with an obsessive interest in something, usually anime, manga and videogames. Has a less negative connotation in the West, where it's been adopted by anime and manga fans to refer to themselves.

rōmaji the representation of written Japanese using the Western Roman alphabet.

rōnin in different contexts, either a masterless samurai (eg Itto Ogami in *Lone Wolf and Cub*) or a student who has failed the college entrance exam (eg Keitaro Urashima in *Love Hina*).

samurai a member of the military nobility and warrior class in feudal-era Japan.

scanlation manga translated by fans, often by scanning in the original pages, digitally removing the Japanese text and replacing it with text in another language.

seinen "young man", used to describe manga aimed at young adult males aged eighteen to thirty.

shōjo "girl", used to describe manga aimed at girls around intermediate or high school age.

shōnen "boy", used to describe manga aimed at boys around intermediate or high school age.

shōnen-ai shōjo manga stories, typically seen in the late 1970s, which featured platonic, sometimes romantic relationships between pubescent boys or young men. See also **boys' love** and **yaoi**.

super deformed (SD) characters drawn in a childlike or squashed manner, usually in comedic sequences. Also known as **chibi**.

tankōbon a paperback collection of manga chapters from a single story that were previously serialized in a weekly or monthly magazine. See also bunkoban.

tachiyomi literally "standing and reading", a practice common in both Japanese and Western manga sections … often to the annoyance of both bookstore employees and other customers.

tokusatsu literally "special effects", Japanese live-action films and TV series that feature transforming costumed superheroes or creatures and the use of such effects.

tsukkomi the straight man in a manzai comedy routine. See also boke.

ukiyo-e print style that rose in prominence in Edo (modern-day Tokyo) in the latter half of the seventeenth century.

world manga see global manga.

yakuza Japanese organized crime groups.

yaoi in Japan, dōjinshi that features suggestive sequences and explicit sex; in Western markets, the term covers all shōnen-ai, yaoi and boys' love material.

yuri describes stories about girls loving girls, whether the target audience is lesbians or straight men and women.

Thumbnail and canon reviews are indicated in **bold**.

from *page* to *screen*

an introduction to the dynamic and addictive
world of Japanese animation

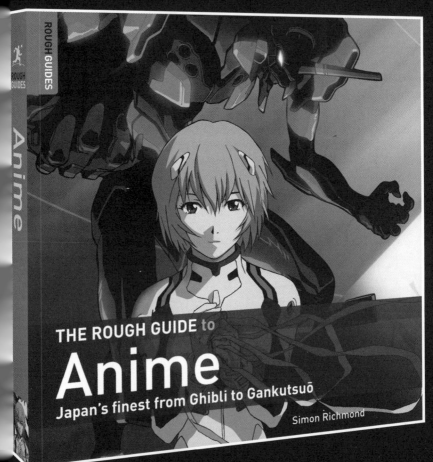

ROUGH GUIDES

Anime

THE ROUGH GUIDE to

Anime

Japan's finest from Ghibli to Gankutsuō

Simon Richmond

www.roughguides.com
MAKE THE MOST OF YOUR TIME ON EARTH

ROUGH
GUIDES